Imaginary Wilds

Architectural interventions for the Thomas Cole National Historic Site

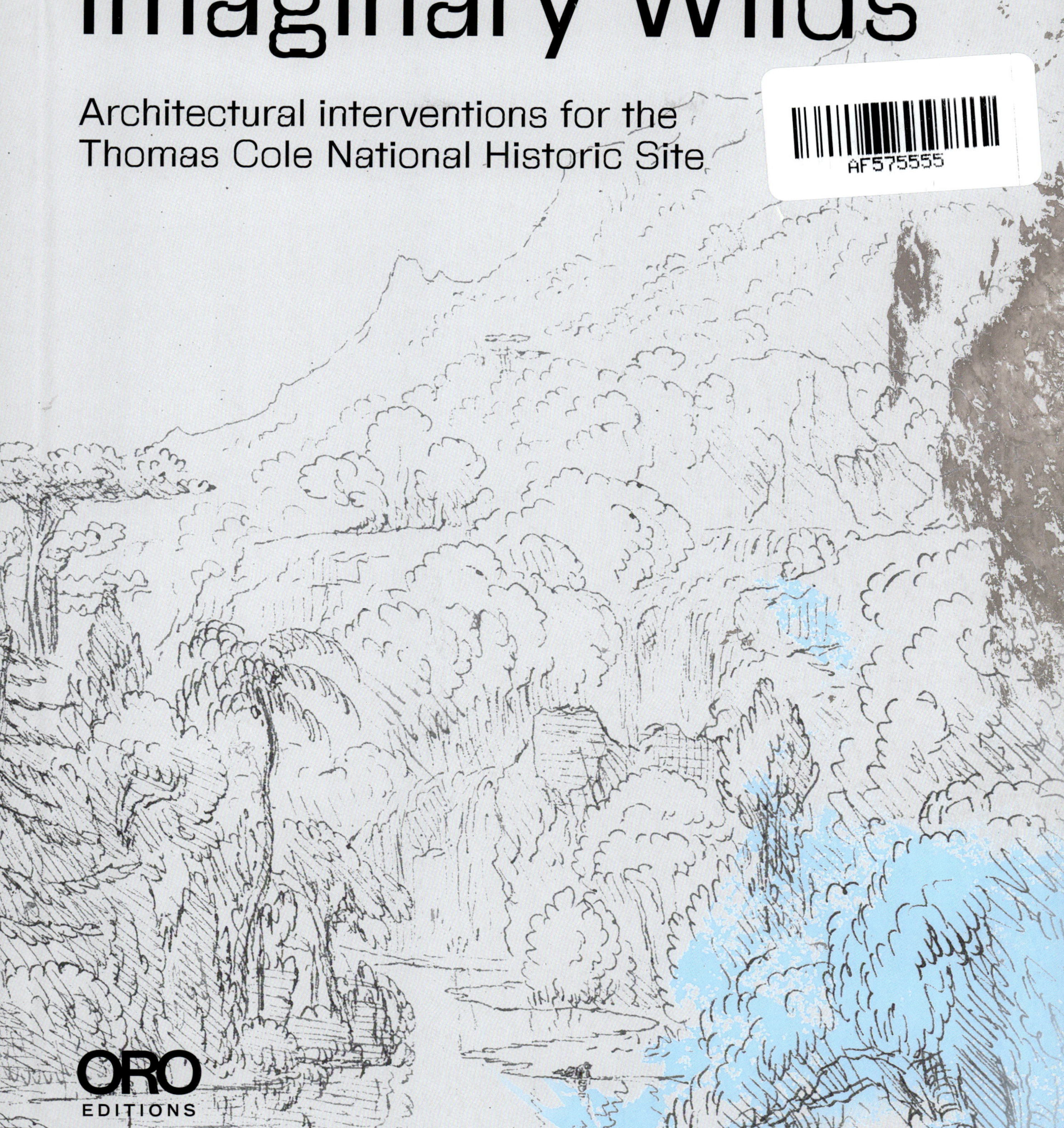

ORO EDITIONS

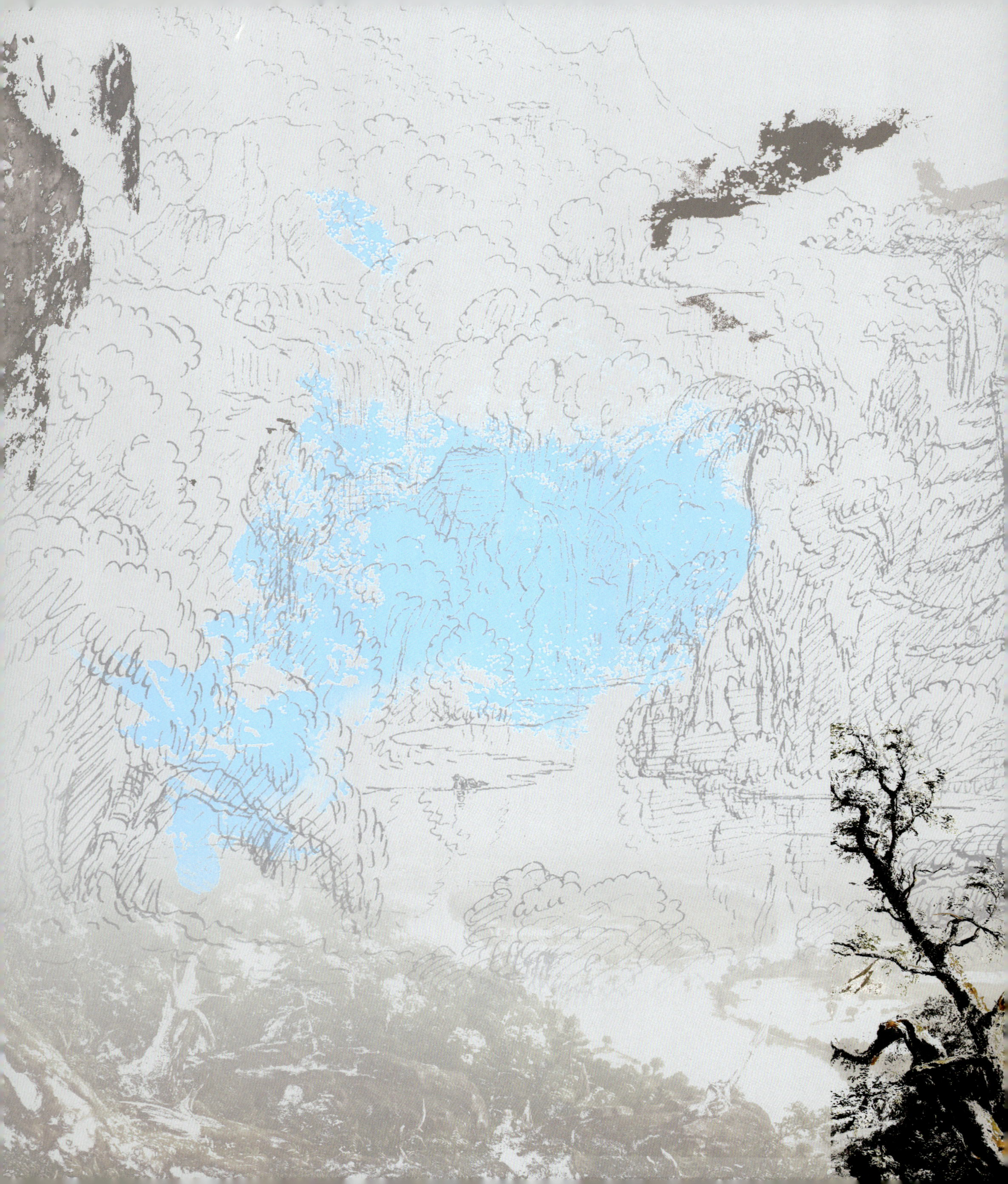

Table of Contents

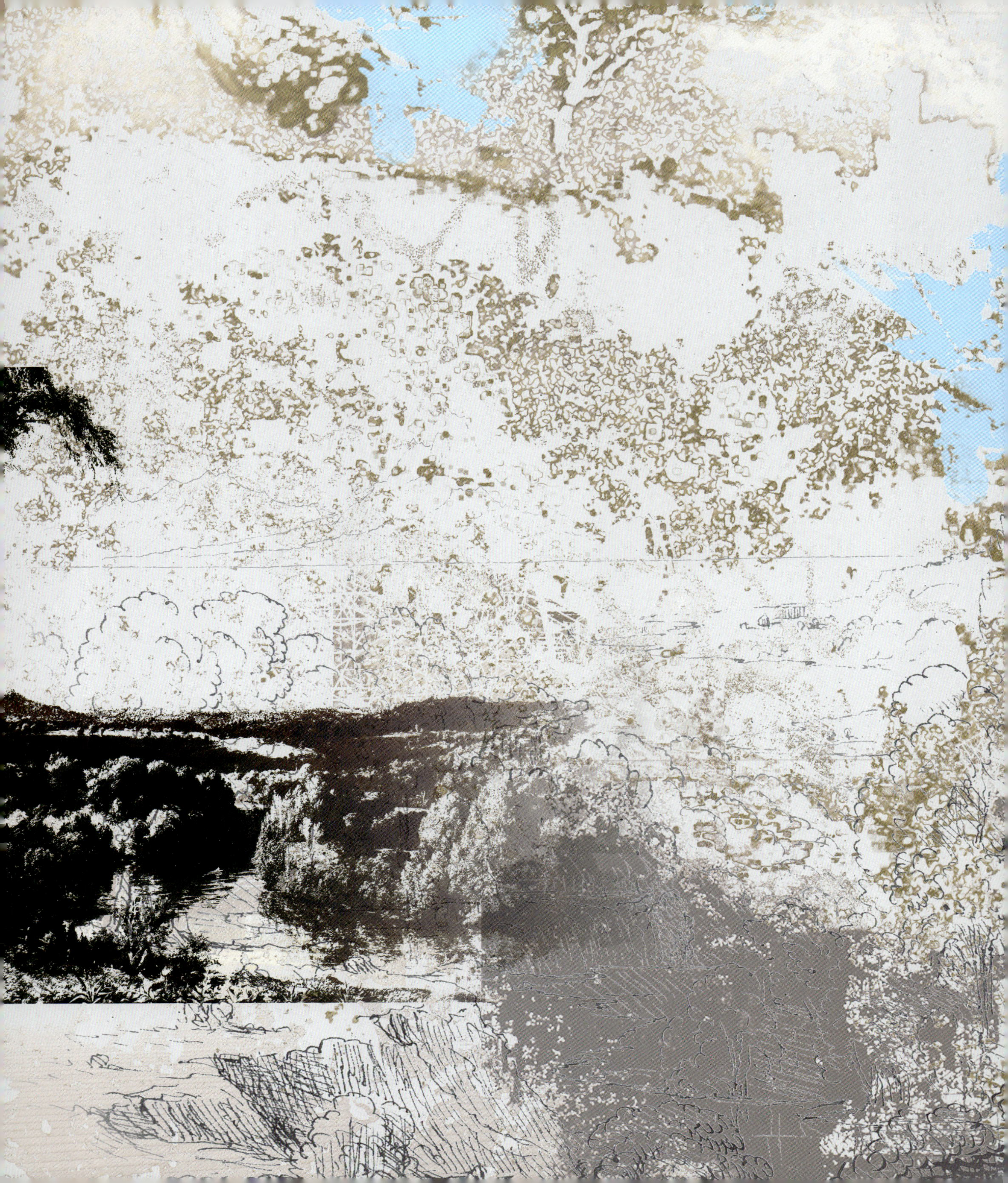

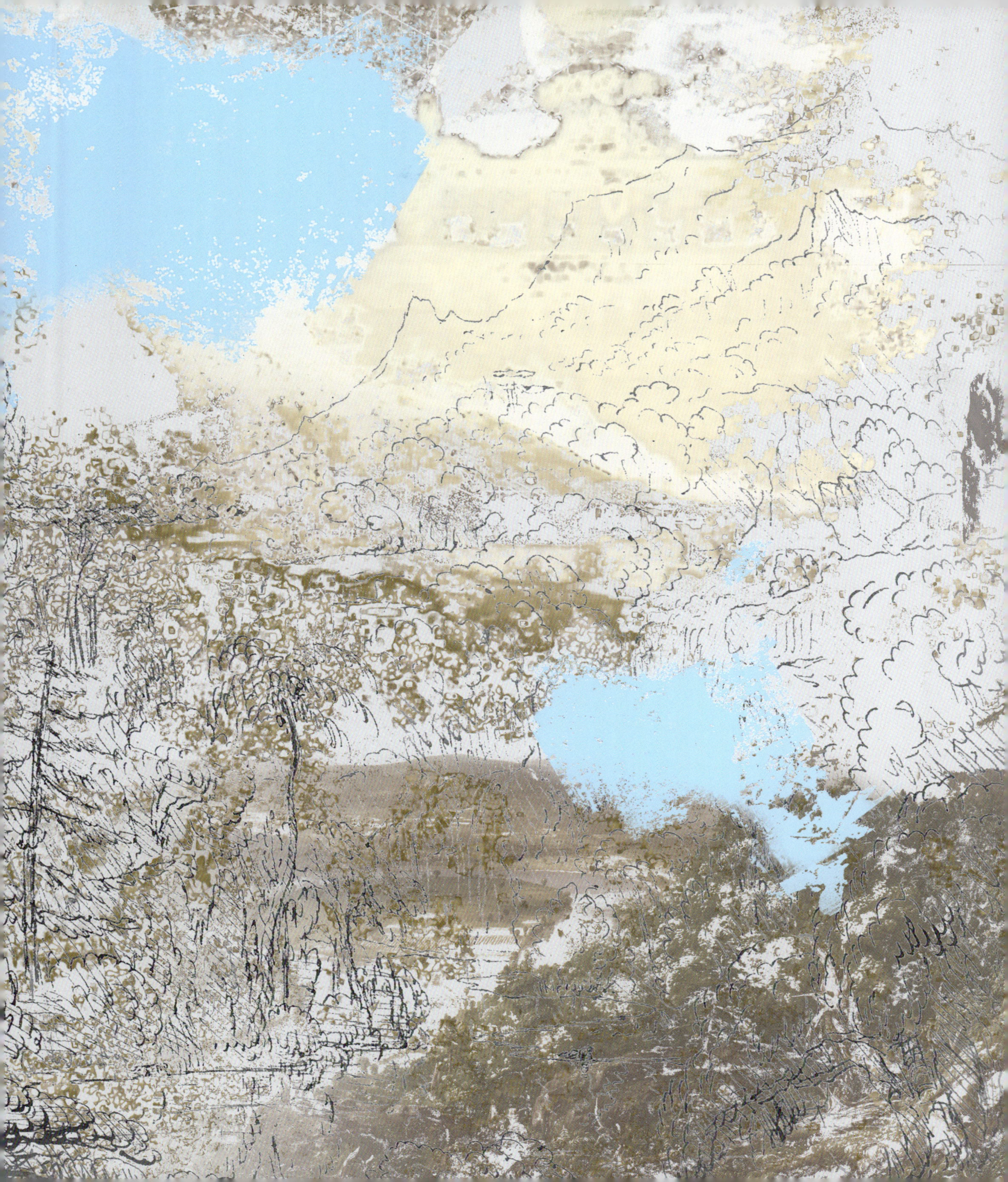

Foreword

Evan Douglis

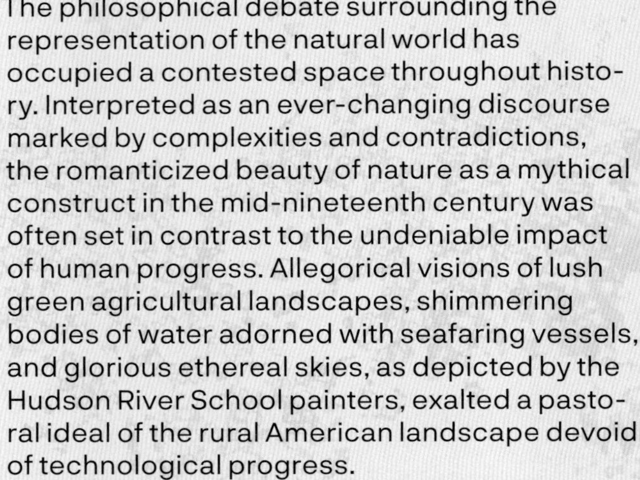

The philosophical debate surrounding the representation of the natural world has occupied a contested space throughout history. Interpreted as an ever-changing discourse marked by complexities and contradictions, the romanticized beauty of nature as a mythical construct in the mid-nineteenth century was often set in contrast to the undeniable impact of human progress. Allegorical visions of lush green agricultural landscapes, shimmering bodies of water adorned with seafaring vessels, and glorious ethereal skies, as depicted by the Hudson River School painters, exalted a pastoral ideal of the rural American landscape devoid of technological progress.

This paradox, vividly exemplified by the works of the legendary American landscape painter Thomas Cole, provides a poignant backdrop to the remarkable collaboration chronicled within the pages of this book. Cole's masterful work, as an enduring source of artistic and cultural relevance, challenges us to reflect on contemporary notions of the natural and built environment in a continuously evolving synergetic partnership.

In the midst of his celebrated odes to the natural world, Thomas Cole was also acutely aware of the encroaching forces of industrialization and the unrelenting sprawl left by building development. He bore witness to the transformative power of human progress, but he recognized that this advancement came at the cost of nature's purity. It was an irreconcilable challenge he grappled with throughout his career, encapsulated in the juxtaposition of the pristine wilderness he so powerfully captured in his paintings and the looming signs of a post-natural world.

As we delve into our students' innovative architectural designs born from the partnership between our esteemed architecture school and the venerable Cole Historic Site, we find ourselves navigating the same intricate terrain that preoccupied Cole himself. Like the Hudson River School painter, we are confronted with a world in transition, where the allure of the natural world in all its splendor now stands in uneasy juxtaposition with the pressing challenges of our contemporary environmental crisis.

Nature today is “neither preordained nor immutable but interconnected and fluid.”[1] It's an ever-changing ecosystem that is both generative and destructive, calling attention to the delicate and precarious balance between human progress and environmental stewardship. In the face of this existential crisis, we are presented not with a choice between beauty and despair but with an opportunity for innovation, where the boundaries of art, science, and the natural world blur, giving birth to a new aesthetic of the sublime in architecture—a fusion of human ingenuity and nature's resilience.

In the bold designs brought to life by the students at the hallowed Cole Historic Site, we discover a creative odyssey of speculative futures: subterranean structures that deftly conceal themselves within the picturesque terrain, amorphic architectural bodies that seemingly meander like imaginary flora figures across the landscape, and unassuming edifices that, beneath their surface, function as memory machines, recalling the timeless beauty of the Hudson River Valley in a bygone era.

Amidst Cole's divine landscapes and the ever-changing tapestry of nature enveloping his estate, these visionary designs emerge. They offer a wondrous journey through the mutable landscapes of architectural thought, serving as a living tribute to the evolving mythos of our relationship with the natural world.

I want to express my gratitude to Betsy Jacks, the executive director of the Thomas Cole National Historic Site, for her unwavering support and enthusiasm during our collaboration. Her efforts to bring Cole to life for a contemporary audience were an invaluable source of inspiration throughout our academic partnership.

I extend my sincere appreciation to Prof. Adam Dayem for his exceptional curatorial oversight during the course of this initiative, where he expertly served as both studio coordinator and the editor of this book. His unwavering commitment to excellence has played a pivotal role in the success of this project.

I want to recognize the scholarly contributions of William L. Colman, Adam Dayem, Cathryn Dwyre-Perry, and David Salomon. Their interpretations have offered valuable insight into this iconic nineteenth-century landscape painter, enabling a new generation to fully appreciate Cole's visionary ideas and masterful artistry.

I want to call attention to the innovative pedagogy of the faculty instructors David Bell, Jillian Crandall, Gustavo Crembil, Adam Dayem, and Leandro Piazzi, who offered important guidance throughout the creative process. They too navigated a complex terrain as educators having to define within their respective studios the proper role of architecture on the sacred ground of the Cole Historic Site.

Finally, I want to celebrate the brilliant work of the students, who contributed important design research into the enduring legacy of Thomas Cole, further confirming his timely value to our contemporary world.

> *In the end, we will conserve only what we love; we will love only what we understand, and we will understand only what we are taught.*
>
> Baba Dioum, Senegalese Ecologist

1 Kusserow, Karl. “Nature ‘Nation’: How American art shaped our environmental perspectives”, Princeton.edu/news, (October 10, 2018)

Preface

Elizabeth B. Jacks,
Executive Director,
Thomas Cole National Historic Site

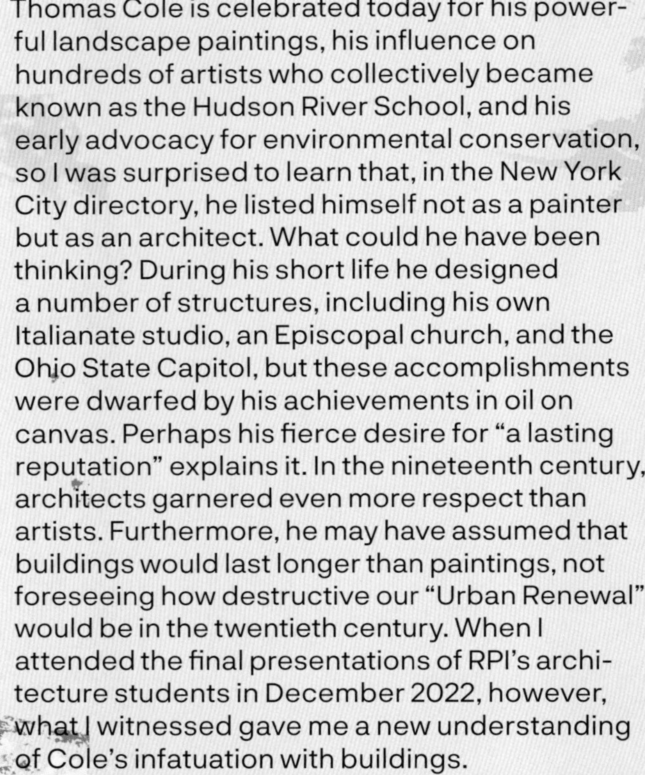

Thomas Cole is celebrated today for his powerful landscape paintings, his influence on hundreds of artists who collectively became known as the Hudson River School, and his early advocacy for environmental conservation, so I was surprised to learn that, in the New York City directory, he listed himself not as a painter but as an architect. What could he have been thinking? During his short life he designed a number of structures, including his own Italianate studio, an Episcopal church, and the Ohio State Capitol, but these accomplishments were dwarfed by his achievements in oil on canvas. Perhaps his fierce desire for "a lasting reputation" explains it. In the nineteenth century, architects garnered even more respect than artists. Furthermore, he may have assumed that buildings would last longer than paintings, not foreseeing how destructive our "Urban Renewal" would be in the twentieth century. When I attended the final presentations of RPI's architecture students in December 2022, however, what I witnessed gave me a new understanding of Cole's infatuation with buildings.

The artist's abiding concern and the subject of both his painting and writing was humans' relationship with land—and isn't that ultimately the role of architecture, to mediate between the two? Cole decried this human / land relationship as it stood in the 1830s and '40s as highly dysfunctional, even criminal, and governed by ignorance and greed. In one of his more optimistic moments he doodled a magnificent villa with wide steps sloping down into gentle waters and labeled it "Palace on the Hudson in the year 2500," calling for a relationship with the waterway that is a far cry from our current reality. Cole's dreamscape with an easy way into the water tells us what he wants us to do: get in there. Put yourself in direct contact with nature. With this directive, he demonstrates the power of architecture to shape our relationship with our surroundings, which is what I saw in the architecture projects at RPI. Will we rise above the landscape in a tall tower? Will we burrow under a hill? Will we sit around a courtyard and look inward? Or open up the ceiling and let in the sky? Each project not only directed the eye in a new direction but also communicated a state of mind, from tumbling into darkness to the aspiration to fly. Never could I have imagined there were so many extraordinarily divergent ways of inhabiting the same place. Before hearing from these students, I had spent the better part of twenty years at the Thomas Cole site, but after seeing and hearing from them that familiar plot of Earth felt entirely new.

How lucky we are that the architect and professor Adam Dayem brought his students to the Thomas Cole site in 2022 and began imagining a partnership, and that the Dean of the School of Architecture Evan Douglis would not only embrace it but run with it, resulting in this publication. The ideas that the students conjured were too extraordinary not to share, and I am overjoyed that we can share them here, now, with you. My heartfelt thanks go to Evan, Adam, and all of the brilliant students whose works I saw, only a subset of which we are able to fit within these pages. Keep bravely creating.

Imaginary Wilds: In Dialogue with Real and Ideal Natures

Adam Dayem

> *If the imagination is shackled, and nothing is described but what we see, seldom will anything great be produced either in Painting or Poetry.*
>
> Thomas Cole[1]

An interpretation of any complex and nuanced artistic legacy is, to some extent, a reflection of the individual making the interpretation—a reflection of their particular time and point of view. And this is the case with the legacy of Thomas Cole, who, as the founder of the Hudson River School, did much to establish the legitimacy of American landscape art. In a relatively short period from the 1820s until his untimely death in 1848, Cole made a series of masterwork paintings on the American landscape. These paintings, along with his limited writings, have left a compelling and sometimes contradictory legacy with regard to natural landscapes, and humans' relationships with them.

Cole's legacy continues to be relevant and worthy of study today, nearly two hundred years after his career, because he approached nature as both material and conceptual conditions. In his essay "Lecture on Art," he says, "by Imitation is not to be understood the vulgar notion, that copying whatever nature presents in her everyday garb...is the perfection of Artistic power." Instead, "True Imitation selects from the great world around us the characteristic, the sublime and the beautiful; in its alembic separates the true from the accidental." The alchemy of the artist is in selecting, editing, and enhancing visions of the natural landscape so that "Art becomes the exponent of Nature's highest qualities."[2] The subjects of many of Cole's paintings include the environment he chose to surround himself with: the Catskill Mountains, the Connecticut River Valley, Kaaterskill Falls, etc., but the aspiration of his art was ultimately to convey an idea about nature, and humans' relationship to it, which he extrapolated from the landscapes he inhabited. As such, Cole was engaging nature as both a real and an ideal condition. And he was doing this in a time of major cultural upheaval, as rapid industrialization in the early nineteenth century was fundamentally changing

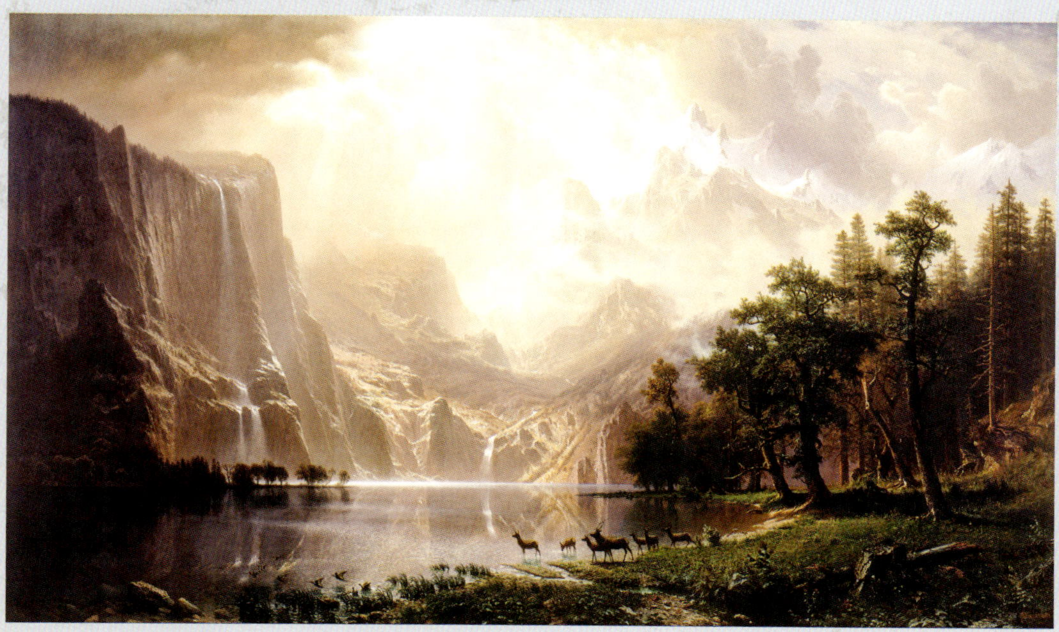

Fig. 1 Albert Bierstadt, *Among the Sierra Nevada, California*, 1868. Oil on canvas, 72 x 120.125 in. Smithsonian American Art Museum, Bequest of Helen Huntington Hull, granddaughter of William Brown Dinsmore, who acquired the painting in 1873 for "The Locusts," the family estate in Dutchess County, New York, 1977.107.1.

humans' ability to inhabit and alter their environments. The result is that his work sustains a level of complexity that can be interpreted in different ways, and these interpretations can offer perspective on the cultural upheavals we are experiencing in our own time, specifically with regard to the environments we inhabit.

The complexity of Cole's legacy, and thus its relevance from a contemporary standpoint, is not necessarily found in the work of his successors in the Hudson River School movement. In the work of Albert Bierstadt for instance (figure 1), who came to prominence in the 1860s, Aaron Sachs finds that "you don't see the nitty-gritty questioning of exactly how American civilization ought to develop; you don't see paintings explicitly asking what the American relationship to the environment ought to be."[3] Complexity is lost, and you see gloriously uncomplicated visions of nature—sanitized and controlled—paving the way for Manifest Destiny. In Cole on the other hand, one sees complex relationships playing out between the utilitarian drive of human development, and the intellectual and spiritual desire to preserve the natural landscape. While Cole generally positioned himself on the side of more preservation, he was not opposed to commerce within limits. What made him uneasy was the erosion of moral, social, and institutional restraints on rampant individualism.[4] This is well represented by the second painting in *The Course of Empire* (1833–1836), a work which consists of five canvases: *The Savage State, The Arcadian or Pastoral State, The Consummation of Empire, Destruction,* and *Desolation,* sequentially depicting five stages of human development in relationship to nature. *The Savage State* represents nature before it is inhabited by humans, the Indigenous people represented in the painting not being fully human in Cole's estimation.[5] *The Arcadian or Pastoral State* (figure 2) represents humans who have begun altering the landscape by adding a limited number of architectural elements and domesticating animals. These interventions are represented in a picturesque manner, and depict humans living in harmony with nature.[6] The subsequent canvas, *Consummation of Empire,* represents the conquest of nature and the pinnacle of human development, which leads to the decline of civilization in *Destruction,* and finally to *Desolation,* where artifacts of human development have been abandoned and overtaken by nature.

While it was not generally received as such, Cole intended *The Course of Empire* to be a parable for the United States.[7] Its message was that unchecked development fueled by greed and disregard for nature would lead to corruption and eventually the destruction of the nation. As Angela Miller describes it, this message could be interpreted as a highly conservative one in favor of maintaining hierarchical power structures capable of limiting development in the face of cultural change, which was being brought about by Jacksonian Democrats.[8] Limiting development of natural landscapes would allow the nation to preserve an arcadian state, and thus avoid the fate depicted in *The Course of Empire.* Cole's conservatism might also be inferred from some of his social relations. In order to maintain his artistic practice, Cole had to behave and produce work in the good graces of wealthy patrons. Preserving status quo power structures would certainly be beneficial to these individuals.[9]

Alternatively, Cole's legacy could be interpreted as a more progressive one which, while not necessarily embracing radical cultural shifts, would at least consider them with a degree of ambivalence and uncertainty. For example, *The Oxbow* (1836) represents a landscape split in half, one side containing a calm, pastoral scene in the Connecticut River Valley, and the other a wild forest and ominous storm (figure 3). The two sides of the painting are held in tension with each other. As Sachs notes, "the wild and calm are never in perfect balance…and no one knows what the next storm will bring." Sachs goes on to observe that the painting engages "with all the complexities of our relationship to nature," and it "is a poignant acknowledgment that in order to live we must constantly use up the resources we depend on…every step toward a seemingly more settled existence also undermines the stability of our habitat."[10] Rather than describing Cole as making a conservative argument for limiting development

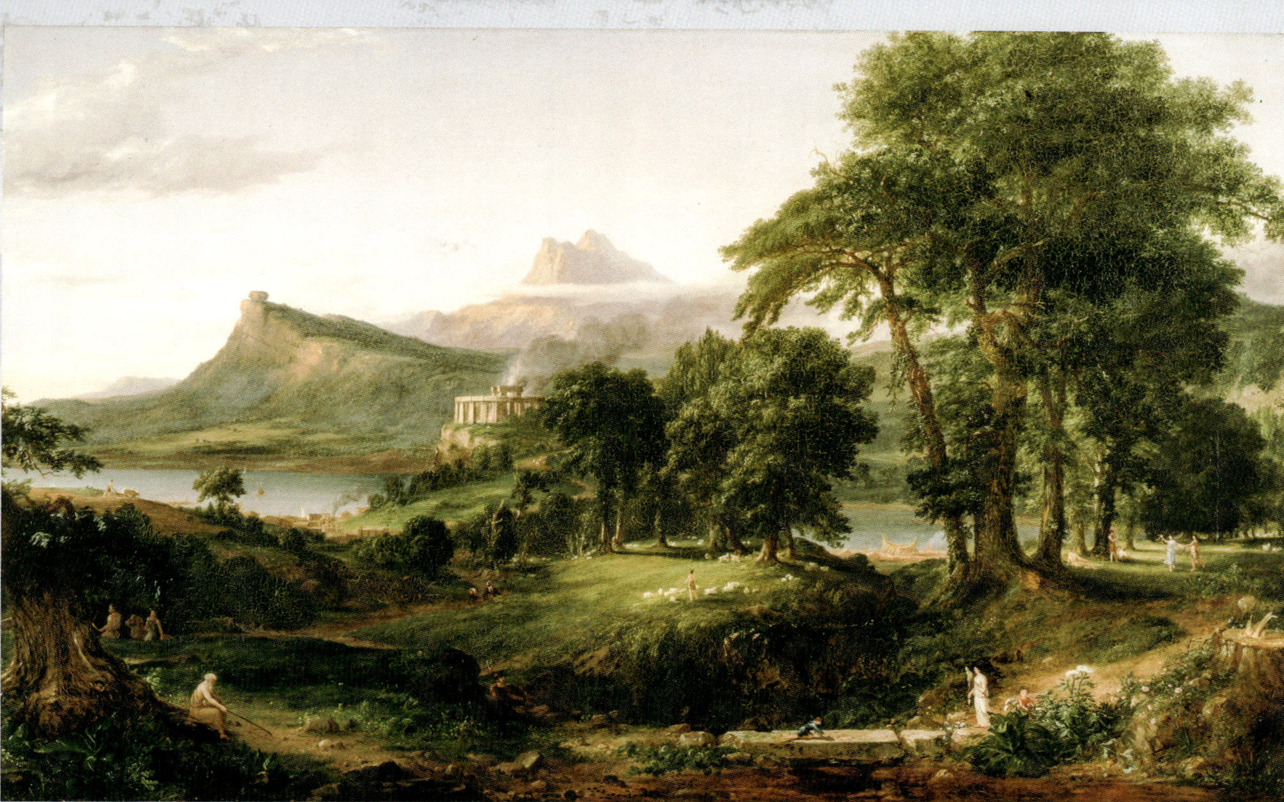

Fig. 2 Thomas Cole, *The Course of Empire, The Arcadian or Pastoral State*, 1834. Oil on canvas, 39.5 x 63.5 in. New York Historical Society, Gift of the New-York Gallery of the Fine Arts, 1858.2.

and preserving an arcadian nation as Miller does, Sachs sees Cole as taking the more progressive position of embracing uncertainty. Sachs's view is reinforced by considering Cole's acquaintances in the art community aside from just his patrons. While his financial situation did necessitate cultivating the patronage of wealthy individuals—often Federalist-leaning individuals—his freely chosen friends were of a decidedly different intellectual makeup. Cole aligned himself with a group of progressive New York artists called the Sketch Club. Matthew DeLaMater has argued that Cole could not have participated in the Sketch Club if he had been seen to be beholden to wealthy Federalist patrons,[11] and goes on to conclude that considering Cole from a more progressive standpoint allows one to read more environmentalist concerns into his work and his belief in the democratization of art.[12]

As may be gleaned from the paragraphs above, the aim of this book is not to make a single definitive reading of Cole's legacy, but to approach his work from different directions, framed within the context of our moment in history. During Cole's career, America was undergoing its fastest rate of urban growth, and revolutions in industry and transportation were fundamentally changing ways of life for many of his contemporaries.[13] In our era, radical changes in the technologic and climatic systems we inhabit are fundamentally changing our way of life. Even though we are experiencing different types of change than Cole did in his time, just like Cole, we can see that our lives and our culture are going to change fundamentally. Exactly how they will change is uncertain. This uncertainty about the future made Cole anxious, and it can certainly produce anxieties in our time. Cole was able to channel his anxiety into a productive artistic practice; the aim of this book is to propose that something similar is possible now.

In the context of uncertainty about the future, particularly as it relates to humans' relationship to the natural world, this book is framed around the concept of *imaginary wilds*. An imaginary wild landscape is a persistent idea in American history. This idea helped Cole define an American identity distinct from European landscapes, which he saw as being more "smoothed" and "tamed"[14] in comparison to much less densely populated expanses of America. Cole's wilderness was imaginary partly because he intentionally made it so by engaging nature as real and ideal in his artistic practice, and partly because he and his contemporaries were largely blind to the fact that the land they felt so much ownership over had been inhabited by humans for millennia prior to the arrival of white European settlers. Today, imaginary wilds continue to have a major influence on attitudes toward landscape and nature. This is often manifested in a nostalgic lament for a version of the biologic and climatic planet we are losing. But more productively, particularly in the context of educating the next generation of architectural students, the imaginary wilds consist of more than just what we typically consider nature—they consist of biologic,

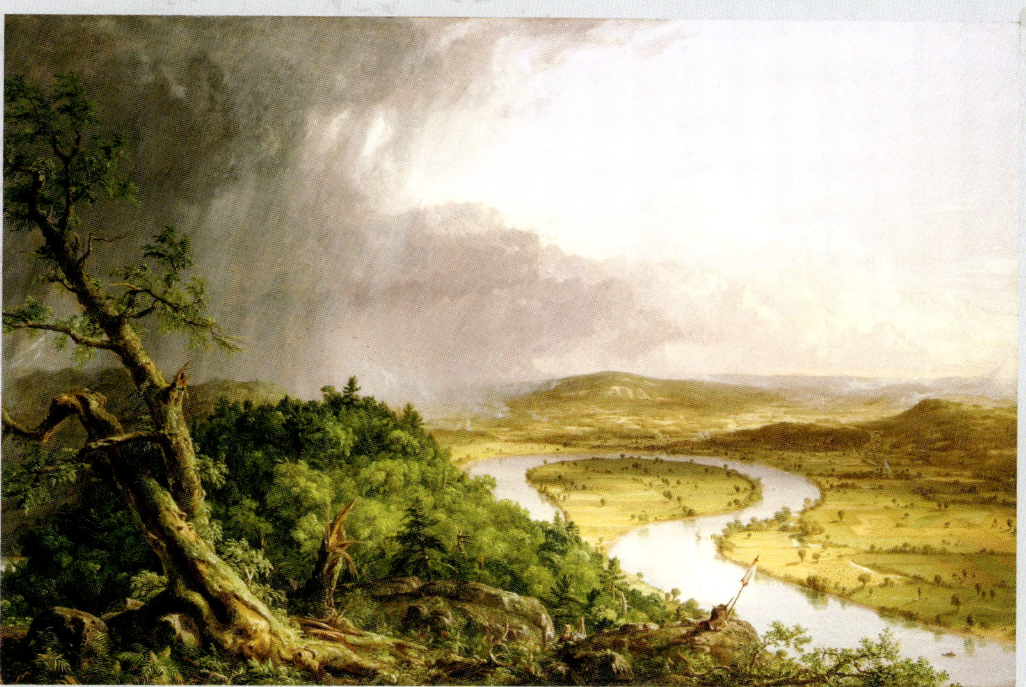

Fig. 3 Thomas Cole, *View from Mount Holyoke, Northhampton, Massachusetts, after a Thunderstorm – The Oxbow*, 1836. Oil on canvas, 51.5 x 76 in. Metropolitan Museum of Art, Gift of Mrs. Russell Sage, 1908, 08.228.

climatic, and technologic worlds taken together as dependent and interacting systems. Imagining these wilds is an acknowledgment of the uncertainties we face, and to embrace them we must imagine possibilities for embracing the uncertainty of the future.

This book presents a series of student-designed architectural projects for a new gallery building sited within the landscape of Cedar Grove, Thomas Cole's historic home and studio in Catskill, New York. Complexities arising from considering landscapes and nature as both real and ideal create a productive frame for exploring how architects might design buildings in relation to landscapes and nature. In the book, these relationships play out in five unique directions under the guidance of five different design studio instructors. The student-designed architectural projects presented here are contextualized in relation to landscape, nature, and Thomas Cole's artistic legacy in a series of essays by a distinguished group of designers and thinkers. The insightful scholarship of William L. Coleman, Cathryn Dwyre-Perry, and David Salomon adds to the wealth of thinking on Cole's legacy from critical and personal perspectives.

Cole was hopeful his work would be widely received and affect people who were not necessarily initiated into the world of art. His most influential written work, "Essay on American Scenery," was delivered as a lecture at the American Lyceum, a venue where

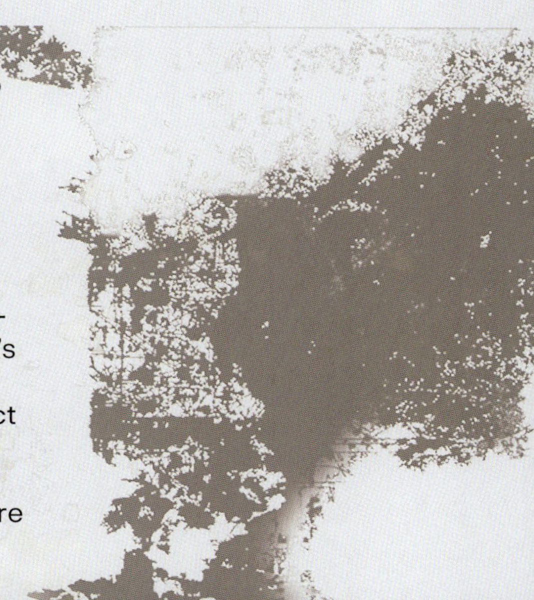

he spoke to educational leaders. Given this opportunity to speak to individuals who could disseminate his message more broadly in schools, he chose to discuss his belief in the need to appreciate *scenery*, as he felt it was being overlooked in favor of industrial development. "In this age, when a meagre utilitarianism seems ready to absorb every feeling and sentiment…it would be well to cultivate the oasis that yet remains to us, and to cherish the impressions that nature is ever ready to give."[15] Perhaps unsurprisingly for a visual artist, part of how Cole envisioned this appreciation evolving was through widespread teaching of drawing in schools, as it gives "precision to the eye and strengthens its perceptive powers."[16]

Hopefully this book, and the work it contains, espouses similar sentiments. While we must look beyond Cole's conception of landscapes as scenery and work to understand the human and nonhuman forces that bring them into being, we can heed Cole's advice to look at technologic development with a critical eye and use visual arts to help strengthen our perceptive powers. The pages that follow channel Cole's legacy in a number of ways. We are creating a pedagogical structure where beginning architecture students acquire professional architectural design skills and test their consequences in a broader cultural context, and where studio instructors can find a compelling architectural project and rich intellectual territory to explore and share with their students. Finally, when combined with writing from contemporary art and architectural thinkers, the design efforts of students and faculty can participate in discourse about Thomas Cole's legacy, humans' relationships to landscape, and architecture's potential roles in this relationship that extends beyond the walls of Rensselaer's architectural design studios, and out into the wider world.

1 Thomas Cole and Louis L. Noble, *The course of empire: Voyage of life, and other pictures of Thomas Cole, N.A., with selections from his letters and miscellaneous writings: illustrative of his life, character, and genius* (New York: Cornish, Lamport & Co., 1853), 93.

2 Thomas Cole, *Lecture on Art* (Catskill, NY: Thomas Cole National Historic Site, 2021), 9.

3 Aaron Sachs, "Downing and American Culture," *Hudson River Valley Review* (Spring 2017): 38.

4 Angela Miller, "Thomas Cole and Jacksonian America: *The Course of Empire* as Political Allegory," *Prospects* (October 1989): 71.

5 Thomas Cole, *Essay on American Scenery* (Catskill, NY: Thomas Cole National Historic Site, 2018), 7.

6 David Schuyler, "Pencil and Pen in Defense of Nature: Thomas Cole and the American Landscape," *Hudson River Valley Review* (Autumn 2014): 27.

7 Miller, 80–81.

8 Miller, 65–66.

9 Matthew DeLaMater, "Thomas Cole's Knickerbocker and Catskill Identity, 1825–1838: A Reconsideration of Cole's 'Englishness' and 'Conservatism' through a Brief Portrait of the Artist who Chose Cedar Grove," *Hudson River Valley Review* (Autumn 2018): 19.

10 Sachs, 33.

11 DeLaMater, 39.

12 DeLaMater, 47.

13 Schuyler, 30–31.

14 Cole, *Essay on American Scenery*, 8.

15 Cole, *Essay on American Scenery*, 5–6.

16 Cole, *Lecture on Art*, 20.

A Nostalgic Future: Thomas Cole, Oil Tanks, and Everyday Monumentality.

David Salomon

I. Introduction

Preserve, restore, transform. These are elastic concepts, equally relevant when considering the future of a building, a city, a landscape, an ecology, or a person. How important is it for an individual, an institution, a nation, a community, or a discipline to preserve their memories, monuments, and histories, no matter how imprecise, inaccurate, or unwanted they are? Such questions are present in the paintings of Thomas Cole. They are also present in the history of the Thomas Cole National Historic Site (TCNHS) in Catskill, New York, and in the everyday and extraordinary landscapes that surround it.[1]

Whereas Cole sought to preserve nature and isolate it from industry and even history,[2] the TCNHS has taken a more synthetic and expansive approach to these and other issues.[3] In keeping with this ethos of inclusion and integration, this essay combines autobiographical reflections, historical analysis, and critical speculations to engage the nostalgia, myths, and the many histories and futures present in Cole's work and homestead. In doing so, the isolation of everyday from extraordinary environments, of personal stories from official narratives, and industrial progress from natural processes will be challenged.[4]

II. My Hudson River School

Pizza, oil tanks, and the Rip van Winkle Bridge. This was how I first came to know Catskill. It was in the 1970s. My dad was from Hudson, which is a few miles north and across the Hudson River from it. We often took the two-hour drive up the New York State Thruway from New Jersey to visit my grandparents. We only went to Catskill once or twice. We went for pizza. I think the place was called Mike's. Our cousin Mark took us. I remember it being near the water and awkwardly close to some oil tanks. These were tattooed with the Citgo logo, or maybe it was Mobil. I noticed them every time we crossed the Rip van Winkle.

Dozens of times we drove within a hundred yards of what is now the TCNHS, aka, Cedar Grove, but it was nowhere to be found on our mental maps. They were filled with orchards and farms where we would pick fruit and buy the ingredients that my grandmother turned into magic down in her dark, damp basement. For decades I have been trying, unsuccessfully, to reproduce it.

The first time I recall paying attention to Cole's beloved Catskill Mountains was on the thruway. It must have been on a Friday night in summer. We had a long, low Oldsmobile station wagon. The back cargo space flipped into a rear-facing seat. I was alone back there; my brother, sister, and parents up front. Somewhere after exit 19 I noticed the sky changing color behind the mountains. It lasted forever. It was spellbinding. I can still see it.

My grandfather was a foreman at a felt factory in Hudson. In my mind's eye there was a gumball machine outside his otherwise gray-on-gray office. When I was little, Hudson still had a functioning downtown. He would take me, and only me, to the bakery, bank, and post office on Saturday mornings. By the time he died, in 1981, Hudson was barely hanging on. It would be a few decades before it would become an outpost for New Yorkers, filled with what my grandmother called "junk stores" but which others call antique shops, galleries, and boutiques. Today, Warren Street is thriving, if not gentrified, and there are signs that Catskill might follow in Hudson's footsteps.[5]

We often visited the train station down by the river to watch the Amtrak and freight trains come and go. We rarely went to the boat launch next door. We certainly never got too close to the water. My dad often lamented how he and his friends swam in the Hudson in the 1940s and '50s, but that it was too dangerous to go in. I would be in college before I found out why. It was because of the PCBs dumped into it by General Electric.

Cole's Hudson Valley and Catskill Mountains were ones of trees, trains, rivers, and pollution. Of industry, agriculture, and art. Of highways, bridges, mountains, and sunsets. Over a hundred years later, it was intermittently mine as well. It was where the wonders and paradoxes of the physical and cultural landscape were also revealed to me. However, it was only when I started to study Cole and Cedar Grove that I realized how what I thought were my own intimate experiences had long ago been scripted by a number of intersecting historical trajectories.

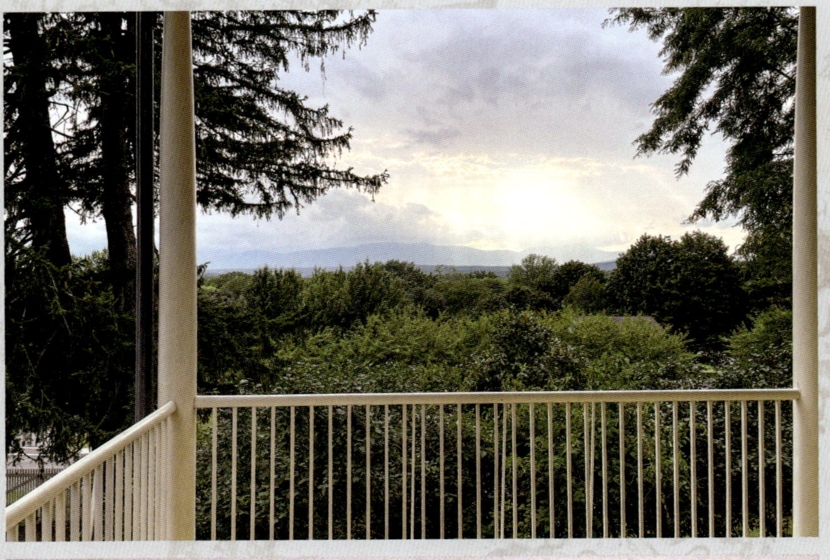

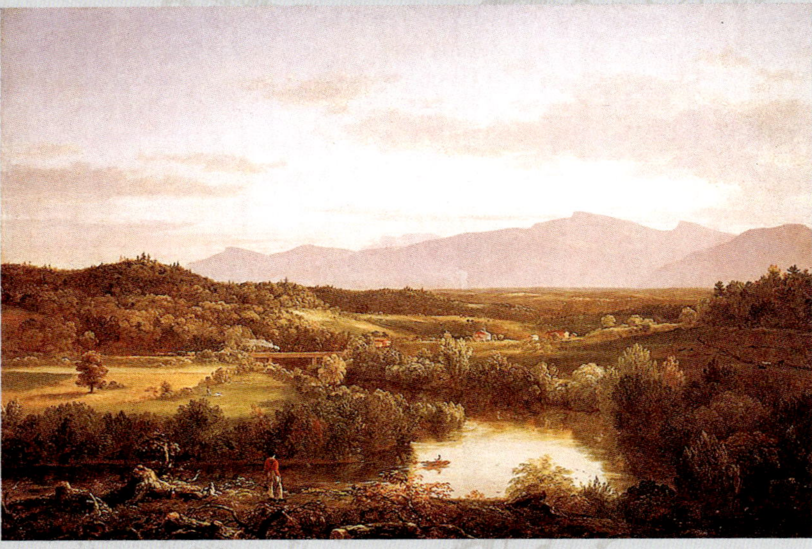

Fig. 1 View from the porch of Thomas Cole's house toward the Catskill Mountains. Photograph by editor, 2023.

Fig. 2 Thomas Cole, *River in the Catskills*, 1868. Oil on canvas, 27.5 x 40.375 in. Museum of Fine Arts, Gift of Martha C. Karolik for the M. and M. Karolik Collection of American Paintings, 1815–1865, 47.1201.

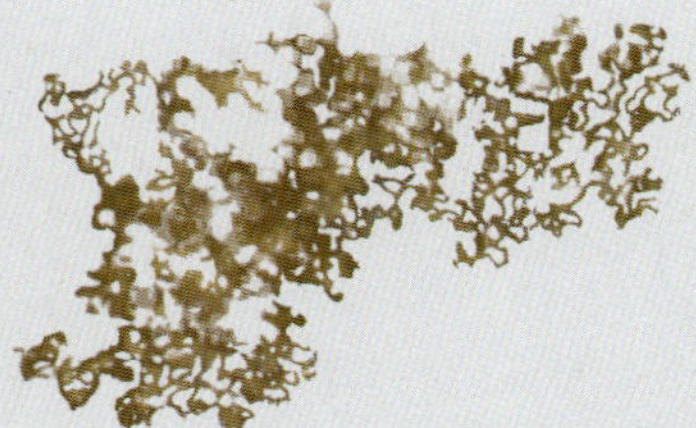

III. Cole, Myth, and the Early Anthropocene

My memories are by no means objective. I'm not even sure how accurate they are. They are rooted in my experience, but they may be false. Are they nostalgic? Probably.

Nostalgia—the longing for a past that never actually existed—could describe Thomas Cole's and the Hudson River School's work. It is also a large part of the myth of the American landscape as an "empty," "wild," "untamed," "savage," "frontier." Understood as such, it could be exploited with moral impunity. But that was only half the myth. The landscape was also understood as a container of the divine.[6] As such it had to be protected and worshiped. Reconciling these two positions required a creative leap. You can't destroy God's work with impunity. In short, it required a myth. A myth that would integrate progress with preservation, exploitation with salvation.

A myth, says Roland Barthes, "could not care less about contradictions so long as it establishes a euphoric security." In the case of the American landscape, the contradiction that is reconciled is "the infinite power of man over nature," with the death of the divine "which man cannot yet do without."[7] This was done by isolating the one from the other. Certain environments were deemed good, true, beautiful, and sacred—the rest was deemed profane. This division, this myth, made it possible for the mortal and the divine, the pragmatic and the spiritual to exist side by side, without one having to pick sides.

Cole's paintings and writing challenged this myth. He took sides. Sixty years after James Watt invented the steam engine, Cole foresaw the coming Anthropocene.[8] His insight was that the unchecked industrialization of the landscape would lead to physical and moral destruction.[9] In a word, things would get ugly. The conception of nature as a resource was combated by depicting it as an Eden, a place of timeless beauty and rapture.

He did so based on empirical evidence. The area around Catskill was neither empty nor pure when Cole first visited in 1825. It was already full of people, culture, beauty, and infrastructure. Native Americans are said to have greeted Henry Hudson along Catskill Creek in 1609. The Catskill Turnpike had been in place since 1804. Robert Fulton's steamships had been making the trip up and down the river since 1807. Tanneries had long lined the Hudson's banks and were depleting the hemlocks and polluting its tributaries. The Erie Canal opened in 1825, supplying the many ships that plied the Hudson with grain and lumber. Catskill was inundated with tourists by the 1820s. Train tracks arrived in the town in the 1830s. Cole's paintings of the region would erase many of these facts. Were they nostalgic? Yes, but that's not all they were.

IV. Preserving / Progress

Cole's preference for the preservation and restoration of nature, and the limiting of industry within it was clear. It was rooted in his own experience as a refugee from industrial England and what he saw happening along the Hudson.[10] He advocated in his letters and his paintings to keep what was not yet harmed that way and to restore what had been damaged back to an "arcadian" state. He conceded that a small portion of the land had to be transformed for practical industrial and agricultural purposes, but that these should be located in places where it did not disrupt both the workings and the image of nature. His efforts, or at least his position, proved partially successful.

In 1885, less than forty years after Cole's death, the Catskill Preserve was created. The New York State Constitution was amended in 1894 to make it "forever wild." Today, the view one gets from the porch at Cedar Grove is consistent with Cole's vision (figure 1). The mountains appear to be free of any past or present industrial interventions. There are no buildings, cell towers, antennae, or utility lines to be seen. Given this scenario, Cole's paintings can be understood both as nostalgic visions of the past and prescient images of the future. One could argue that his paintings helped create our present.

Still, the peaceful scene from the porch is somewhat undermined by the noise of the traffic on New York Route 23 headed to and from the bridge, or from the freight trains that run just a quarter of a mile to the west. They don't get in the way of the view, but they do remind us that this place is still enmeshed with the networks of transportation and commerce that Cole typically excluded from his work.

Enmeshed but not integrated. Rail lines, highways, signage, power line rights of way, quarries, etc., are copiously present outside of the officially preserved lands. Once off of them, anything can happen to the mountains, forests, and rivers, including their being developed as dumping grounds for toxic chemicals and agricultural runoff. The bound duality of a forever wild landscape juxtaposed with the forever wild of commerce, trade, and infrastructure do not balance each other out, they accelerate their division.[11]

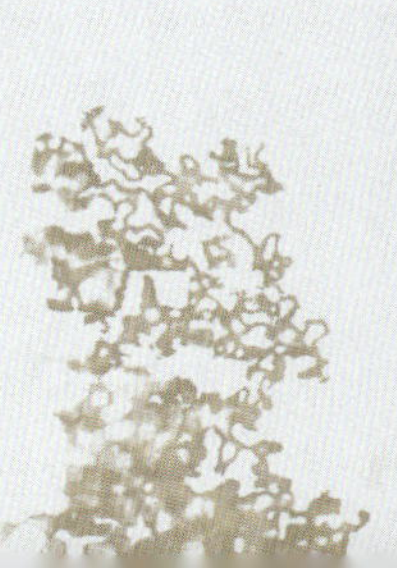

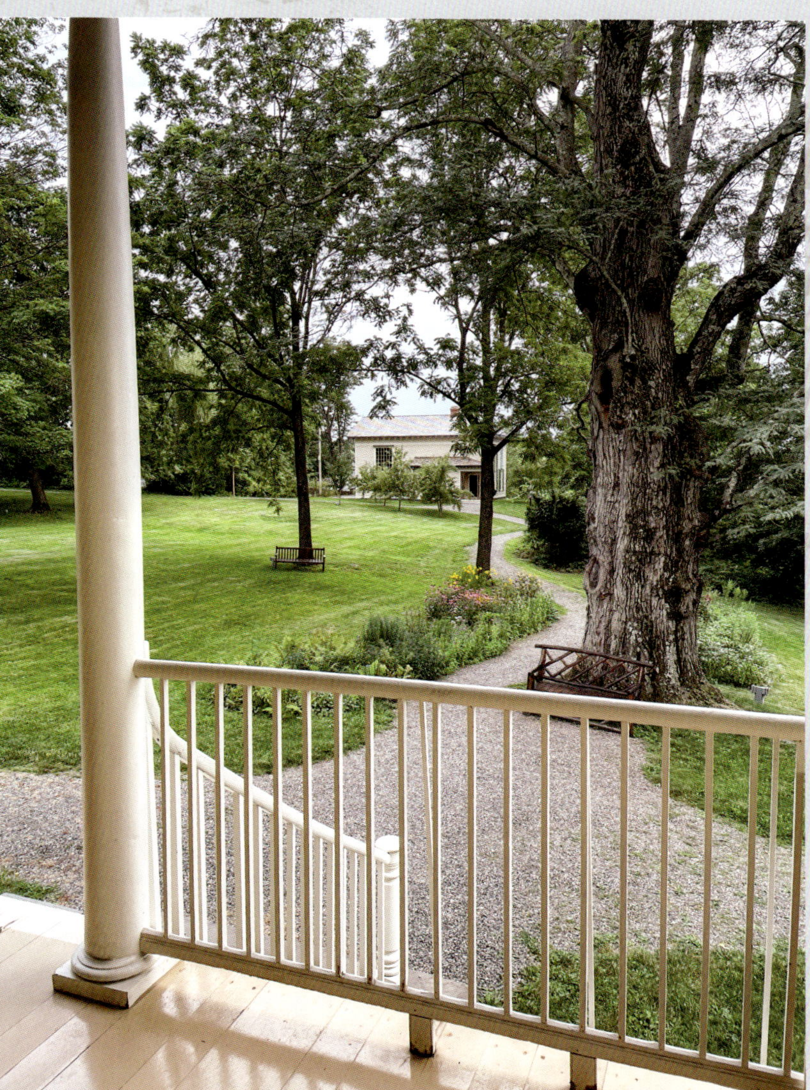

Fig. 3: View from the porch of Thomas Cole's house to the New Studio. Photograph by editor, 2023.

V. Reforming / History

If the isolation of nature into a “preserve” only pushes development and pollution somewhere else—somewhere deemed less special—a similar thing can be said about history. The establishment of a place as historic can have the effect of making everything around it nonhistoric, and thus up for grabs. The act of historic preservation can also divide the landscape in two.

Potentially, the physical and institutional transformation of Cedar Grove into the Thomas Cole National Historic Site could at once isolate it from its local context and help transform that context. Such changes may not be the institution’s intention, but it would also be beyond its control. The economic and social changes happening up and down the Hudson Valley, i.e., its gentrification, are the results of a myriad of factors. Still, TCNHS could exacerbate and accelerate them by reinforcing the division between history and everyday life.

Importantly, it is distinctly *not* doing this. Its vision of preservation and restoration and history is an inclusive one. Recent curatorial efforts foreground the presence of the many until now marginalized actors and agents who envisioned, occupied, built, and maintained the buildings and landscapes of Cedar Grove. Instead of creating a nostalgic image of an unchanging, pristine, and aestheticized world, it is exposing and highlighting the intersection of different worlds. This is happening in the displays within the main house, but also in the contemporary exhibitions it curates and the research it sponsors.[12] In other words, it is focusing on the history of the site, not its myth.

This means telling a series of individual stories about the many people who had contact with the site. Stories that include those of the sisters, servants, and slaves of the men who owned Cedar Grove and made it famous. This means locating the construction of the Main House within a network of settler colonialism, slavery, and industrialization, as this is where the capital for its creation came from.[13] In addition to actively taking part in triangular trade, Cole’s in-laws, the Thomsons, managed ferry and cargo ships on the Hudson, and invested in railroads that would link Catskill to the rest of the region (figure 2).[14]

In short, the Thomson family’s business dealings were in direct conflict with Cole’s stated position on the relationship between nature and commerce. Yet he lived under their roof.[15] How to account for this? Was he a hypocrite, benefiting from practices he otherwise maligned? Was he a pragmatist, working to change minds from inside a place of privilege? Was his presentation of a pure landscape an attempt to reconcile these contradictions at the level of myth? Or did he compartmentalize these contradictions? Did the presence of these forces in his daily life inspire him to create a vision of the future where both worlds could exist, but in isolation from one another?

These are relevant questions. Answering them exposes one to the risk of nostalgia—that is, the risk of presenting a past that we long to expose but cannot be completely sure ever happened. Some histories are hard to prove. They lack enough artifactual and archival evidence. Describing them requires speculative narratives and leaps of scholarly interpretation to complement the facts at hand. They require fiction—not as a lie but as a synthetic narrative that links fragmented facts with one another.[16] The need for such stories suggests that undermining an entrenched myth cannot be achieved simply by exposing the truth. It might also require the establishment of a new myth.

The inclusive history being done at the TCNHS is based on facts found in textual and physical archives. Bringing these facts to life has generated a new set of stories about Cedar Grove, and has produced questions about Cole's relationship to it and its environs. These narratives not only present an expanded notion of the past, but, like Cole's work, they come with a longing for a different, more diverse, and just future. Call them speculative nostalgias, that is, a *future anterior* that may or may not come to pass.

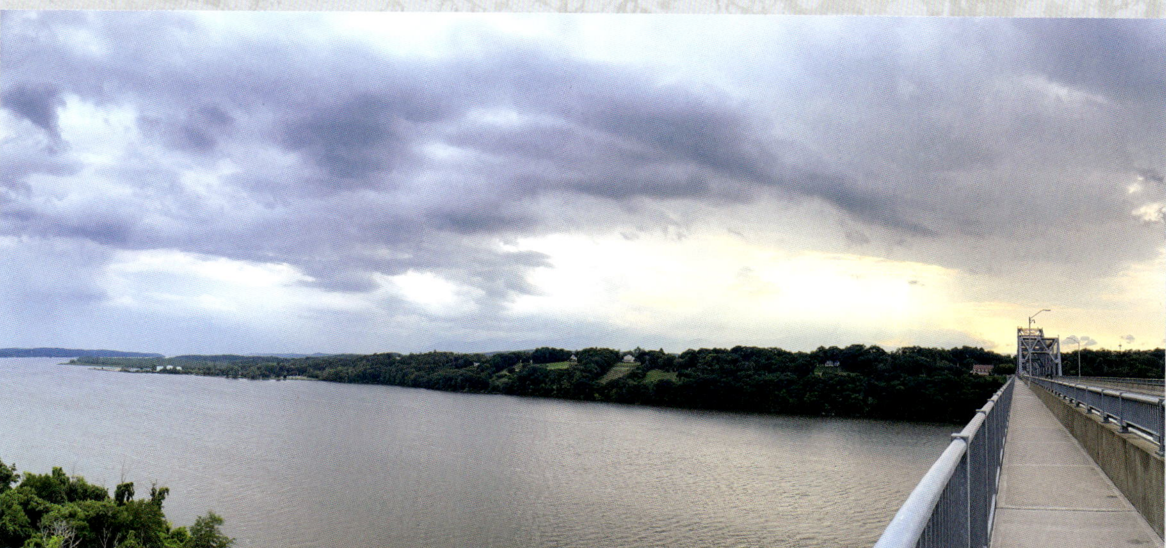

Fig. 4: View from the Rip Van Winkle Bridge toward the oil tanks and Catskill Mountains beyond. Photograph by editor, 2023.

VI. Transforming / Architecture

The TCNHS engages preservation, restoration, and transformation simultaneously. It has preserved the Main House. It has restored the Old Studio and rebuilt the New Studio. It has restored the place of the many women and men who lived with Cole at Cedar Grove. It has transformed the site into a thriving contemporary cultural institution, one engaged in the production and dissemination of knowledge. Its openness and willingness to entertain change is manifested in the curatorial efforts that bring new voices and sensibilities and histories onto the site. Voices from the past and voices from the present. In doing so it does something rare—it simultaneously celebrates and critiques the same thing. It at once champions Cole, Cedar Grove, and their legacies, and it prods its strengths and weaknesses.

One could say the same about the three main buildings at the TCNHS, namely, the Main House, and the Old and New Studios (figure 3). They are significant for who owned, used, and built them. They are not the "best" examples of architecture from their era. As such they have been renovated, rebuilt, and repurposed both by Cole and by TCNHS.[17] This willingness to change things, to not keep things as sacred, and the general tension between preservation and transformation is also present in the designs produced for a new gallery on the site made by second-year students from Rensselaer's School of Architecture. Their proposals would transform the site, some quite dramatically. Some proposals are humbly tucked along the northern or eastern edge of the site. Some dig into the ground and have an almost geological presence on the western edge of the site. Others are more aggressive. Some take over the "quad" between the three main buildings on the grounds. Some are tall belvederes that create new viewing portals. None attempt to mimic the architecture currently there. Or, if they do, it is via their scale not their style. In general, the work, like the histories being done there, is focused on mining the past to create a very different future.

All the projects speak to the individuality of their creators. Each student is searching for their own design voice within the context of their peers, the structure and history of the discipline, and contemporary environmental and social concerns. This is one goal of a design education. Taken as a whole, the variety of solutions echoes the many different voices that have, are, and will be present on this site. They also ask the speculative question: how would transforming the physical site of the TCNHS influence what histories and myths could be told, and how would it change their telling?

VII. Multiple Futures

Over the years, I visited Hudson and its environs less and less. We'd go for group birthday parties in February. We camped in the Catskills once or twice. We took trips in October to see the leaves, pick the apples, and visit our cousins. We visited friends from another part of our lives. Some things haven't changed, many things have. The mountains are still there. The trains still run up the river. The oil tanks in Catskill still get filled. The banks of the Hudson are still strewn with harbors, bridges, quarries, power lines, and power plants. Some are in operation and some are in ruin. Despite the cafes, galleries, and real estate prices, poverty persists in Hudson and Catskill; class and racial divides remain easy to recognize.

Thomas Cole also wanted some things to change and some things to stay the same. He wanted our understanding and use of the landscape to change. He wanted power to stay in the hands of the elites.[18] The changes his paintings depict may look ancient, but in fact they helped to create a new era, an age where managed wilderness and laissez-faire development were to be productively isolated from one another.[19]

Perhaps this is why the presence of those oil tanks along the banks of the river, the bridge that soars above them, and the sound of the cars and trains continue to draw my attention (figure 4). They disrupt the image (both literally and figuratively) of the landscape as a human-free zone. They break the rules of isolation by competing for our aesthetic attention. They are not quite integrated with their surroundings, but they don't quite undermine the overall picturesque effect. They are not subtle, but they are not like the toxic sublime sites one finds elsewhere along the river.[20] They don't follow the aesthetic or isolationist script. They are something else. They have a different sensibility—call it an everyday monumentality, a concept that might also describe the work being done at the TCNHS.

The tanks are particularly intriguing. It is hard to imagine anyone fighting to preserve them. One of them has already been removed. They are not a part of the golden age of Catskill when tourists and painters disembarked on its landings to explore the nearby wilderness. They are part of another story, the story of the river, of the landscape, as an infrastructural point within the large network of resource extraction and exchange. They are part of a story many would like to terminate and forget.

The history of where those tanks sit is complex. They are located in the part of Catskill where an Indigenous settlement stood before it was "purchased" by Dutch settlers. It is the place where Henry Hudson was said to have landed and met these people. They sit at the mouth of Catskill Creek, Cole's favorite place to walk and sketch and paint. It is the place where passenger and cargo ships docked. Well, not exactly. The tanks actually sit on landfill that extended the bank of the river out to a small island. It is a relatively new, artificial landscape.

A 2009 revitalization plan for Catskill would have them removed to create a purely recreational zone.[21] The tanks, like other more obvious monuments to settler colonialism, could be dismantled in the name of a cleaner environment and a decolonized history. And yet, their presence does disrupt the (past and future) vision of the site as pure. Like the stories of women, slaves, and freed Blacks being incorporated into the history of the TCNHS, should these tanks be included in the living history of Catskill? As long as they remain, they deny the reading of the landscape as either one thing or another, as either wild or spoiled. Such unseemly and unwanted disruptions seem necessary to remind us that history is present. Of course, these objects are also part of my own story, they contribute to my own nostalgia. I am not an impartial judge. When it comes to history, memory, and myth, who is?

1 For an introduction to the TCNHS, see United States National Park Service, *Thomas Cole National Historic Site General Management Plan and Environmental Assessment*, 2004 (Boston, MA: National Park Service, Northeast Region, Park Planning & Special Studies Division, 2004), https://purl.fdlp.gov/GPO/LPS54769; see also https://thomascole.org/.

2 Sophie Lynford, "Idyllic and Industrial Visions: Thomas Cole, William Guy Wall, and the Hudson River," in T. J. Barringer and Gillian Forrester, *Picturesque and Sublime: Thomas Cole's Trans-Atlantic Inheritance* (Catskill, NY: Thomas Cole National Historic Site; New Haven, CT: Yale University Press, 2018), 66–81; Alan Wallach, "Thomas Cole's River in the Catskills as Antipastoral," *Art Bulletin* 84 (June 2002): 334–50; William Coleman, "Painting the 'Baronial Castle': Thomas Cole at Featherston Park," *Huntington Library Quarterly* 80, no. 4 (Winter 2017): 635–65.

3 The Cole Fellowship Program has done much work to open the lens on this topic, see the "2023 Cole Research Scholars Presentations" (April 15, 2023), https://www.youtube.com/watch?v=uZwN-vOyOkw, made by Beth Wynne, Kristen Marchetti, and Sofia Thieu D'Amico. For a complete list of topics and presentations done in the program, see https://thomascole.org/fellowships/.

4 Bruno Latour, *We Have Never Been Modern* (Cambridge, MA: Harvard University Press, 1992).

5 "Catskill, N.Y.: A Place Where 'People Are Jazzed About Making Art,'" *New York Times* (May 18, 2022), https://www.nytimes.com/2022/05/18/realestate/catskill-ny-a-place-where-people-are-jazzed-about-making-art.html.

6 Lynford, "Idyllic and Industrial Visions"; Wallach, "Thomas Cole's River"; Tzu-I Chung, "Frontier Exceptionalism: The Representation of Nature and Race in Thomas Cole's Art and PBS's Frontier House," *Tamkang Review: A Quarterly of Literary and Cultural Studies* 39 (December 1, 2008): 67–94, https://discovery-ebsco-com.proxy.library.cornell.edu/linkprocessor/plink?id=84bdc19e-e541-3d03-9b0f-45c819356f5f.

7 Roland Barthes, *Mythologies* (New York: Noonday Press, 1972), 70.

8 Lynford, "Idyllic and Industrial Visions"; Wallach, "Thomas Cole's River."

9 Thomas Cole, "Essay on American Scenery," *American Monthly Magazine* 1 (January 1836), retrieved from https://thomascole.org/wp-content/uploads/Essay-on-American-Scenery.pdf.

10 Lynford, "Idyllic and Industrial Visions."

11 William Cronon, "The Trouble with Wilderness: Or, Getting Back to the Wrong Nature," *Environmental History* 1 (January 1996): 7–28.

12 See note 3 above: Thomas Cole National Historic Site, "Programs and Events," http://thomascole.org/events/.

13 Beth Wynne, "Cedar Grove Foundations: Demerara Exploits and Catskill Beginnings," talk given at 2023 Cole Research Scholars Presentations (April 15, 2023), https://www.youtube.com/watch?v=uZwN-vOyOkw. Slaves lived with the Thomson family in Catskill before Cole arrived. The archive is unclear about Cole's view on slavery and Black lives).

14 Kenneth W. Maddox, "Thomas Cole and the Railroad: Gentle Maledictions," *Archives of American Art Journal* 30, no. 1 (1990): 146–54; New York State Archives Digital Collection, *John A. Thomson Papers*, https://digitalcollections.archives.nysed.gov/index.php/Detail/collections/71.

15 William Coleman, "Painting the 'Baronial Castle': Thomas Cole at Featherston Park," *Huntington Library Quarterly* 80, no. 4 (2017): 635–65; Lynford, "Idyllic and Industrial Visions"; Wallach, "Thomas Cole's River."

16 Zoë Anne Laks, "Projecting a Nostalgic Future: Nostalgia as Time Machine," *Cinémas* 29 (Summer 2022): 33–51, https://id.erudit.org/iderudit/1079803ar.

17 William L. Coleman, "From Villa to Studio: Thomas Cole's Drawings for Cedar Grove," *Bulletin of the Detroit Institute of Arts* 90, no. 4 (2016): 16–31.

18 Ross Barrett, "Violent Prophecies: Thomas Cole, Republican Aesthetics, and the Political Jeremiad" *American Art* 27 (March 2013): 24–49; Wallach, "Thomas Cole's River"; Coleman, "Painting"; William L. Coleman, *Something of an Architect: Thomas Cole and the Country House Ideal* (PhD diss., UC Berkeley, 2015), https://discovery-ebsco-com.proxy.library.cornell.edu/linkprocessor/plink?id=07668794-dc9d-3f20-a184-1333e83a3706.

19 William Cronon, "The Trouble with Wilderness: Or, Getting Back to the Wrong Nature," *Environmental History* 1 (January 1996): 7–28.

20 The Center for Land Use Interpretation, "A Trip up the Hudson: From the Battery to Troy," https://clui.org/projects/more-programs-projects/river-points-interest-hudson/a-journey-hudson-river-battery-troy.

21 Greene County, "Village of Catskill Downtown and Waterfront Revitalization Plan," 2009, https://www.greenegovernment.com/departments/planning-and-economic-development/planning/downtown-plan.

A Meditation on Thomas Cole: Breaking Ground

Cathryn Dwyre-Perry

Somewhere among the wastes of the World, is the key that will bring us back to our Earth and to our freedom.
Thomas Pynchon, *Gravity's Rainbow*

Thomas Cole, the celebrated American landscape painter and founder of the Hudson River School of painting, was an immigrant. In 1818, at the age of seventeen, he arrived with his family from Bolton, Lancashire, in northwestern England, part of a trend of economic refugees from the craft and skilled trades in Europe. The still relatively recent invention of the steam engine and consequent automation left skilled tradespeople, makers, and artisans out of gainful employment. He was also a millennial child, a creative with drawing and pattern-making skills, an outsider to the US, and eventually, a man of great ambition. We can imagine that for his first seventeen years of life, Cole had a front-row seat to the massive and rapid effects of industrialization on urban and rural England—what was in effect a dramatic reshuffling of cities and landscape.

Recent urban exodus has put new value on a "return to nature." During the COVID-19 pandemic, 33,394[1] people relocated to the Hudson River Valley from New York City, many in search of a simpler life. It feels more relevant than ever to consider a historic homestead such as Cole's Cedar Grove, an artist's prospect that was established just as the United States had broken free of the Crown, and unbeknownst to itself, was careening into a new geological epoch of our own making.[2] Close to the Hudson River and characterized by its orientation toward the western prospect of the Catskill Mountains, how the Bartow family came to own and work this land is a microcosm of the United States' first institutions of private property, from a colonial land grant in 1684, to a subdivision in 1773.

In his approach to landscape painting, Cole used some of the most relevant contemporary tools of today's architectural and landscape designers, including spatial imagination of atmosphere,[3] and development of a uniquely referential language, but perhaps most relevant to our current moment, the capacity to tell an urgent story[4] about the future, foretold from a cautionary tale of "progress." Where he was troubled by the loss of wilderness in the nineteenth century, in the twenty-first we are troubled by the possible obliteration of *Homo sapiens* by either climate change or artificial intelligence. At the time of writing in the summer of 2023, Earth is experiencing a heat wave gripping three continents, what the US special envoy for climate called "a threat to all of humankind," just two weeks after scientists recorded Earth's hottest days in recorded history.[5] The climate refugee is now a common newcomer to the Hudson Valley region, from California expats fleeing forest fires, to Arizona retirees escaping from melting pavement. One way in which many of us collectively deal with this doom is a reappraisal of how we live, and for many, this means relocation.

As the steam engine proliferated across Europe in the eighteenth century, England was also undergoing its first shift toward parliamentary democracy alongside the accelerated privatization of previously common lands through "enclosure,"[6] a dissonant pairing of newly public discourse alongside newly private land resources. This precipitous loss of commons also destroyed the "concrete collective intelligence attached to these commons" on which people depended.[7] With hindsight, we now know that this period was also a global geological crux, shifting from one epoch to another (in this case, from the *Holocene* to the yet-to-be-officially-announced *Anthropocene*). Globally, scientists have registered the massive shift in atmospheric carbon produced by the steam engine and by the extraction and burning of fossil fuel that powered the Industrial Revolution. In short, the geologic record of the eighteenth century itself registers the evidence of the barbarous effects of capitalism, which is why the new epoch is alternately and frequently referred to as the *Capitalocene*.[8]

Nostalgia for "nature" was congealing into a style while untouched territory was becoming increasingly rare. As the existing contours of unimproved land vanished, so too did the human experience of the landscape *as it was*. Nostalgia can, if wielded as a manipulative device, facilitate the demise of precisely that which it is appreciating. An unfortunate example of this is Cole's painting *Scene from "The Last of the Mohicans," Cora Kneeling at the Feet of Tamenund.* Painted one year after the popular book was published in 1826, it had the effect of reifying an already very well-known story in which Indigenous Americans die off "as nature would have it, with the 'last Mohican' handing the continent over to Hawkeye, the nativized settler, his adopted son."[9] James Fenimore Cooper's fictional tale was taken as fact, creating a devastatingly false impression that Indigenous people were already a part of America's past. In actuality, the Indigenous population at the turn of the century was approximately six hundred thousand, down from estimates of between one and ten million pre-European contact,[10] but the success of this novel signaled that they'd already been excluded "from the process of formation of American society and culture."[11]

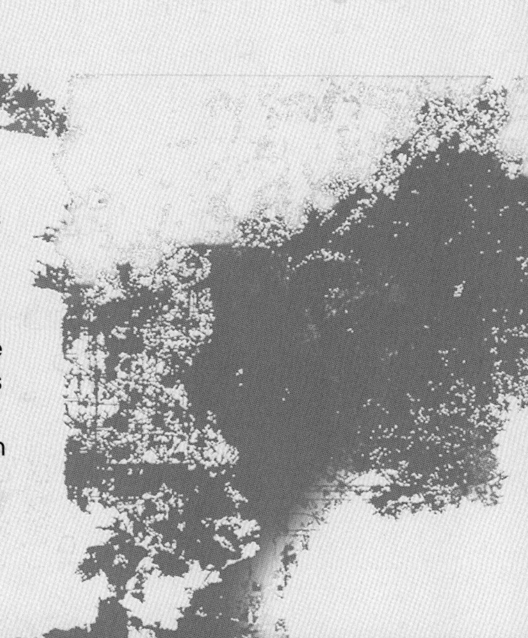

It's a cyclical tale. A sense of impending loss, and in this case, looming cultural and ecologic trauma, drives nostalgia for that which is vanishing. In the social media universe, we are haunted by photographic histories and reminders of time's strange coils with algorithmic predictability. This is all evidence of the human imperative to capture, whether through portraiture (which is how Cole started out), landscape painting that omitted or altered "modern" elements (like the train), or, in a new bend in the time loop altogether, the twentieth-century photographic documentation of the ruins of nineteenth- and twentieth-century industrialization and the space race, including Edward Burtynsky, Lynn Davis, and Richard Misrach, among others. These photographers engage in zero nostalgia, but rather, show us the world-as-it-is, and in effect produce meditations on the ruins of culture. In particular, Davis's *Space Project* captures both their contraband nature as well as the fickleness of perception and memory. She recounts, "Often I found myself in front of an amazing structure when I would be informed that what I was looking at didn't exist, which was a way of saying, 'Do not under any circumstances photograph this forbidden site.'" Burtynsky's photograph *Salt River Pima-Maricopa Indian Reservation/Suburb* reveals a stark comparison of land-based practices between the suburban and Indigenous Americans in one of the most arid places in the United States. The image forces us to consider whether we, too, might be caught in a maze of our own creation.

When Cole arrived in America in 1818, settler colonialism and its tactics, from unlimited warfare to land grants, had advanced the Jeffersonian objective of pushing Indigenous peoples west of the Mississippi. These actions also drove wealth generation for the few through agrarian and capital-based land practices. The Scots-Irish and other European settlers were falsely promised land in exchange for their barbarism against Indigenous Americans, yet rarely benefited from their citizen army deployments. In an echo of the poor, uneducated white Republicans of 2023 who support Trump yet have seen little material change to their circumstances, the populism of Jackson, despite his two terms in office, resulted in very few landless settlers acquiring land themselves.

It was just eighteen years after Cole's arrival in the United States that he wrote his "Essay on American Scenery." We can presume that he witnessed many changes to the land, specifically ecosystem loss, evidenced by his early painting *Lake with Dead Trees*. It troubled him deeply that this acceleration of "progress" was already leading toward the consumption of the natural world. As an outsider from industrial England where the rampaging forces of industry were decades ahead of the United States, he had perspective on what was coming. In the concluding section to his essay, he says morosely, "I cannot but express my sorrow that the beauty of such landscapes are quickly passing away—the ravages of the axe are daily increasing—the most noble scenes

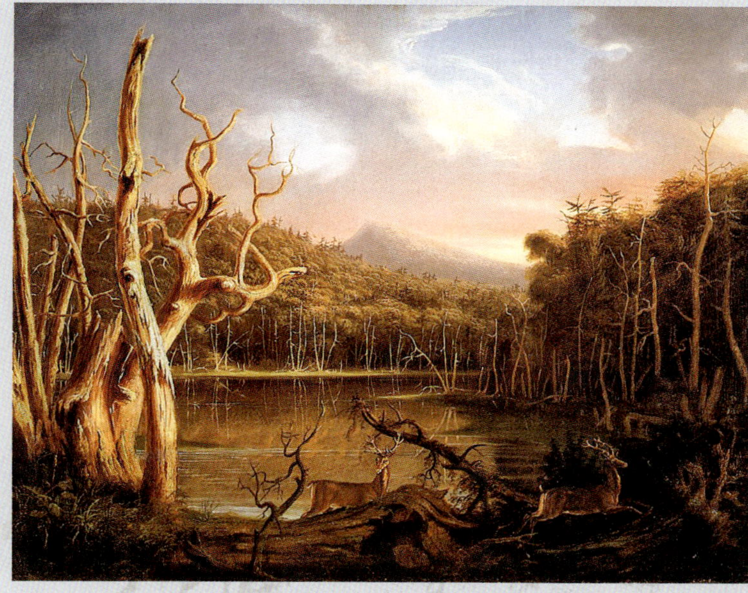

Fig. 1 Thomas Cole, *Lake with Dead Trees*, 1825. Oil on canvas, 27 x 33 in. Allen Memorial Art Museum, Gift of Charles F. Olney, 1904.1183. The painting's Eastern Hemlocks (*Tsuga canadensis*) have been denuded of their bark, harvested for the tanning of leather. In the 19th century, 64 tanneries were operating in the Catskills and 70 million hemlock trees were harvested for their bark. The Nature Conservancy's first preserve, the Mianus River Gorge is a hemlock-hardwood forest and home to 350-year-old *Tsuga canadensis*; this valuable native forest ecology is yet still threatened.

are made desolate, and oftentimes with a wantonness and barbarism scarcely credible in a civilized nation. The wayside is becoming shade-less, and another generation will behold spots, now rife with beauty, desecrated by what is called improvement."[12] And so it goes that the *scenery*, much like nostalgia itself, is rendered increasingly thin.

The new modern ideal characterizing Cole's coming of age, across politics and landscape thinking, despite its apparent barbarism driven by the "ravages of the axe," called for a radically more balanced relationship with context. In politics, this manifested as democratic ideals in America, a transition to parliamentary democracy in England, and in landscape, if not actually a productive balance with ecology, topography, and hydrology, the *appearance* of it. This new ideal was one in which "nature was no longer subservient to (hu)man(s), but a friendly and equal partner in landscape design," according to Sir Geoffrey Jellicoe, an ambassador for the art of landscape and the subconscious in its design.

So then what is the significance, in Cole's famous essay, often cited as representative of his environmentalism, of the word "scenery" to talk about environment? The word, according to the Oxford English Dictionary, first comes into use around the turn of the eighteenth century. Initially, it referred to the synopsis of the plot of a play, and within a few years, in 1707, it encompassed something more spatial, so, the actual setting in which a play takes place, a built set, furniture, painted backdrops, etc. It was another ten or so years before the word registered as a landscape idea *per se*, defined as "the features of a place, landscape, or view considered in terms of their appearance or attractiveness, e.g., picturesque natural landscapes." The use of *scenery* for landscape was not coincidentally coming into some form of feverish use while picturesque theory is being actively debated and written. Any way you think about this idea, it suggests a landscape that has been "designed" for human experience and perception. And the act of framing a landscape, whether by a human eye, artist's canvas, the god's-eye view, the house window or the camera lens, was called upon to value specific qualities of environment.

Among other things, the phrase reveals a view of environment as a construction or invention (and particularly during this period, "evidence" of God's creation)—a richly ornamented setting for the human drama. This lush yet ultimately fixed scenography, a kind of living, growing landscape painting, was a guiding principle of Frederick Law Olmsted and others at the time, that the (designed) experience of "nature" was essential psychological and spiritual medicine. This mode of talking about the natural world, a world in which humans are one small and recent species inhabitant, as *scenery*, vexes the contemporary ear. The linguistic distancing trick sets up a disjunction not unlike the boundary between a stage and an audience, placing the human as spectator rather than *inside and part of the environment in which we are enmeshed*. This separation of human from environment is also likely an undesired effect of Cole's sublime agenda. Rather than raising awareness about the imperative to protect natural resources, the massively distancing effect of the sublime can stop us in our tracks, and in effect, well short of the kind of probing questions that are demanded of the present-day collapse in human-Earth relations.

If Cole's sublime, and the Romantic literary pieces it sometimes illustrated, aimed to convey warnings about natural destruction, it framed ecological destruction through longing for a past natural balance never to be recovered. That environmental upheavals brought about by human exploitation should be paralleled with outbursts of violent weather reinforced their association as two sorts of interventions over which present viewers would have no influence or control. Ecologist and writer Aaron Ellison summarized this aspect in an essay by stressing that "the suffocating embrace of romantically-infused notions of landscape has cut humans off from nature and from the world."[13]

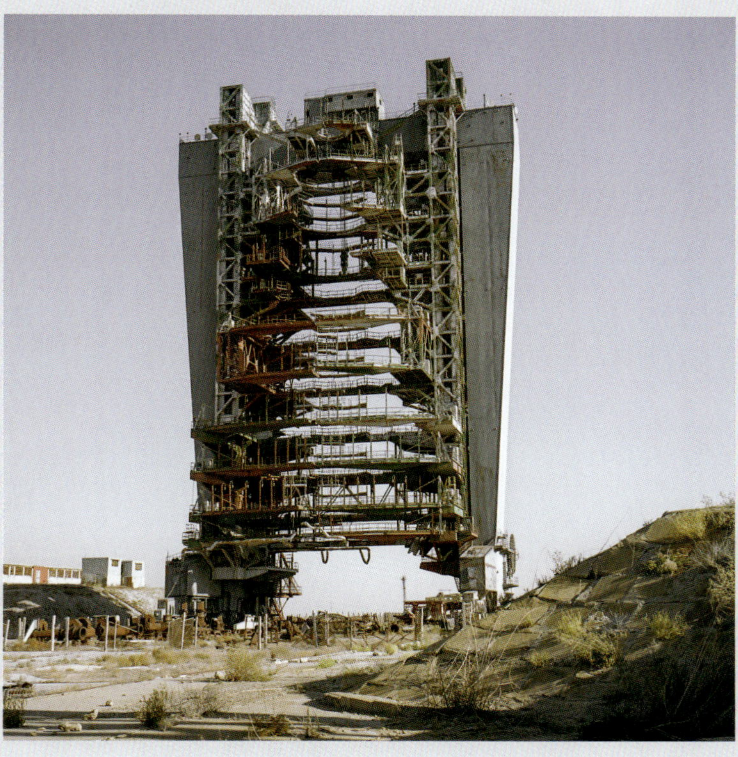

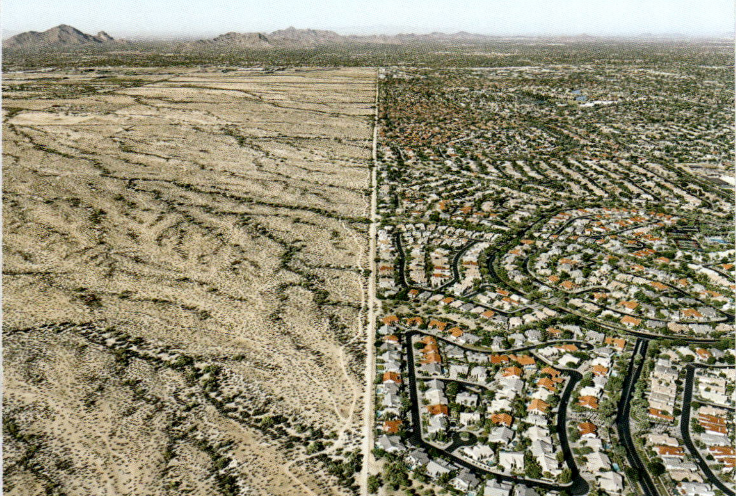

Fig. 2 Lynn Davis, *Baikonur Cosmodrome*, Kazakhstan, 2005. Photograph. *Launch platform: Abandoned Launch Site*. The world's largest launch site, Baikonur, reveals a tug-of war between the Earth and space. Alongside present launches one can find rusting techno-detritus of the Soviet-Russian space program slowly being reclaimed by steppe vegetation.

Fig. 3 Edward Burtynsky, *Salt River Pima-Maricopa Indian Reservation*, Scottsdale, Arizona, U.S.A., 2011. This landscape is a conspicuous example of territory-making and terraforming in an arid desert suffering from ongoing and worsening drought.

Cole's mode of appreciation for "wild nature" was itself "an invention of the late eighteenth century, of the Romantics—and more specifically, an invention of people who lived in cities."[14] The prevalence of writing and pictures about *scenery* in the eighteenth and nineteenth centuries was built on the back of another ultimately nefarious word with multiple layers of significance—*improvement*. The philosophical basis for *improvement* was laid down by Sir Francis Bacon in the previous century, and "his goal of making nature subservient to human needs was at its heart."[15] The idea of improvement also drove the enclosure movement in England, in the name of agrarian "progress." Cole wrote about reorganization of land in England critically as "when a meager utilitarianism seems ready to absorb every feeling and sentiment, and when what is sometimes called improvement in its march makes us fear that the bright and tender flowers of the imagination shall all be crushed beneath its iron tramp."[16] He understood firsthand that "improvement" was a contradictory term.

During midcareer study travel in France and Italy, Cole became fascinated by how great civilizations rose and fell and believed that industry would be responsible for the decline of his own "new" landscape of North America. His early years in industrial England had set the stage both for escapist retreat into the comparative wilderness of the United States, as well as a certain feeling of urgency to document it before it vanished. Increasingly, "Cole foresaw inevitable doom for the republic, as with Rome before it."[17] In part, this sense of impending cataclysm propelled him to paint epic narrative scenes and narrative series with recognizable symbols as a form of mass communication, a fair warning about greed and consumption, particularly of the land. These ideals also presented a dilemma and consequent compromise; Cole had an ongoing need for patrons and very relatable money problems. In most cases, those patrons were active accelerators of industrialization and the denuding of landscape, and he knew it. Unlike his acclaimed student Frederic Church just across the Hudson River at Olana in Hudson, he didn't have his own generational wealth to fall back on.

None of this stopped him from producing potentially uncomfortable paintings. Cole's *River in the Catskills* depicted the train weaving through a pastoral landscape, and it failed to sell. *Lake with Dead Trees* of 1825, an early work that led to his "discovery" as a talent, depicted the denuded native Eastern Hemlock (*Tsuga canadensis*) trees, stripped of their bark, which had been harvested *en masse* and boiled for the local tannery industry. As a result, along the Hudson River Valley, this once thriving native ecology was decimated in a short time period. And then his 1843 painting *Catskill Mountain House: The Four Elements*, deploys a kind of extreme weather sublime reminiscent of J.M.W. Turner, whom Cole admired. This painting is not only a meditation on extreme weather but also a moratorium on the

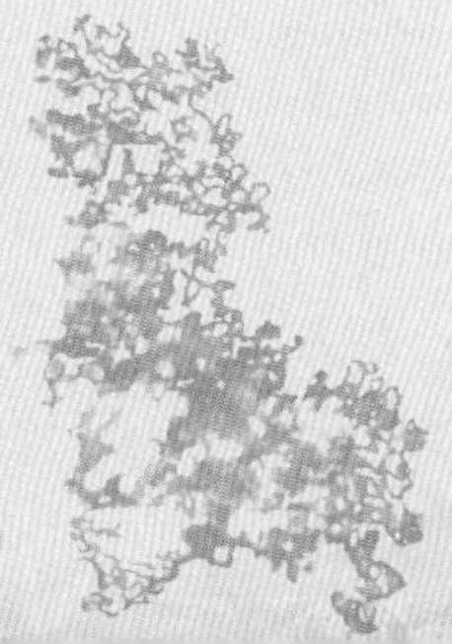

irresponsible consumption of land brought by the tourist industry and a potent prophecy given the recent tragic destruction of Maui. Each painting in its own way asks us to pay attention to the effects of capitalism on landscape and ecology. These scenes also remind us of Cole's poem *The Lament of the Forest*, itself bemoaning the smoke rising through the trees, but "even as Cole laments, he does not lose faith. If anything, he seems ever more intent on summoning the power of art to pass judgment on the world around it."[18]

As tastes were changing toward the end of his life, Cole's work had begun falling out of favor in preference for the more "truthful" works (as opposed to the allegoric and imaginary) espoused by John Ruskin. One of the main precepts of Ruskinian theory was that a landscape could only possess "vital truth" when it simultaneously conveys information about its past, present, and future, as well as a kind of scientific veracity. This interest in truthfulness to nature, as well as multiple temporal consciousness, predicts the significant role of twentieth-century American photography[19]—replacing painting as the dominant fine art landscape medium—most notably for those with an environmental agenda.

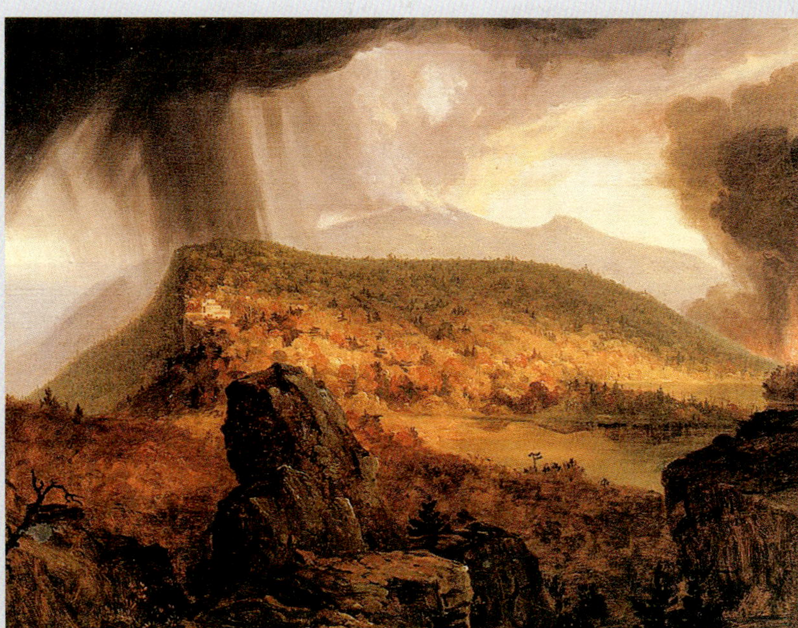

Fig. 4 Thomas Cole, *Catskill Mountain House: The Four Elements*, 1843. Oil on canvas. Private Collection. A meditation on extreme weather as well as a moratorium on the irresponsible consumption of land brought by the tourist industry.

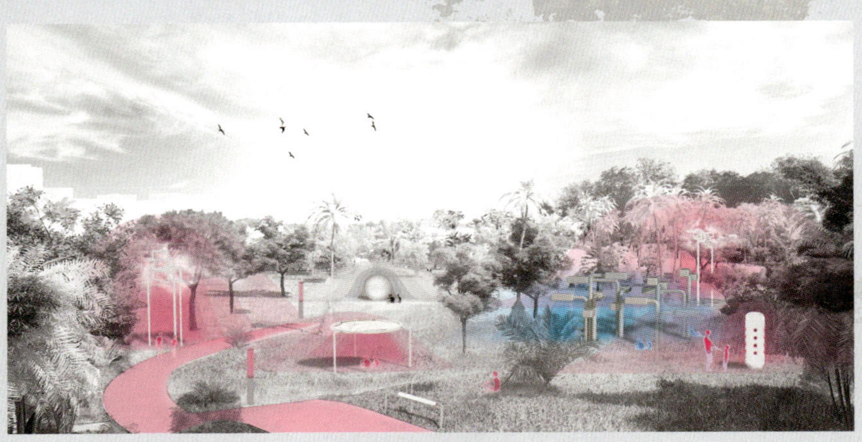

Fig. 5 Philippe Rahm architectes, mosbach paysagistes, Ricky Liu & Associates, *Central Park*, Taichung, Taiwan. *Central Park* is an example of architecture deploying spatial imagination in the production of atmosphere with micro-climate devices, niche plantings, and infrastructural earth and water works.

Certain landscape themes persist throughout the modes and centuries of art history, and one of the most conspicuous is the use of ruin as an activist device of meaning. The ruin in its various forms asks us to consider the passage of time and the questionable results of humans' long (and short!—it's all relative—*Homo sapiens* have been around for only 0.007% percent of the entire history of the planet) durational changes to the planet, whether the temples of Rome or the lithium mines of the twenty-first century. Americans may have always had a taste for ruin imagery, even before they had architectural ruins of their own. The popularity of Cole's ambitious allegorical series *The Course of Empire* indicated that Americans were captivated by its story of decline, an ominous tale of the likely pitfalls ahead for Jacksonian democracy and a civilization that viewed nature solely as a vehicle through which to acquire wealth. One might suggest that twentieth-century photographers built on the legacy of Cole and others by turning "a cold eye on the pastoral imagery of ruins (making) visible the entropic narrative of industrial civilization, compelling us to contemplate ruins as the detritus left behind in the headlong, at times reckless, rush to the future that otherwise drives our culture."[20]

Any American ruin of the twenty-first century grapples with the extent of environmental destruction and appropriation of land resources toward the accumulation of wealth in the name of "progress." Despite the seemingly inclusive ideals of democracy, it has never systematically provided a voice for the land itself upon which it was built, the Rights of Nature, much less the Indigenous Americans who occupied this land for thousands of years before the arrival of Europeans.[21]

Few early settlers' hands were clean in the process of securing and working land, and Maria Bartow's family were no exception. The Federal-style house at Cedar Grove in which they lived together from 1833 until his death in 1848 was built in 1815 by a group of people that likely included enslaved laborers. Sandy Thomson, Maria's uncle and owner, enslaved people from at least 1790 until 1820, when they were eventually freed through gradual emancipation.

On the one hand, the COVID-19 pandemic instigated urban exodus around the country. Another trend saw the proliferation of farm-like houses, mostly in America's subdivisions. This recent excerpt from the *New York Times* about the country's most popular new building style, *Modern Farmhouse*, relates:

> *Now, at a moment when populism has taken hold amid deep political divisions, the style of the day is one that imagines a romanticized and fantastical agrarian past—a real farmhouse doesn't have a walk-in shower with a waterfall showerhead or a sliding barn door to hide a well-appointed laundry room with a weathered placard that says, "wash and dry." As the country grapples with existential questions about its identity and its future, the house of choice makes you think about spinning wool into yarn.*

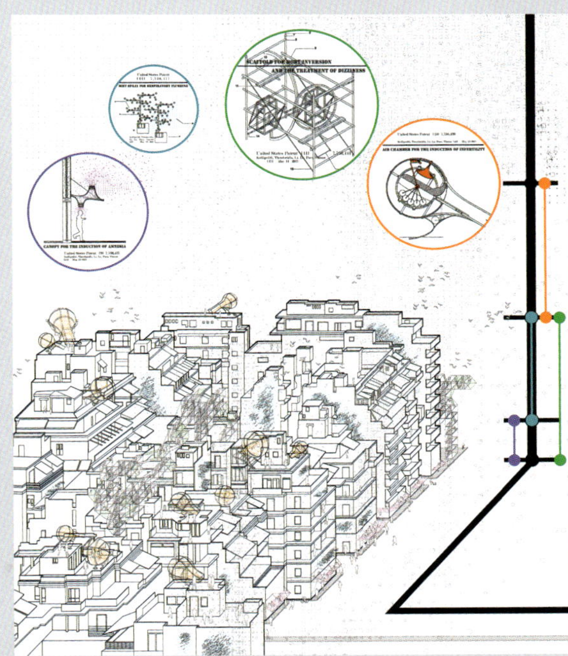

Fig. 6 Lydia Kallipoliti and Andreas Theodoridis, *Air Shake*, 2017. An example of contemporary architects using atmosphere as their 'material', *Air Shake* designs with predicted 2027 air pollutants in Athens, Greece to imagine an array of future diseases and cures.

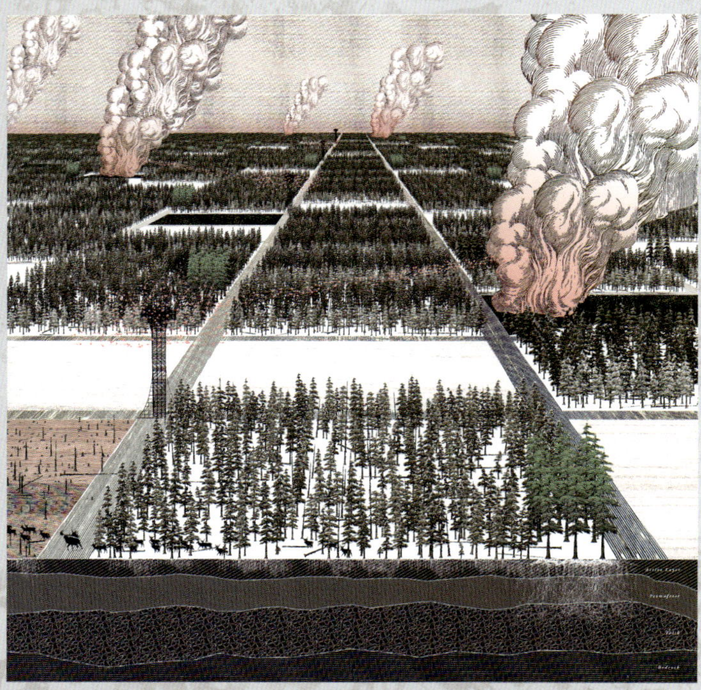

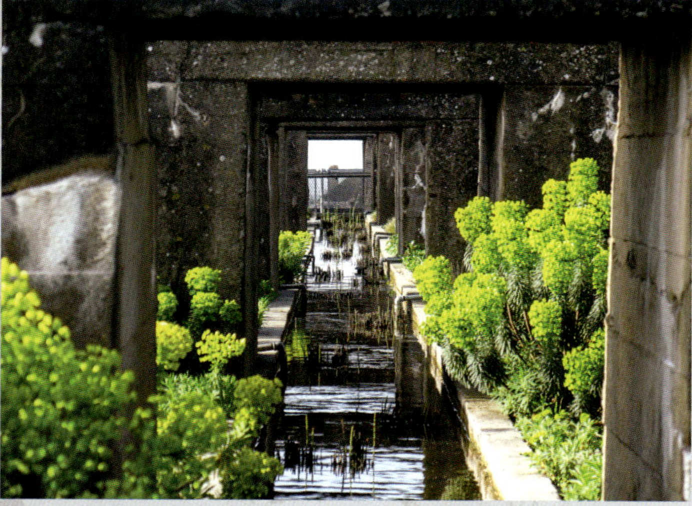

Fig. 7 Design Earth (Rania Ghosn and El Hadi Jazairy), *The Planet After Geoengineeering*, 2021. Design Earth is a research practice that produces speculative architecture through storytelling, ultimately to raise public awareness about the climate crisis. Their work, *The Planet After Geoengineering* explores geoengineering as planetary management through five visual narratives. Conceived as a series of sectional drawings, the project explores a continuum between deep earth and outer space.

Fig. 8 Gilles Clement's *Tiers Paysage Jardin*. Saint Nazaire, France, ongoing. Photograph by Meryl Septier. Clement planted here minimally, allowing the vegetal kingdom to self-seed through a combination of birds and wind, producing a vibrant hybrid ecology from both intent and chance in an otherwise dejected landscape.

It may be useful to consider this pseudo-farmhouse a ruin of the real one, like the one worthy of preservation, Cedar Grove. This is the kind of "ruin relationship" set up by Rebecca Solnit in her seminal book *The Ruins of Memory*, about San Francisco's ongoing reshaping by humans, interrupted catastrophically by recurrent earthquakes as a powerful agent of chaos. Solnit's theory of ruination suggests that Amazon is a ruin of the independent bookstore. Following this line of thought, the modern farmhouse might well be a *ruin of the actual one*, in which barn doors are for appearances (and humans) only, and little is being farmed beyond the lawn.

The kind of nostalgia that generates something like this modern farmhouse is a bit of a trap. This new style is just that, a style, and in its imitative gestures, fails to carry with it the land ethics and productive problems of an actual farmhouse. This trap is one to which Cole himself fell prey. Even when he intended to make a strong moralizing commentary on so-called improvement and environmental destruction by incorporating the train into a painting, it was done with such a delicate and pastoral hand that the train appears to seamlessly complete the scene in *River in the Catskills*, rather than rending it asunder.

Whether romanticizing on one hand or moralizing on the other, each presents a bit of a communication dilemma. Most experience happens in the ambiguity of mediated space, leaving designers facing a predicament not unlike the one Cole confronted. Given the scale and expense of most architectural and landscape projects, especially public works, constraints such as capital and the needs of the client impose limits on the creative process. Yet the seat of these two disciplines is traditionally shaped in academic design studios that encourage students to experiment widely, question, and rethink everything. It's typical to spend a semester (and sometimes two), exploring an avenue: concept development, experimentation, critical questions, program and site, how design might arise from site ecology and generally, through long-duration research, modeling, and drawing, how an idea might take hold in the ground in a meaningful way. All of this suggests a privileging of site-specific concepts as an essential springboard to explore the discursive side of design practice. At the same time, upon graduation, the expectation is that the educated professional will ultimately provide what in many cases is a problem-solving service in the context of professional practice, a mode of working often removed from the conceptual springboard. While this might feel out of sync with its academic counterpart, a few rare practices manage the simultaneous sponsorship of wild experimentation within a context of professional production.

Similarly, Cole's work wrestled with the competing functions of, on the one hand, pleasing patrons with irresistible new work, while on the other, deeply investing in societal critique as another kind of "service" which contributed to a larger discussion of nature and culture. In this way, Cole's practice, like that of architectural and landscape architectural design studios, aims to navigate the constraints of a professional service and the stuff it produces, while sponsoring invention of thought and deed. Regardless of the context, asking critical questions is essential to the practice of each.

For architectural and landscape architectural education, such critical questioning includes asking what experiences are being facilitated by works of design, on the spectrum from fulfilling basic needs, to creating public contexts, or spaces of monastic retreat? And what would it mean to do no harm to the land? To be light on the land, and use minimal engineering and impact, or even just *a bit less*? Americans in particular are not known for their ability to tread lightly upon the ground.[22] This reflection and critique may be the most important of all, and what climate action might look like for contemporary designers. If an architect consulted with a permaculture specialist on breaking ground, they'd advise "*Wait one year.*" Live on-site, observe its seasons, materials, ecologies, species, and light. Not only are we called upon to understand the character of a place itself, its contours, its geology and species diversity, but also its human history and, specifically in the United States, its settler colonial legacy; the way it's been worked (or not) and the ways in which it might come to heal from a tough past of misuse or other dark engagements.

Once we "break ground" or "level the site" we are engaged in an act of destruction, however controlled and conscious. The building process itself initiates a kind of first-order ruin, of the site ecologies and existing logics. The sister site(s) from which the materials are extracted, whether wood, stone, or glass, are yet another and lead to further questions, for instance, what would it mean to locally source architecture? Asking such questions may be in its own way a form of climate action, both a way to work and state of mind while deliberating the prospect of breaking ground.

Embracing these ideals suggests a need to re-evaluate how we organize ourselves relative to land resources. Isabelle Stengers looks at user movements with a small measure of optimism regarding how we move forward. She observes that "those who unite around a 'common,' a river or a forest, with the ambition of thwarting the sinister diagnosis of the 'tragedy of the commons'" have a tendency to succeed.[23] After all, it is common knowledge that none of us, no matter how self-reliant we may be, can survive alone for an extended period of time. The functions of architecture and landscape architecture will always include spaces of collectivity, eating and sleeping, land and food cultivation but surely it's much more than this. And here again we can take a cue from Cole; a great work of contemporary design, like one of Cole's paintings, asks us to think, see, and inhabit the world a little bit differently.

1 Statistics come from an article by John Jordan published on July 18, 2022, in www.realestateindepth.com.

2 The "Anthropocene" is a term widely used since its coining by Paul Crutzen and Eugene Stoermer in 2000 to denote the present geological time interval, in which many conditions and processes on Earth are profoundly altered by human impact, which has intensified significantly since the onset of industrialization, taking us out of the Holocene epoch that postdates the last glaciation. See http://quaternary.stratigraphy.org/working-groups/anthropocene/.

3 Experimental practices such as those of Sean Lally, Francois Roche, and Phillippe Rahm explore the immaterial of atmosphere and climate as the "material" of design. A 2022 exhibition at The Clark Art Institute entitled *On the Horizon: Art and Atmosphere in the Nineteenth Century* highlighted the previous century's attempts at depicting the invisible.

4 Design Earth is a research practice founded by Rania Ghosn and El Hadi Jazairy that deploys urgent storytelling to sound the alarm for the frailty of *Homo sapiens*, using the medium of a speculative architectural project to make public the climate crisis.

5 Alan Yuhas, "Heat Waves Grip 3 Continents as Climate Change Warms Earth," *New York Times* (July 18, 2023), updated 4:12 p.m.

6 Between 1760 and 1870, about seven million acres (about one-sixth the area of England) were changed, by some four thousand acts of Parliament, from common land to enclosed land. Many considered this outright theft. G. Slater, "Historical Outline of Land Ownership in England," in The Land, The Report of the Land Enquiry Committee (London: Hodder and Stoughton, 1913).

7 Isabelle Stengers, *In Catastrophic Times: Resisting the Coming Barbarism* (Open Humanities Press and Meson Press, 2015), 84.

8 The term "Capitalocene" was originated by Andreas Malm. It is a counterproposal for the geologic name of our current epoch (Anthropocene) and connects the world-economy to the world-ecology and seeks to understand human relations of power, production, and environment-making in, and in relation to, the web of life.

9 Roxanne Dunbar-Ortiz, *An Indigenous People's History of the United States* (Boston: Beacon Press, 2014), 104.

10 J. David Hacker and Michael R. Haines, "American Indian Mortality in the Late Nineteenth Century: The Impact of Federal Assimilation Policies on a Vulnerable Population," *Annales de Demographie Historique*, no. 110 (2005/2): 1.

11 Ibid., 104. Historian Francis Jennings describes US exceptionalism relative to the Indigenous in the origin stories of the "new" country.

12 Thomas Cole, "Essay on American Scenery," *American Monthly Magazine* 1 (January 1836): 12.

13 Thomas Busciglio-Ritter, "Behold the White Storm," *Antennae: The Journal of Nature in Visual Culture* 60 (2022/3): 25.

14 Michael Pollan, "Beyond Wilderness and Lawn," *Harvard Design Magazine* 4 (Winter/Spring 1998).

15 Vittoria di Palma, *Wasteland: A History* (New Haven, CT: Yale University Press, 2014), 46.

16 Cole, "Essay on American Scenery."

17 Alexandra Wolfe, "A New Way of Seeing Artist Thomas Cole," Wall Street Journal (January 12, 2018). A quote from Tim Barringer, co-author of "Thomas Cole and the Aesthetics of Landscape," in *Picturesque and Sublime: Thomas Cole's Trans-Atlantic Inheritance* (New Haven, CT: Yale University Press, 2018).

18 Tim Barringer and Jennifer Raab, "An Inheritance in Print: Thomas Cole and the Aesthetics of Landscape," in *Picturesque and Sublime: Thomas Cole's Trans-Atlantic Inheritance* (Thomas Cole National Historic Site in association with Yale University Press, 2018), 44.

19 "Americans may have begun by imagining and perhaps yearning for ruins, as part of a romantic nostalgia in the nineteenth century...it was the function of photography in the twentieth century to turn a cold eye on the pastoral imagery of ruins," from Miles Orvell, "America in Ruins: Photography as Cultural Narrative," *American Art* 29, no. 1 (Spring 2015): 14.

20 Miles Orvell, "America in Ruins: Photography as Cultural Narrative," *American Art* 29, no. 1 (Spring 2015).

21 "Rights of Nature (RoN) is a legal instrument that enables nature, wholly or partly, i.e., ecosystems or species, to have inherent rights and legally should have the same protection as people and corporations; that ecosystems and species have legal rights to exist, thrive and regenerate. It enables the defense of the environment in court—not only for the benefit of people, but for the sake of nature itself." From IPBES, the Intergovernmental Science Policy Platform on Biodiversity and Ecosystem Services.

22 "Americans have never trodden lightly on the land. We want to leave our mark. We are not shy. When we erect a missile silo in a cornfield, it assumes the mythic grandeur of a Mayan pyramid. There is nothing more spectacular, more monstrous – and more truly American—than Mount Rushmore." Witold Rybczynski, "Really, Really Big," introductory essay to *American Monument*, by Lynn Davis (New York: Monacelli Press, 2004), vii.

23 Stengers, *In Catastrophic Times*, 87.

Thomas Cole's Built Landscape

William L. Coleman

On February 21, 1837, Theodore Allen wrote to the prominent American landscape painter Thomas Cole (1801–1848) with a request: "If all goes well with me, I may want in the course of the summer a plan for a country residence. And as you have succeeded so well in your architecture, I venture to tax one of your leisure hours if you have any."[1] Allen, the son-in-law of Cole's most important patron of the period, Luman Reed, proceeded to list the dimensions of rooms he had in mind and to sketch the proposed site in Hyde Park, New York, along with a possible floor plan, in the hope that the artist could do a better job than the best "my poor head can produce." While no reply from Cole has surfaced, this episode is tantalizing evidence that this now canonical artist was a serious and skilled student of architecture, and that he was known in particular for his attention to the question of how best to live in the country.

On the occasion of the response of a rising generation of architects from Rensselaer to the possibilities of Thomas Cole's domestic environment, once known as Cedar Grove and now the Thomas Cole National Historic Site, we have an opportunity to reflect on the ways in which Cole's legacy is uniquely suited to such a project. In his painting practice, we find an artist who was especially attuned to the built environment, and to the idea of houses as the essential building blocks for a nation that was very young and fragile in his lifetime. The fact that he even enjoyed some success in the practice of architecture in a period when amateurism was the norm, before the standardization of the rigorous training these students have received, lends further significance to this exciting initiative. All evidence indicates that Cole recognized the power of architecture as the most public of the arts, and that he would have been thrilled by the original designs which follow in this book.

Thomas Cole, commonly called "the father of the Hudson River School," or even "the father of American landscape," was born in Lancashire in 1801, and immigrated with his family to the United States at the age of seventeen.[2] After only rudimentary training and preliminary efforts as an itinerant portrait painter in Ohio, a group of landscape paintings he displayed in New York in the fall of 1825 found favor with an influential group of artists and writers, thereby launching his career.[3] This young art-world star went on to fame for poetic visions of the meeting of wilderness and civilization like *View from Mount Holyoke, Northampton, Massachusetts, after a Thunderstorm—The Oxbow* (1836, Metropolitan Museum of Art); and learned allegorical cycles like *The Course of Empire* (1833–1836, New-York Historical Society) and *The Voyage of Life* (1839–1840 first version, Munson). Architecture is key to these allegories and becomes the explicit subject in *The Architect's Dream* (1840, Toledo Museum of Art) (figure 1).

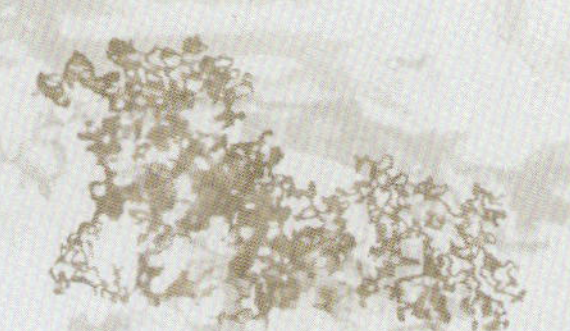

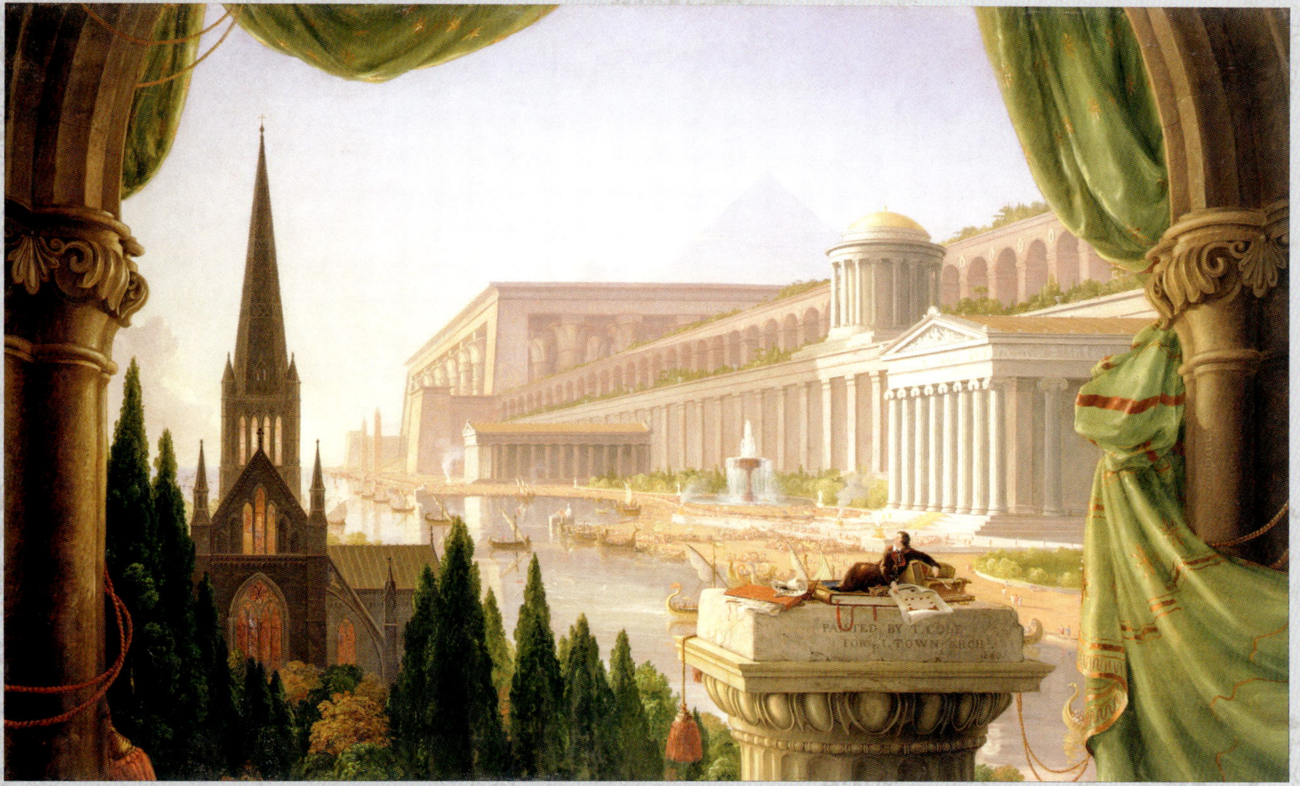

Fig. 1 Thomas Cole, Architect's Dream, 1840. Oil on canvas, 54 x 84 in. Toledo Museum of Art, Purchased with funds from the Florence Scott Libbey Bequest in Memory of her Father, Maurice A. Scott, 1949.162.

This remarkable canvas lays out a vision of architectural possibilities, and makes a statement about the breadth of the artist's own studies of the subject from Egyptian to Greek and Gothic. Moreover, it includes traces of at least two built projects to which Cole contributed: the Ohio Statehouse (in the cupola at right) and St. Luke's Church in Catskill, New York (which bears a strong resemblance to the church at left) in this supposed fantasy painting.[4] In the words of Reverend Louis Legrand Noble, Cole's pastor and first biographer: "Profound in all the science necessary to be an accomplished builder he was not. To be so he had neither time nor occasion. But in all that raises architecture from mere science to an art he was a very fine architect."[5]

Of the many times Cole painted real or fictive houses in the landscape, the story of the first landscape painting commission he received stands out for the ways it crystallizes some of the issues that were central to his short but productive and exceedingly influential career before his early death at the age of forty-seven in 1848. Shortly after his 1825 moment of discovery, Cole received an invitation to spend the winter of 1825–1826 near Schenectady at "Featherston Park," the 1,500-acre estate of George William Featherstonhaugh, a pioneering agriculturalist and railroad entrepreneur. There, Cole painted views of the stately mansion in its setting in exchange for room, board, and a small stipend.[6] The house at the center of these expansive grounds was a grandiose wood-frame structure, vaguely Palladian in style, so large that one friend of Featherstonhaugh jestingly called it his "Baronial Castle."[7] That this early project required him to engage with the form and meaning of a country house is significant; it would be one of many times he did so over the course of his career, and it was an exercise that contributed to the artist's thinking about how he might design a country house of his own, a preoccupation throughout his life.

Of the three surviving canvases Cole made for Featherstonhaugh, the most accomplished illustrates the challenges the artist's house portraits present.[8] *Landscape, the Seat of Mr. Featherstonhaugh in the Distance* (figure 2) at first appears to have much in common with other of his early landscapes. The basic components and composition are typical of his work, including foreground animals and dead trees, water in the middle distance, and dense forests in the back ground. However, the "country seat" included in the title changed considerably the resonance of this view: Cole reduced the massive house to a tiny speck of white, silhouetted against distant, misty hills and illuminated by a beam of sunlight, precisely painted, and significant despite the structure's diminutive size. Dark clouds whirl past overhead, dappling the foreground with shadows, and a flock of sheep graze amid boulders and blasted stumps, while one gnarled tree that clings to life rises nearly to the top of the canvas.

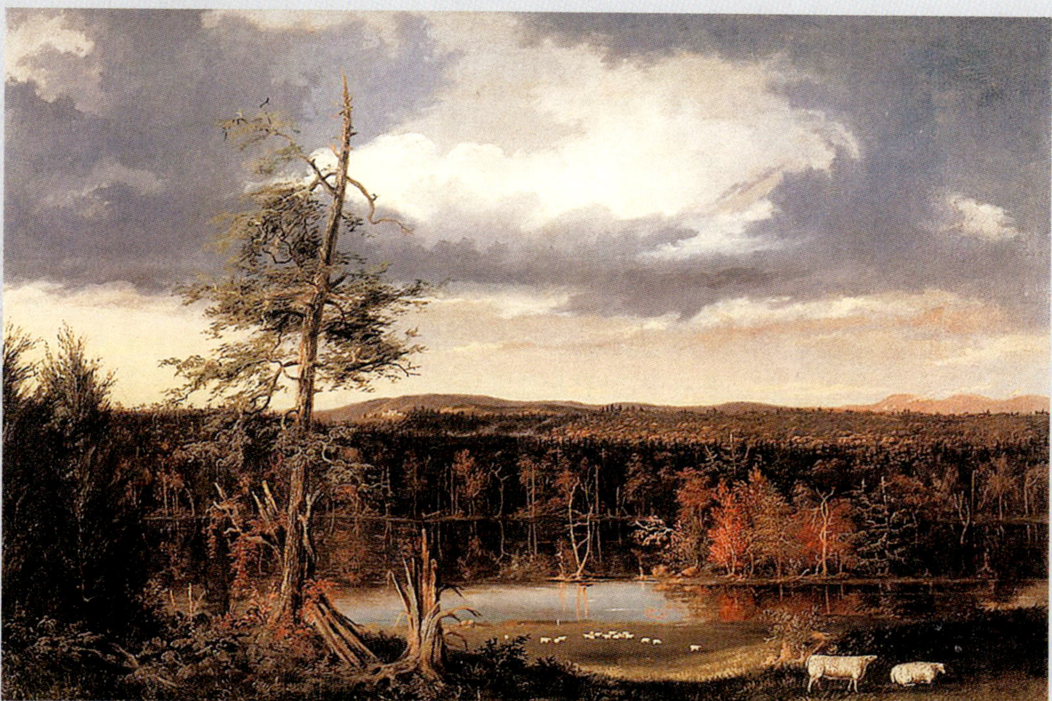

Fig. 2 Thomas Cole, Landscape, *The Seat of Mr. Featherstonhaugh in the Distance*, 1826. Oil on canvas, 33 x 48 in. Philadelphia Museum of Art, 125th Anniversary Acquisition. Gift of the McNeil Americana Collection, 2004-115-4.

In this composition, Cole makes some important choices. He immerses the house into its setting in order to naturalize it and make a more satisfying landscape painting and, second, depicts the estate as a place of virtuous democratic citizenship rather than self-satisfied luxury by foregrounding the industrious spirit of inquiry and improvement that allowed Featherstonhaugh's private wealth to be considered public-spirited. The house stood out as a beacon of urbanity conveying wisdom and grace to a dark land of writhing stumps and untold dangers, far from the capitals of culture. The rocks visible allude to Featherstonhaugh's role as a pioneering geologist. The products of the sophisticated breeding program on which the reputation of the estate rested, in this case Border Leicester sheep for which Featherstonhaugh gained national recognition, supplant the routine arcadian staffage of most English house portraits. Instead of suggesting dynastic permanence, Featherstonhaugh's "Baronial Castle" blazes white and new on the land, a first trace of a civilization still in the process of being hewn from wilderness. According to Cole's canvas, Featherston Park was the country seat not of an American decadent but of an intellectual leader who put his privilege to use for the good of the nation.

Throughout the years when Cole painted houses in the landscape and traveled to the villas and country houses of Europe, he also developed plans for a country house of his own that would express his taste and attainment. By doing so, the artist consciously participated in a tradition of artists' houses with both American and European precedents. While few of his designs for expressly Italianate construction on his wife's family's property in Catskill, New York, were executed, his plans and elevations are vivid evidence of his concept of the country house ideal in the final decade of his life, his ability as a designer of domestic architecture, and his thwarted ambition to become the social equal of his patrons on the basis of his talent. Considering the surviving drawings for his Italianate villa at Cedar Grove in the context of his house portraiture reveals the ways in which those encounters with three distinctly different modes of country life affected his plans.

Unlike the country houses that were Cole's inspiration, Cedar Grove never belonged to the artist alone. Despite his lofty plans for the site, the potential to realize his architectural ideas there was limited. Although he came to own a few acres of the larger property by the end of his life and worked diligently toward the goal of constructing a villa of his own on that plot, he lived out his days as a tenant in the main house that belonged to his wife's family. Because subsequent artists, including Frederic Edwin Church, Albert Bierstadt, and Jasper Francis Cropsey were inspired by Cole's work at Cedar Grove to build country houses of their own, it is difficult to imagine Cole living with his in-laws and painting in a rustic storeroom, rather than happily ensconced in a private country place that would better befit our notion of "the father of the Hudson River School." The story of Cole's work at Cedar Grove is one of ambition, negotiation, and frustration, and rather less about execution. Only on paper did he realize his dreams of an ideal country house.

Amid national economic upheaval in 1837, Cole came to own two acres at the southern edge of the Cedar Grove property himself.[9] Holding the title to this property inspired him to commence an intensive period of architectural draftsmanship for an elegant country house of his own on the plot. In a letter of October 30, 1839, to a regular correspondent on architectural matters, Cole wrote: "I am about building a house. It will be a sort of Italian looking thing. If times are favourable I expect to finish it next summer."[10] Clearly this was no mere fantasy project if he could speak with such confidence about its completion date, and the sheer number of plans and elevations for new construction on the site, now preserved in the Detroit Institute of Arts, testify to his commitment to the endeavor.[11] While he quickly scaled back his ambition even on paper and never succeeded in constructing the villa he envisioned, what seems to be the first and most

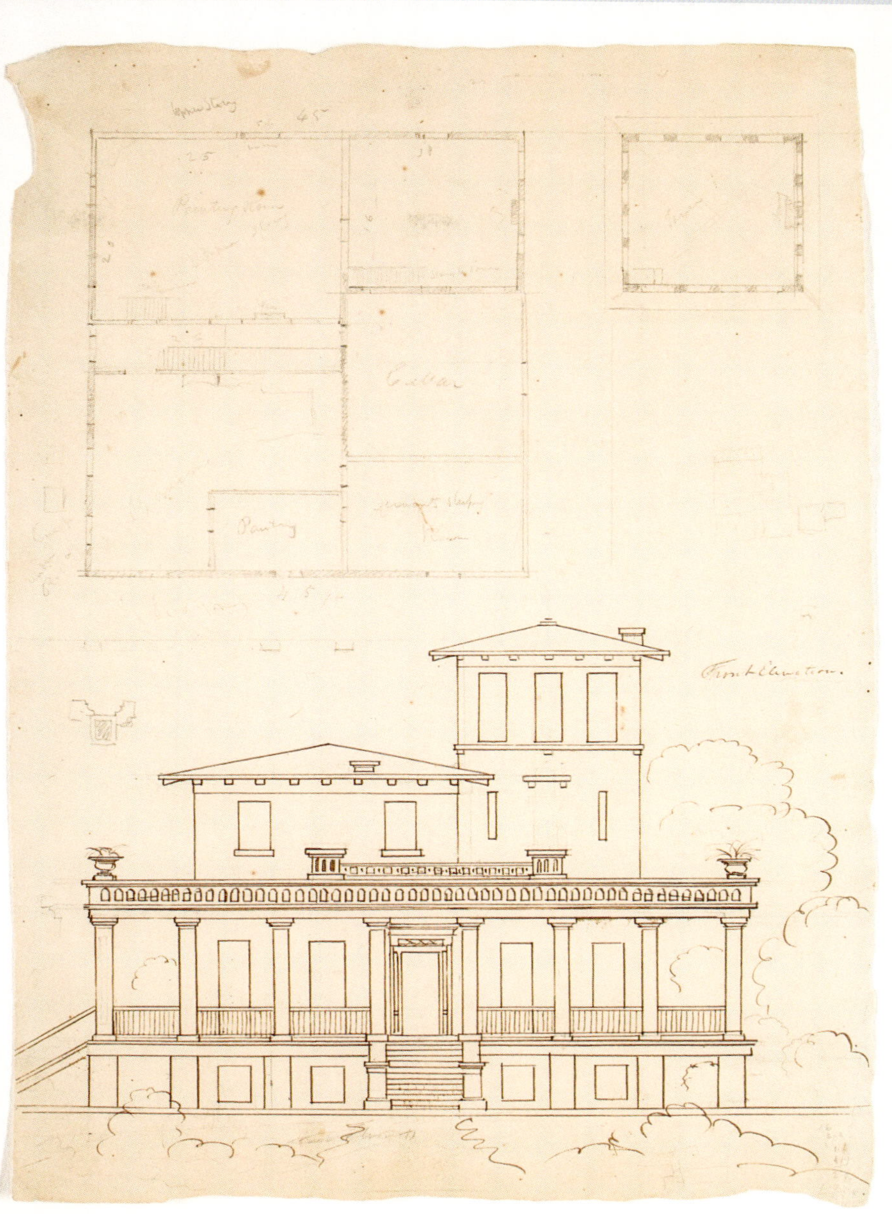

Fig. 3 Thomas Cole, *Front Elevation of Proposed Villa at Catskill*, nineteenth century, pen and brown ink over graphite pencil on beige wove paper. Detroit Institute of Arts, Founders Society Purchase, William H. Murphy Fund, 39.510.

ambitious of his designs is an eloquent document of lessons learned from painting various modes of American country life (figure 3). The broad porch, which wraps fully around the western side of the building to embrace the view of the Catskill Mountains, included an ornate balustrade topped with urns from which plants sprout. On the plan indicated above this elevation, Cole granted himself a generous twenty-by-twenty-five-foot "Painting Room" that took advantage of northern light from an upper story. In a western elevation of the same state of the design, he included a touching vignette of Maria with one of their children in her arms on the porch, enjoying the view from this family home.[12]

While financial realities intervened and made it impossible to build on so grand a scale, in 1846 Cole succeeded in building an outlying studio building that was the only built trace there of his design thinking. He would die just two years later. Cole's earlier vision of a tower commanding a grand view would be realized by his star pupil, the artist Frederic Church, whose 250-acre estate just across the Hudson River is in no small part a tribute to Cole's abiding influence and the role of architecture in his posthumous reputation. The Thomas Cole National Historic Site's reconstruction of the "New Studio," completed in 2016, was an important first step in taking Cole's built legacy seriously, and has continued through exhibitions, publications, and other building efforts. The current creative collaboration with a rising class of architects is an innovative continuation of a rich history. Those of us who treasure the story of this fascinating American painter-architect can only hope that his story lives on through this new generation.

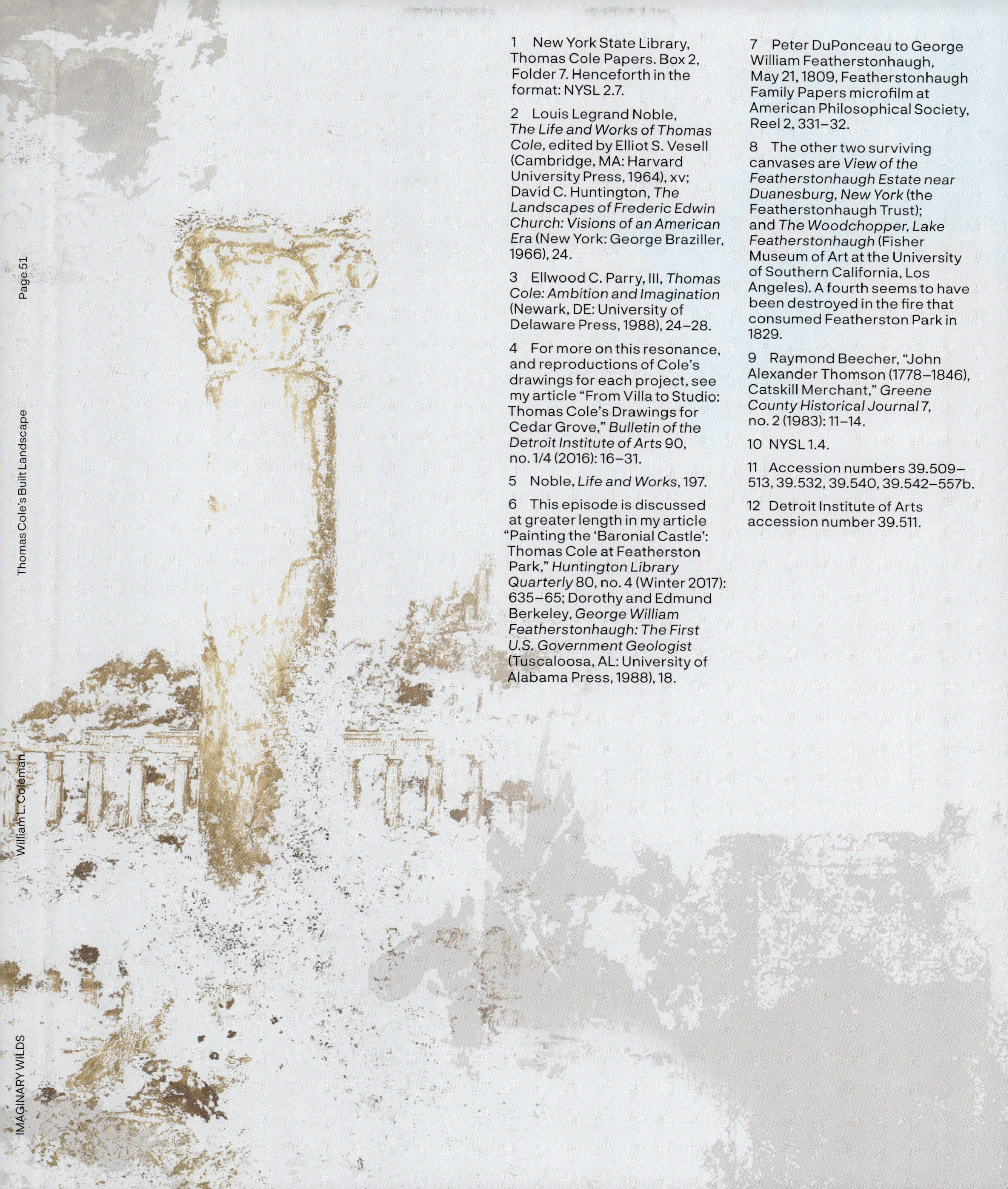

1 New York State Library, Thomas Cole Papers. Box 2, Folder 7. Henceforth in the format: NYSL 2.7.

2 Louis Legrand Noble, *The Life and Works of Thomas Cole*, edited by Elliot S. Vesell (Cambridge, MA: Harvard University Press, 1964), xv; David C. Huntington, *The Landscapes of Frederic Edwin Church: Visions of an American Era* (New York: George Braziller, 1966), 24.

3 Ellwood C. Parry, III, *Thomas Cole: Ambition and Imagination* (Newark, DE: University of Delaware Press, 1988), 24–28.

4 For more on this resonance, and reproductions of Cole's drawings for each project, see my article "From Villa to Studio: Thomas Cole's Drawings for Cedar Grove," *Bulletin of the Detroit Institute of Arts* 90, no. 1/4 (2016): 16–31.

5 Noble, *Life and Works*, 197.

6 This episode is discussed at greater length in my article "Painting the 'Baronial Castle': Thomas Cole at Featherston Park," *Huntington Library Quarterly* 80, no. 4 (Winter 2017): 635–65; Dorothy and Edmund Berkeley, *George William Featherstonhaugh: The First U.S. Government Geologist* (Tuscaloosa, AL: University of Alabama Press, 1988), 18.

7 Peter DuPonceau to George William Featherstonhaugh, May 21, 1809, Featherstonhaugh Family Papers microfilm at American Philosophical Society, Reel 2, 331–32.

8 The other two surviving canvases are *View of the Featherstonhaugh Estate near Duanesburg, New York* (the Featherstonhaugh Trust); and *The Woodchopper, Lake Featherstonhaugh* (Fisher Museum of Art at the University of Southern California, Los Angeles). A fourth seems to have been destroyed in the fire that consumed Featherston Park in 1829.

9 Raymond Beecher, "John Alexander Thomson (1778–1846), Catskill Merchant," *Greene County Historical Journal* 7, no. 2 (1983): 11–14.

10 NYSL 1.4.

11 Accession numbers 39.509–513, 39.532, 39.540, 39.542–557b.

12 Detroit Institute of Arts accession number 39.511.

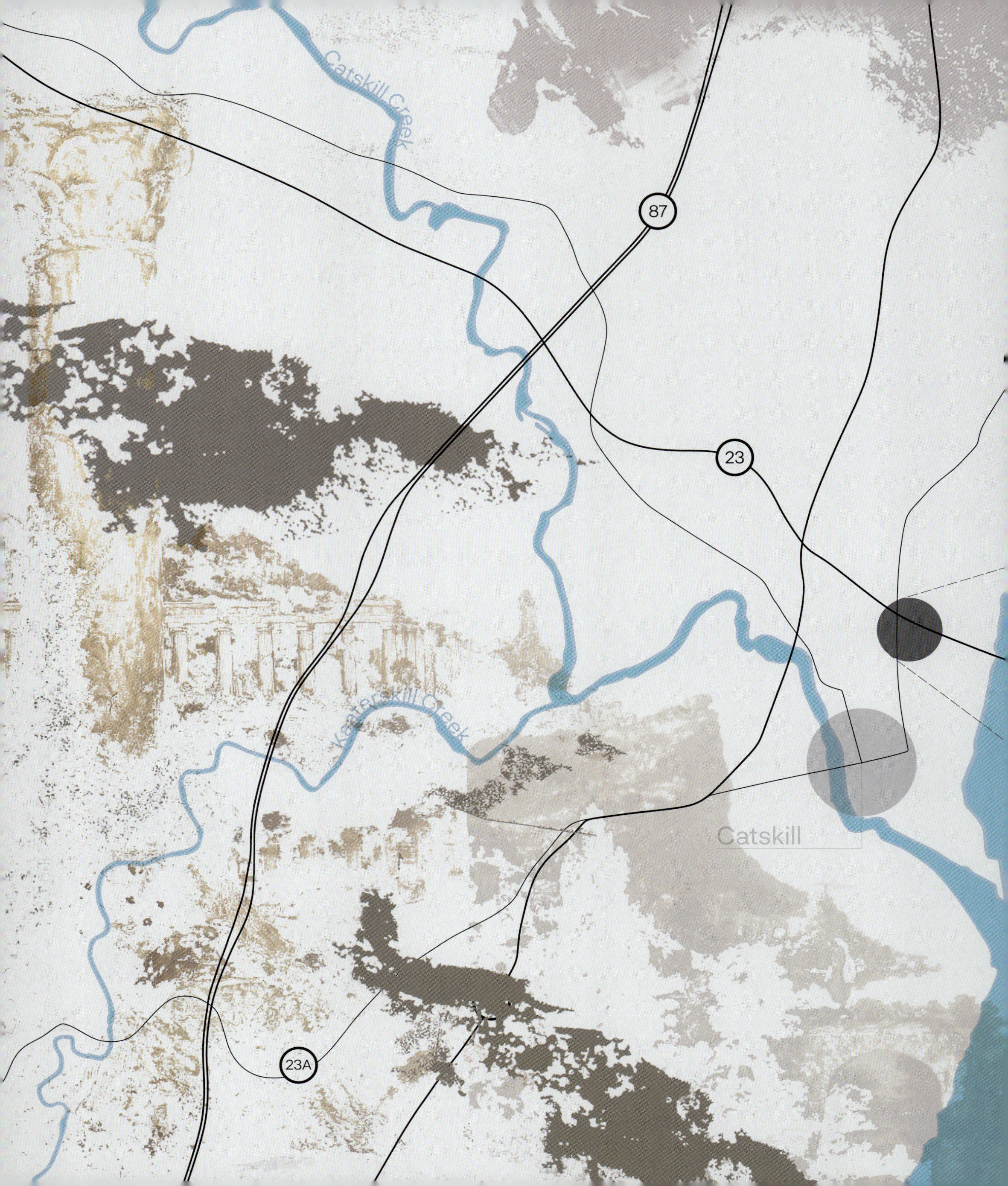
Catskill Creek
87
23
Kaaterskill Creek
Catskill
23A

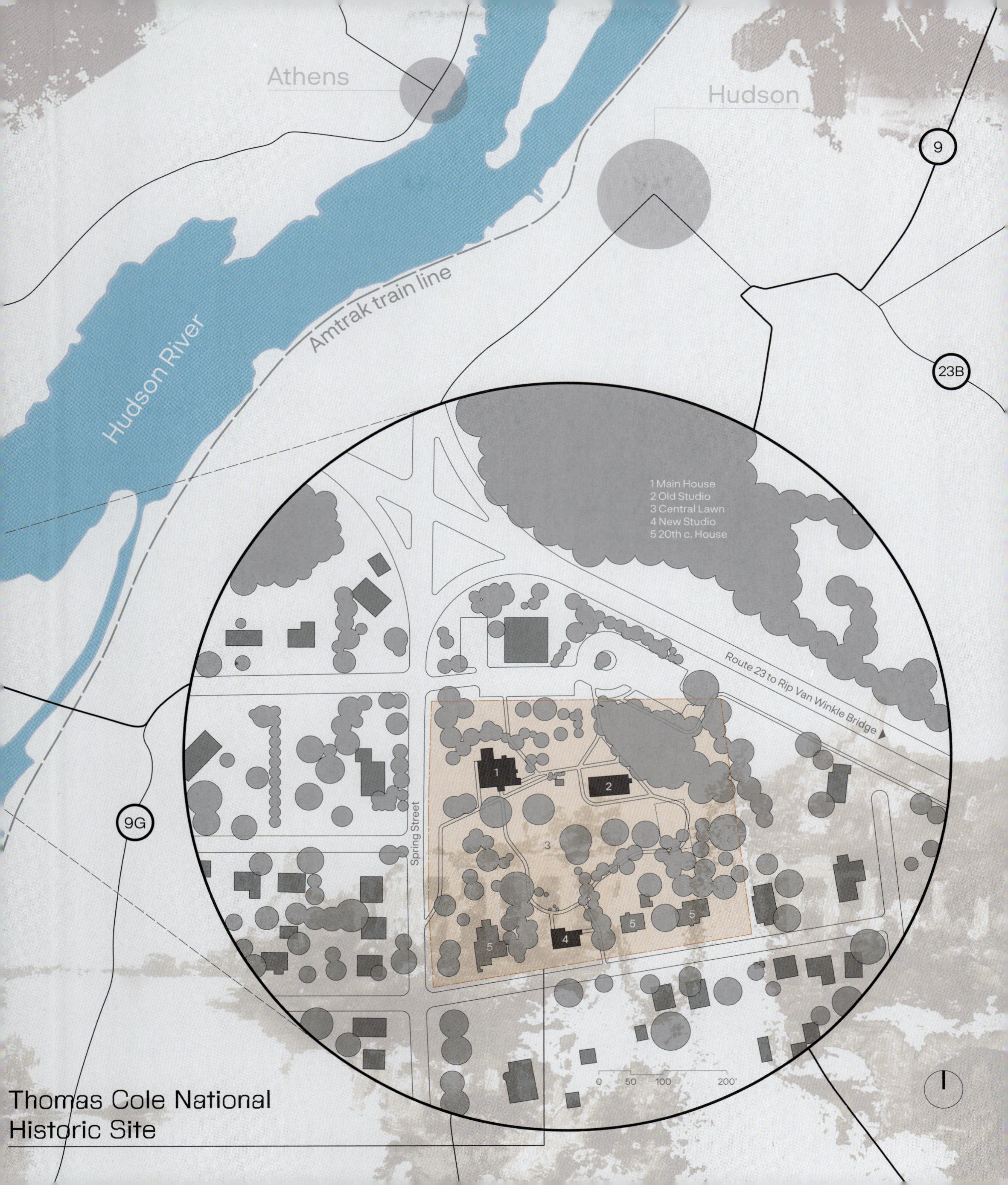
Athens
Hudson
9
23B
Amtrak train line
Hudson River
1 Main House
2 Old Studio
3 Central Lawn
4 New Studio
5 20th c. House
Route 23 to Rip Van Winkle Bridge
9G
Spring Street
0 50 100 200'
Thomas Cole National
Historic Site

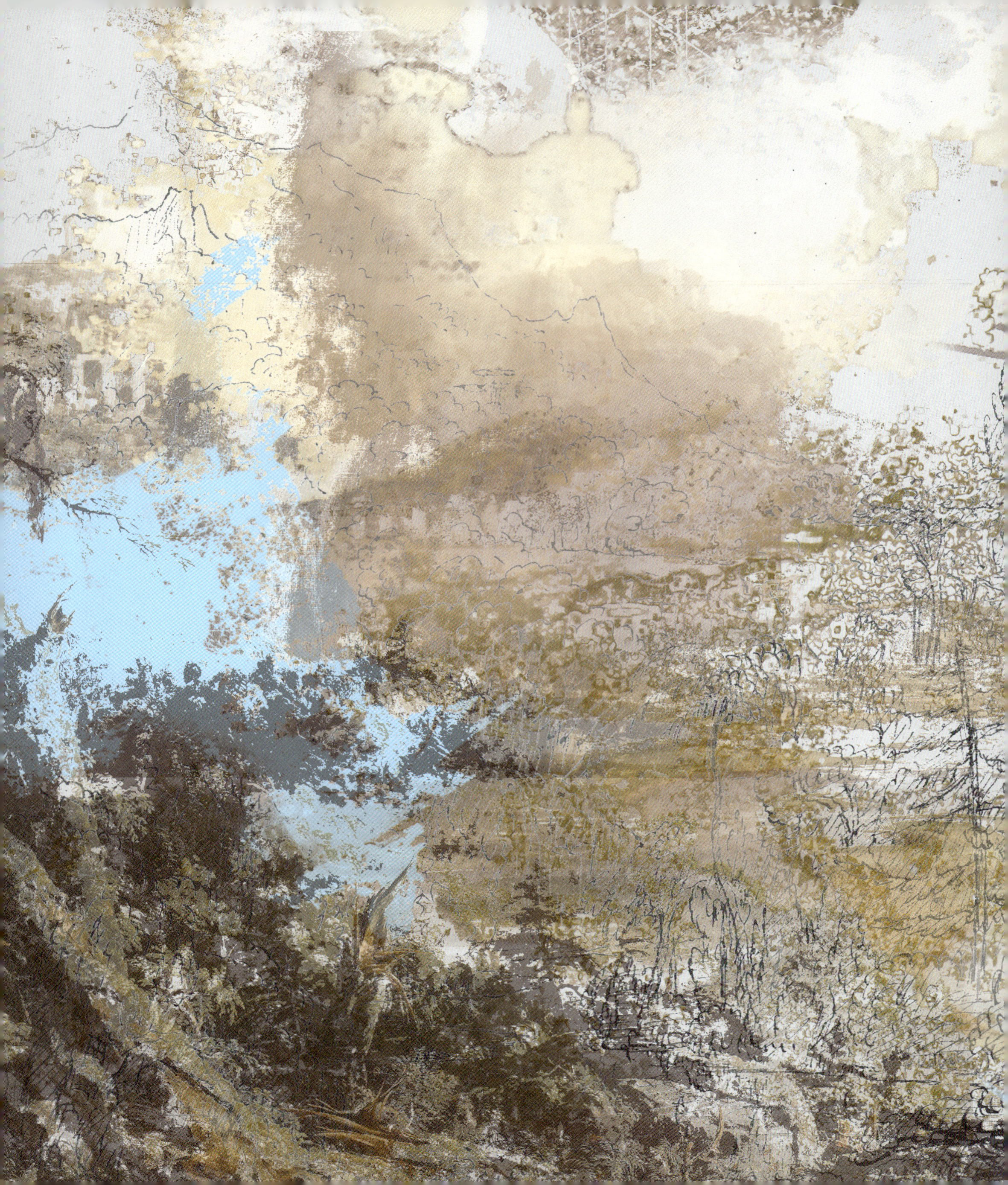

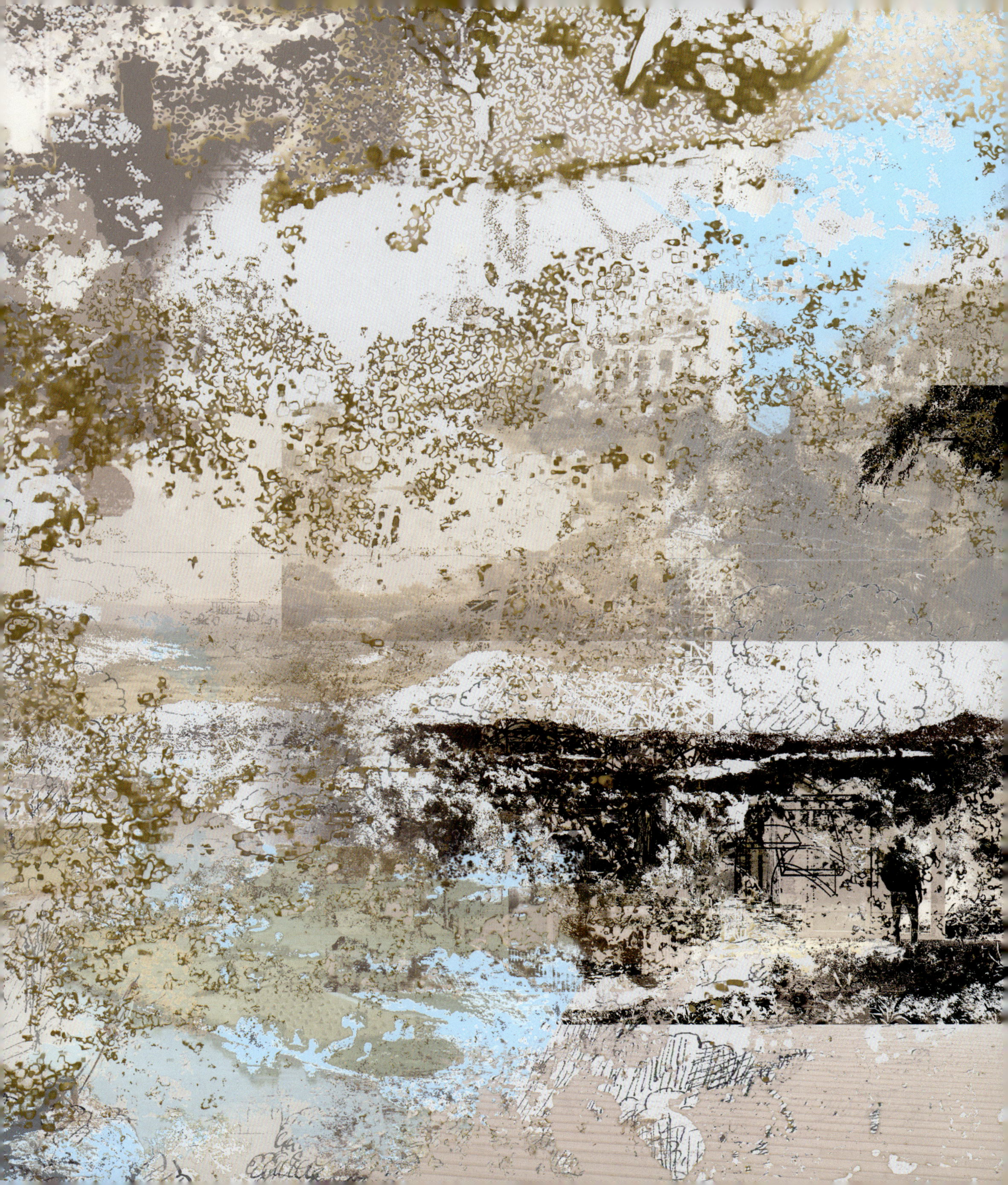

Design and the (De)construction of Nature

Design Studio Instructor

Jillian Crandall

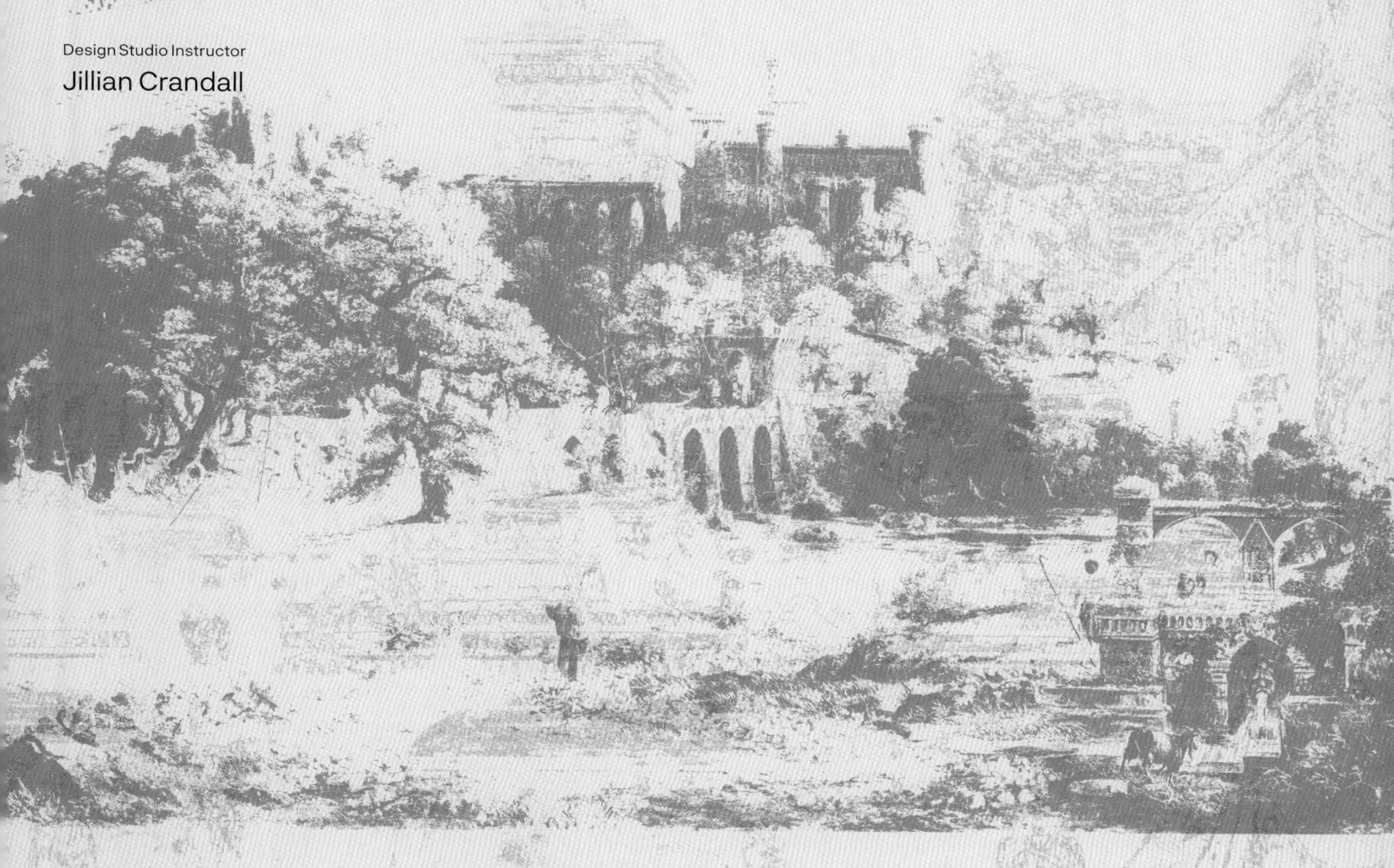

The design of the constructed environment is a continual collective process. What we understand as "nature" is both socially constructed and shaped by forces outside of human control. Engaging these premises, this studio section undertook a careful reading of the Thomas Cole National Historic Site through a contemporary lens. Today, the Cole site shows rather than tells the story of its own creation myth, cordoned off from the adjacent urban context with gates and walls, revealing an image of "pristine nature" conserved from its "unnatural" developed surroundings, host to its own tourists and local artists. In this studio section, students questioned how the site contends with fraught social histories and contemporary challenges, responding to Cole's invitation to think critically about the role of art / artist in constructing the environment.

In *The Course of Empire* series, Cole depicts the process of reshaping the land under American nationalism, passing from untamed wilderness to pastoral republic to urban extravagance, and ending in prophetic decline. Unlike his successors in the Hudson River School, Cole was skeptical of the notion that industrial / imperial expansion was a natural, benign process necessary for America's "national destiny."[1] Yet despite his proto-environmentalist attitude and criticism of profit-driven Jacksonian development in the 1830s, Cole was still responsible for perpetuating the settler-colonial myth that Europeans were the original "civilized" stewards of North America, transforming the land "from the first state of savage rudeness."[2] As art historian Angela Miller contends, these scenes also "cannot be understood apart from the sectional polemic concerning free labor and slavery"[3] being waged at the time. In this design studio, I challenged students to question both art and the museum typology and their cultural roles. Whose histories are preserved, and whose are missing? One may consider this project an "un-museum"—unbuilding preconceived notions of nature, landscape, and museum to explore what this could mean programmatically, materially, aesthetically, and spatially. Cole believed in the social agency of the artist, acknowledging the power of art as a medium to communicate sociopolitical narratives. In *The Oxbow*, a minuscule human figure is depicted: a partially concealed painter, spectator/documenter of the sublime under transition, but simultaneously—in looking back at the audience—acknowledging that he is a conscious participant in the process of the landscape's making. Cole's work invites us to consider that artists, curators, architects, designers, and educators are all actors and contributors to broader social issues with which we have a responsibility to contend.

For this studio section, research was paramount, informing the creation of a "muse collage" from which generative rule sets were established and critical conceptual positions were developed. The projects were highly varied: challenging dichotomies of urban vs. rural / man vs. nature, envisioning ways the site could become more porous to the surrounding city and residents; revealing pre-anthropocentric geological timescales by excavating the earth to form walls; producing uncanny visualizations to reveal nature as a manufactured hyperreality; using daylighting and net-zero strategies; proposing programmatic interventions such as an Indigenous artist-in-residence program; returning the land to Indigenous food sovereignty movements; confronting violence and dispossession, the erasure of slaves in Hudson River School depictions, proposing site as monument to underacknowledged Black laborers; and more. Ultimately this process invites a self-reflective look at the very institutions (including the university and the museum) that judge good aesthetics and inculcate certain values, while acknowledging our power to potentially impact our environment and society for the better.

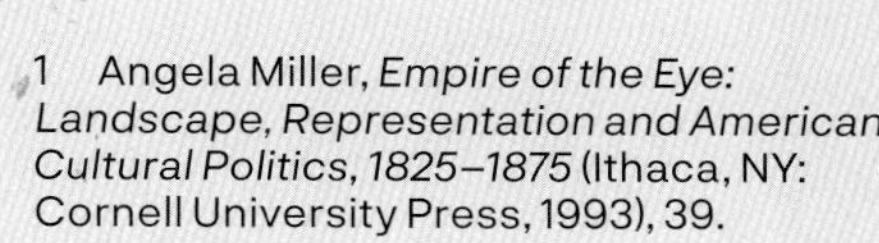

1 Angela Miller, *Empire of the Eye: Landscape, Representation and American Cultural Politics, 1825–1875* (Ithaca, NY: Cornell University Press, 1993), 39.

2 Ibid., 23.

3 Ibid., 5.

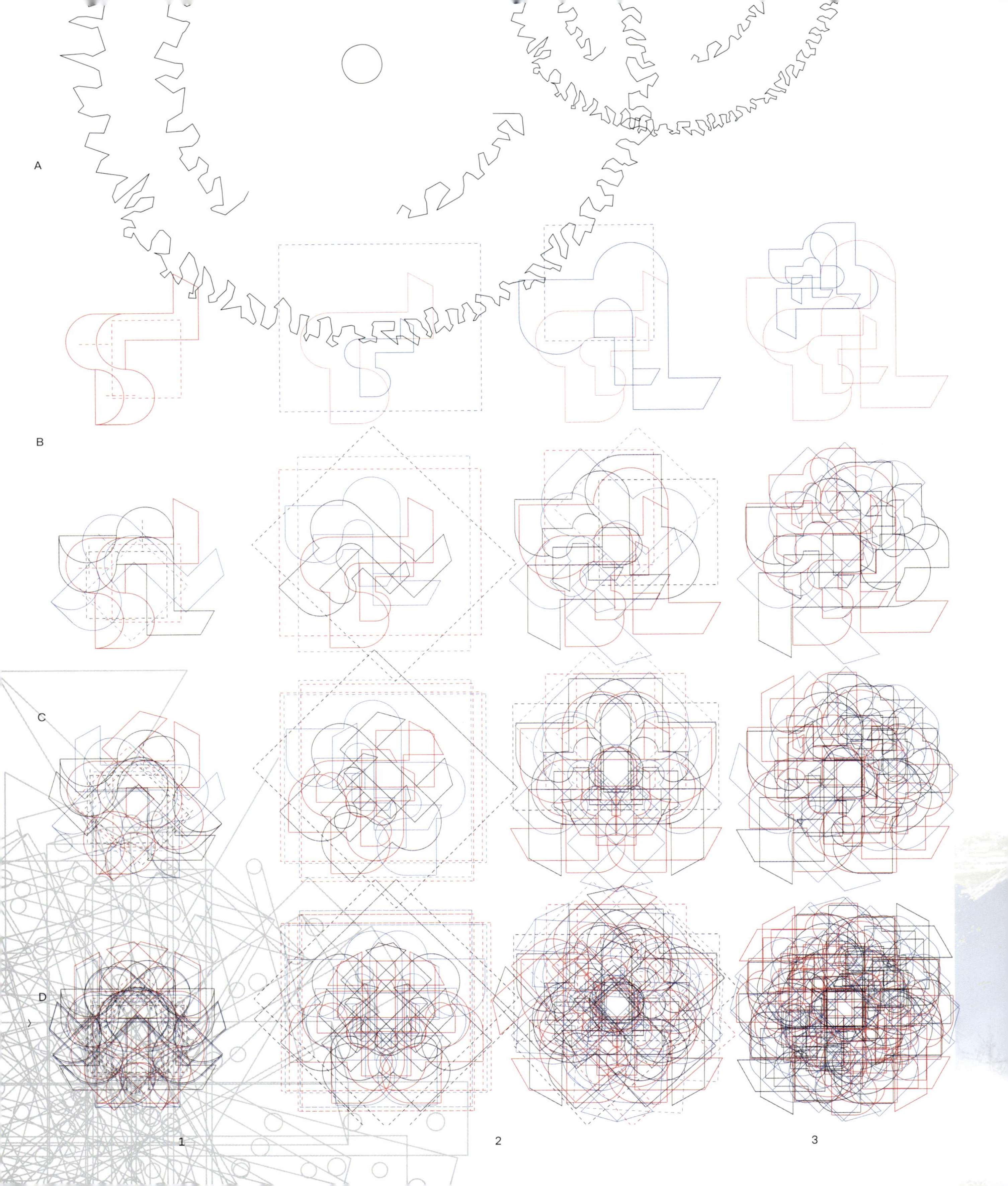

A
B
C
D
1
2
3

D1 Benen Pominville
B2 Jillian Lin
C5 Carson Oliver
B6 Marcus Morgan

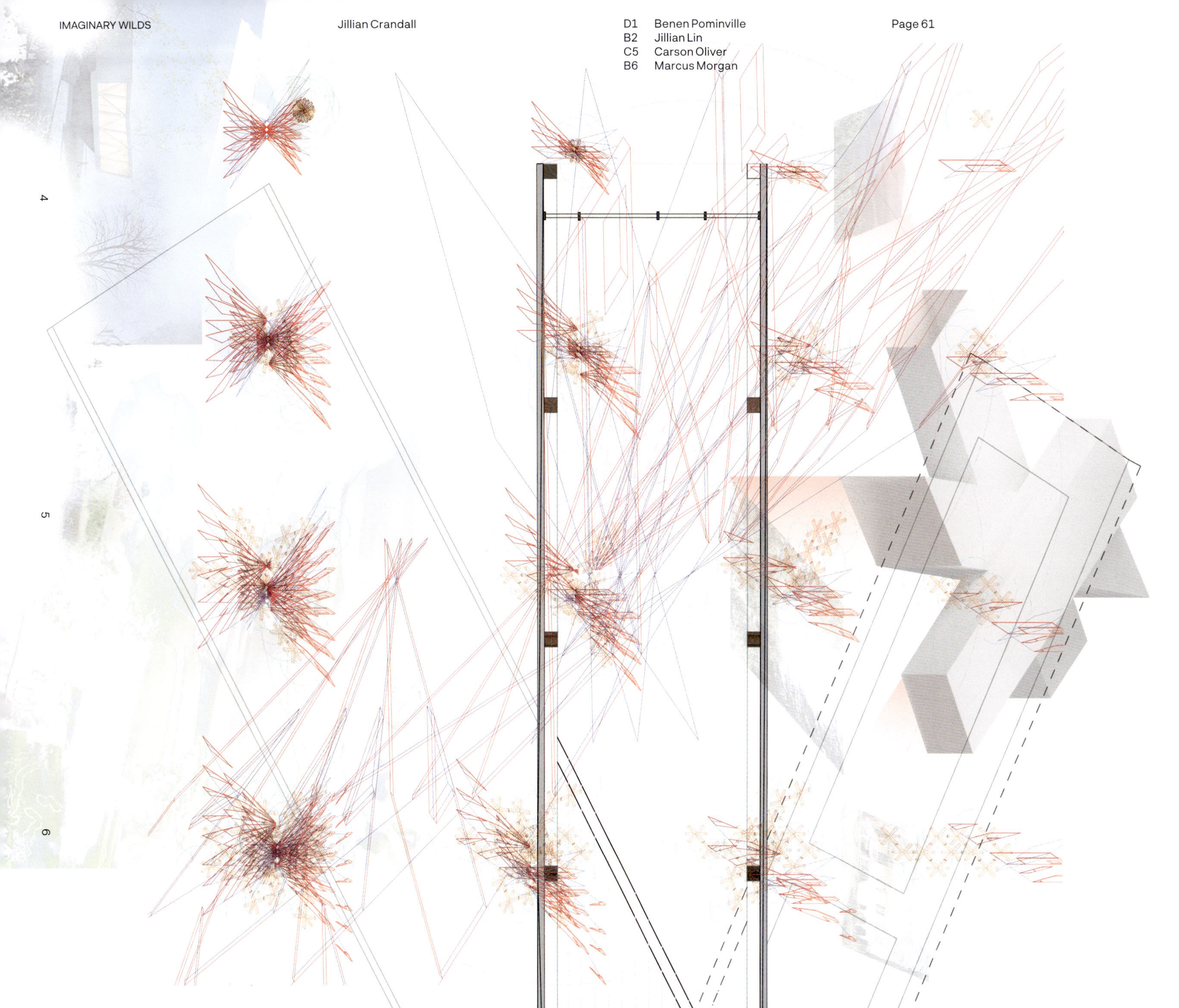

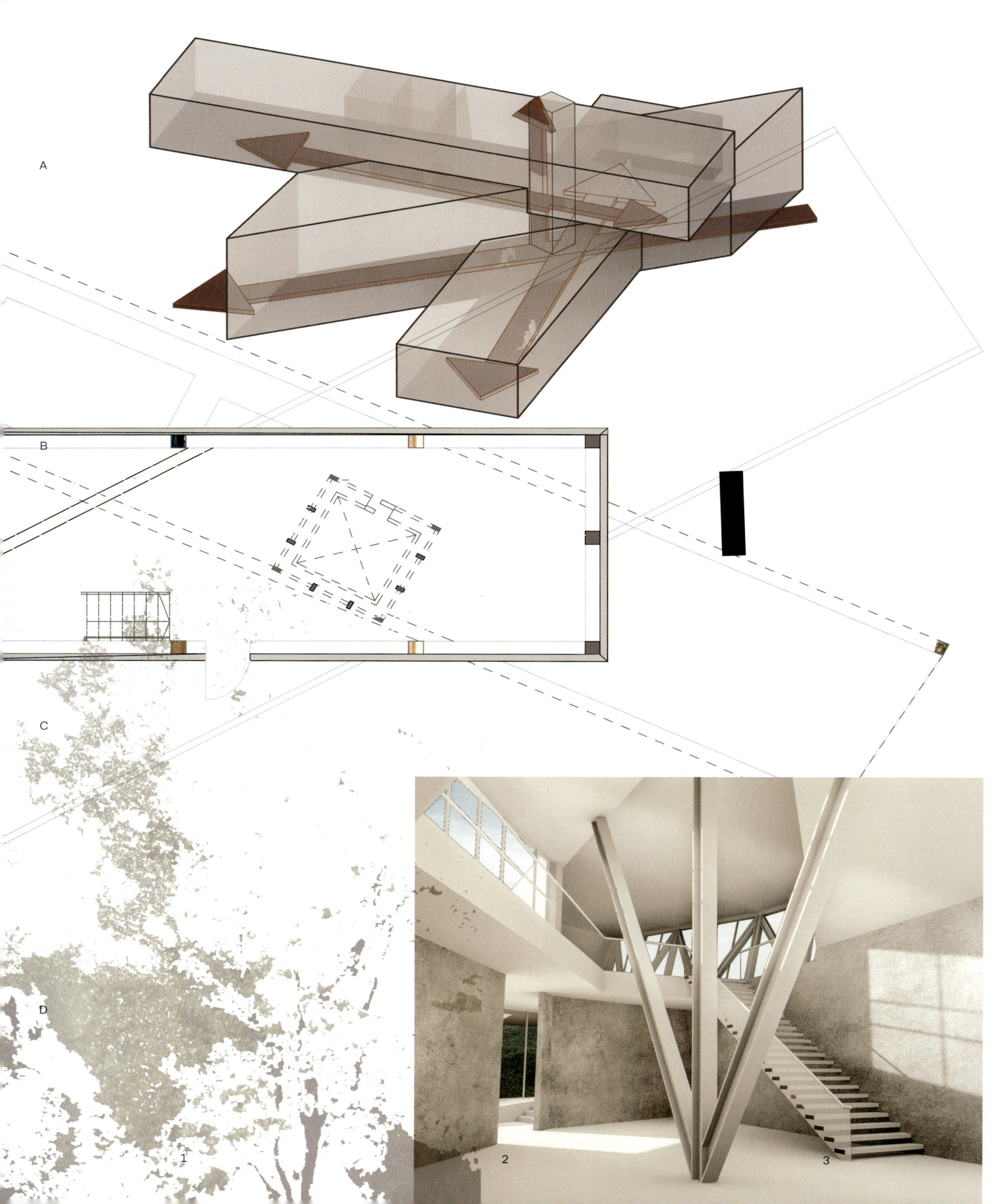
A
B
C
D
1
2
3

A2 Marcus Morgan
B1 Marcus Morgan
D3 Bryn Peterson
B5 Bryn Peterson

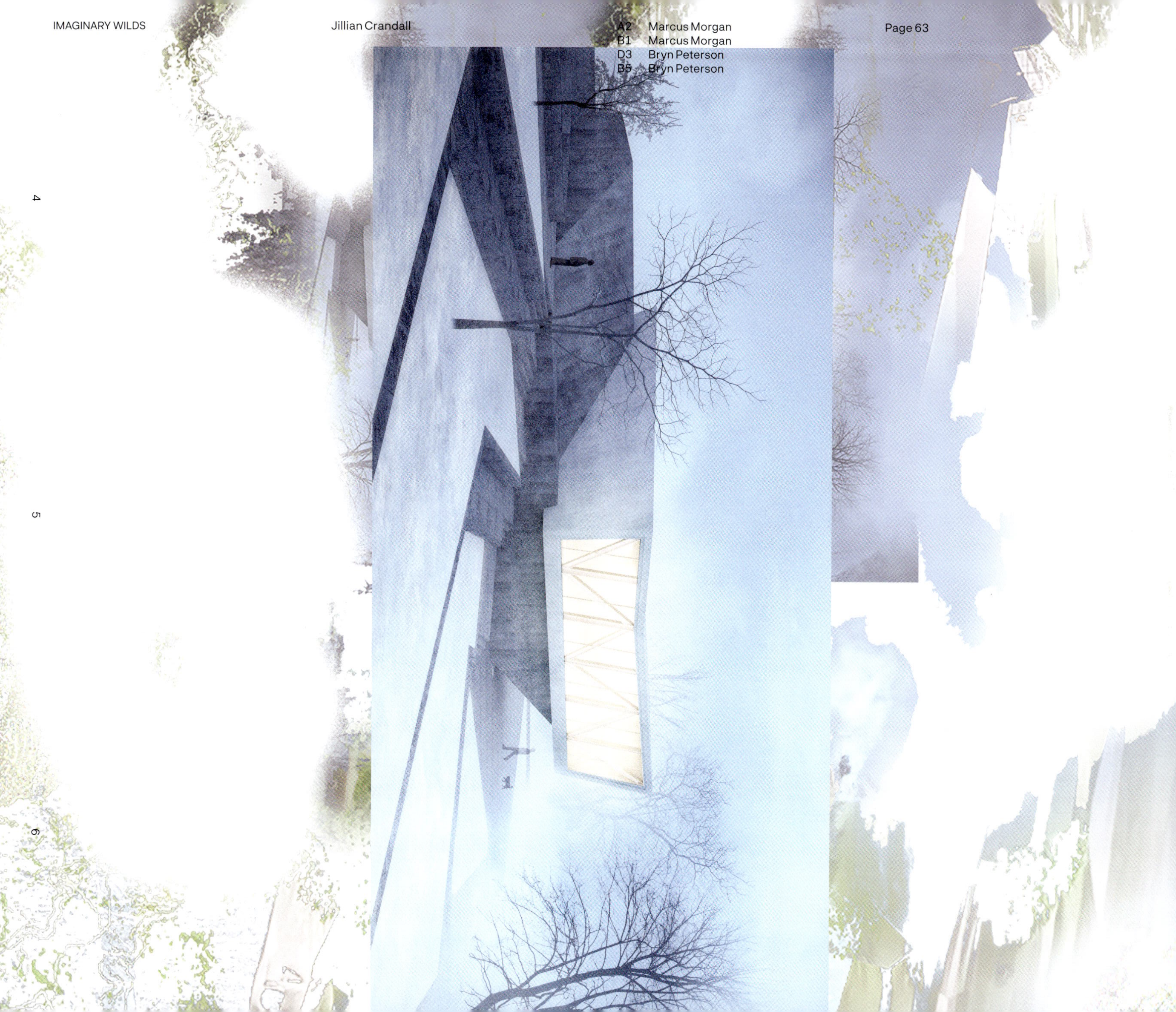

4
5
6

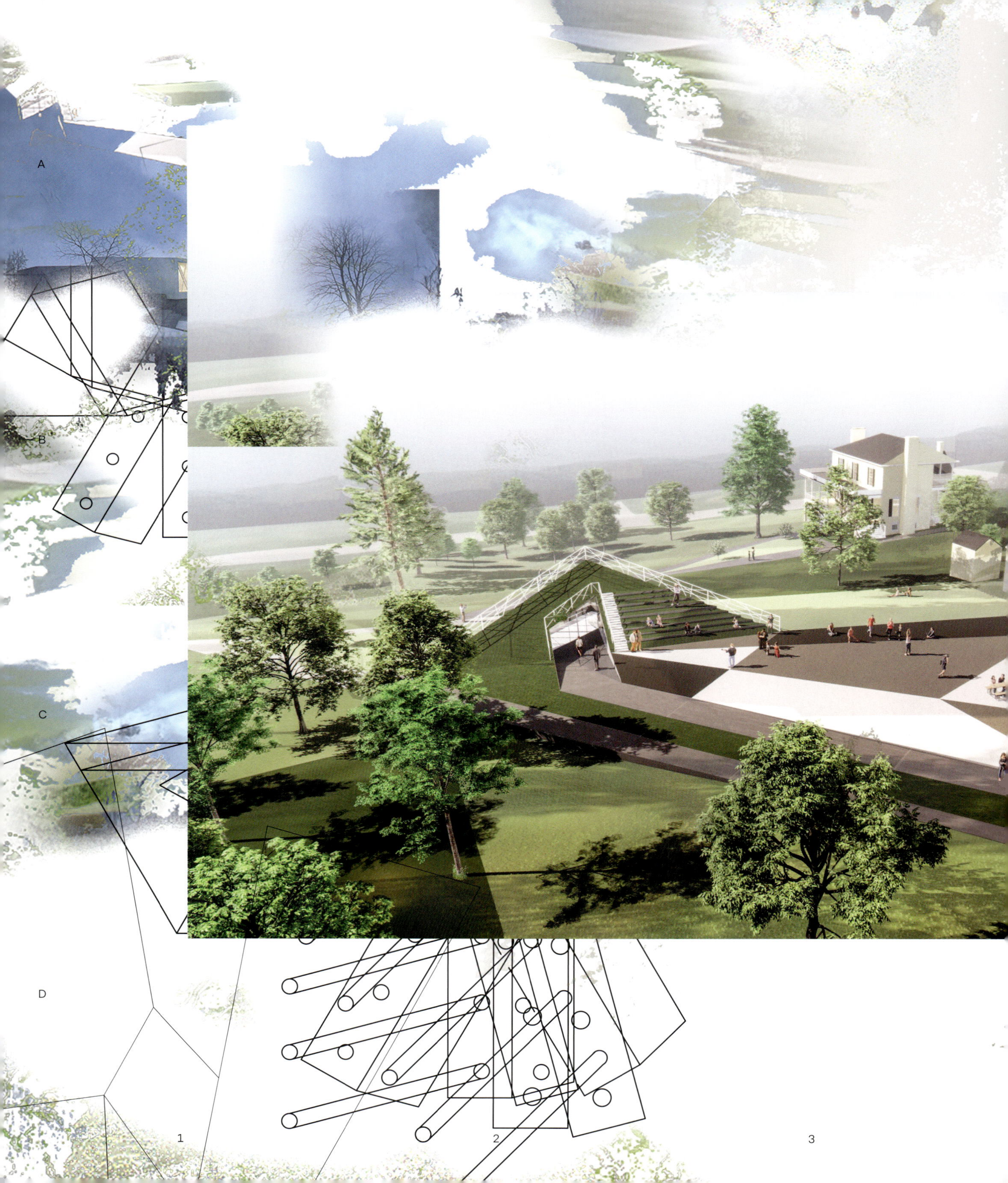
A
B
C
D
1
2
3

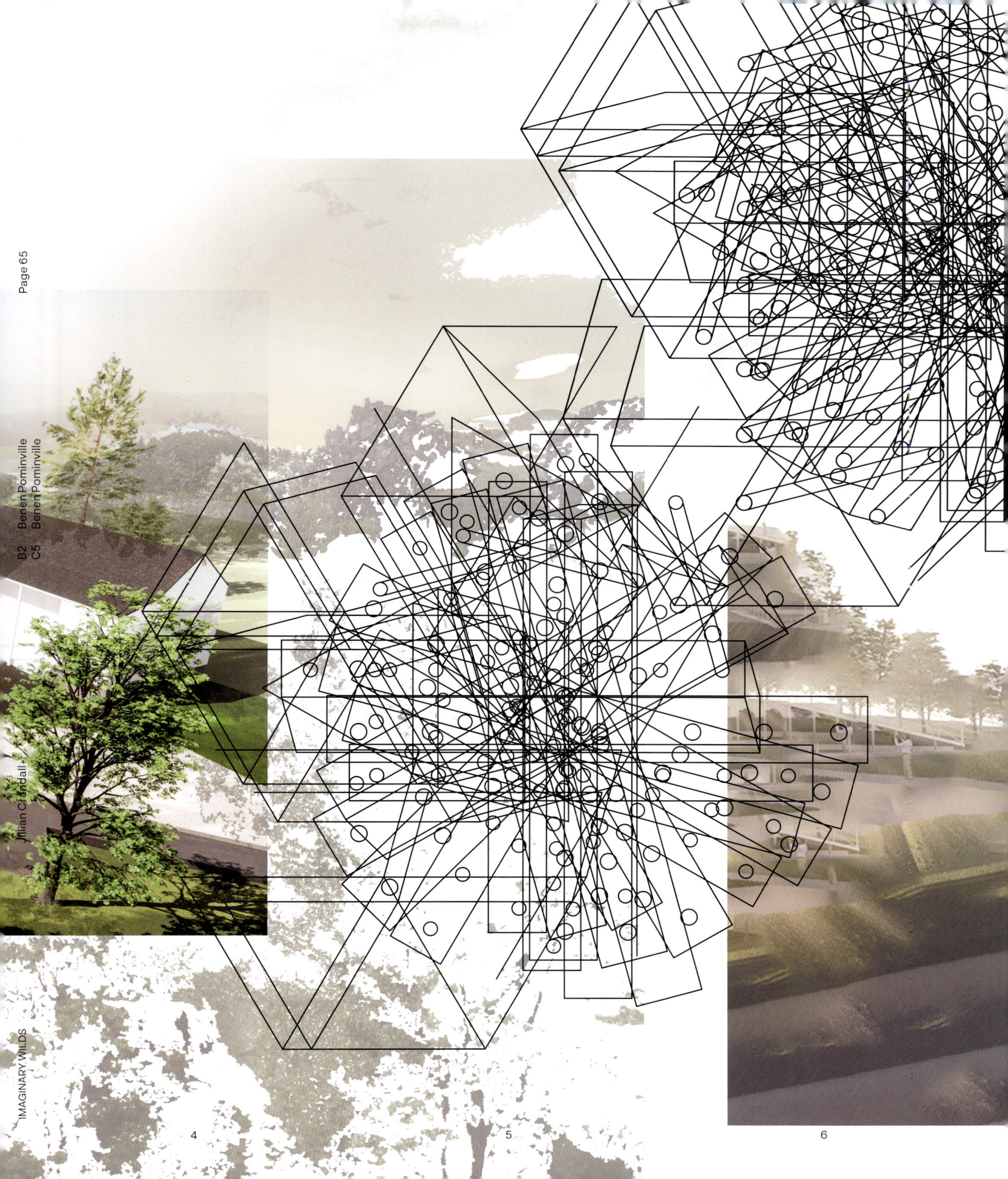

Jillian Crandall
B2 Benen Pominville
C5 Benen Pominville

4

5

6

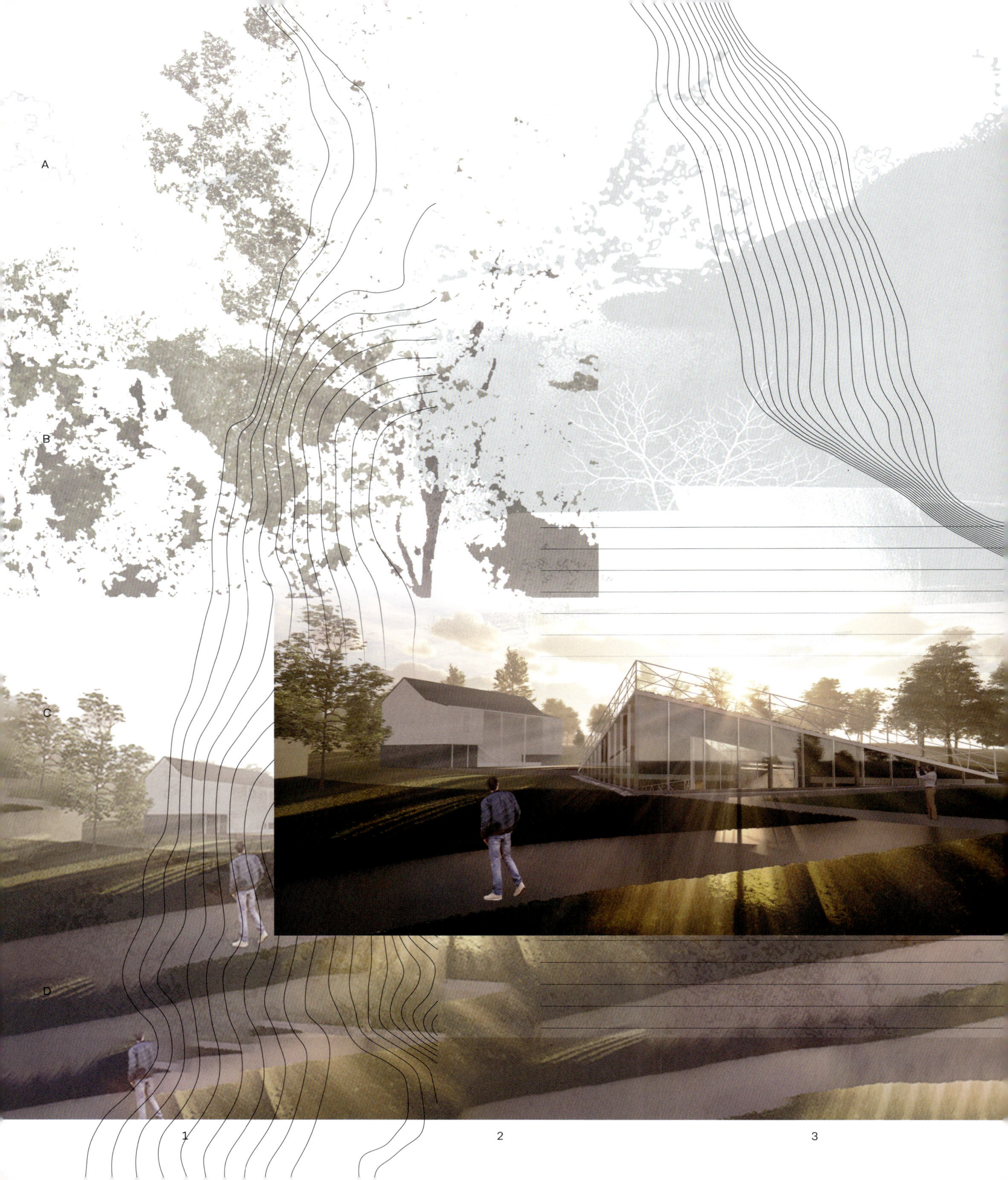
A
B
C
D
1
2
3

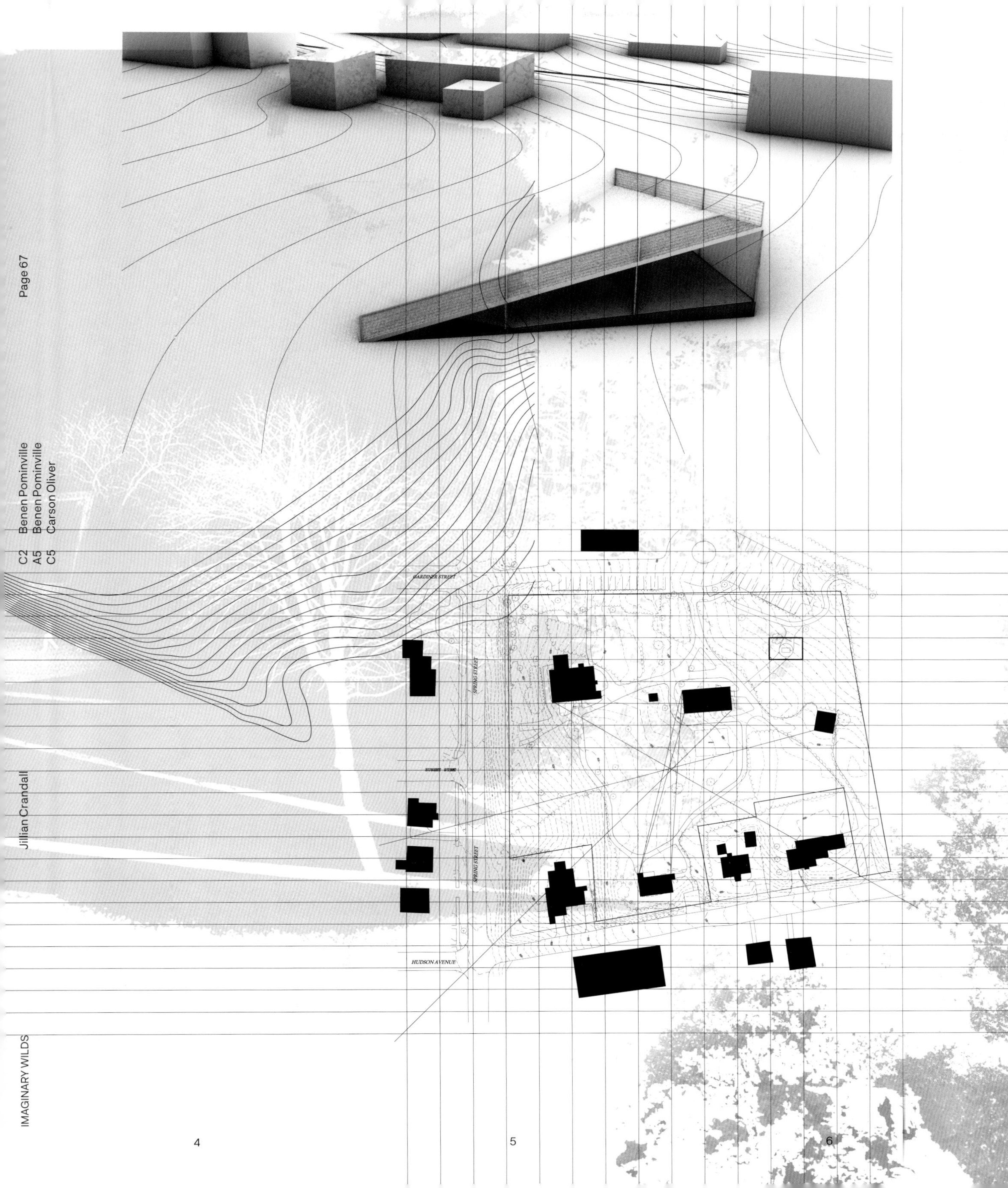
GARDINER STREET
SPRING STREET
SPRING STREET
HUDSON AVENUE
4
5
6

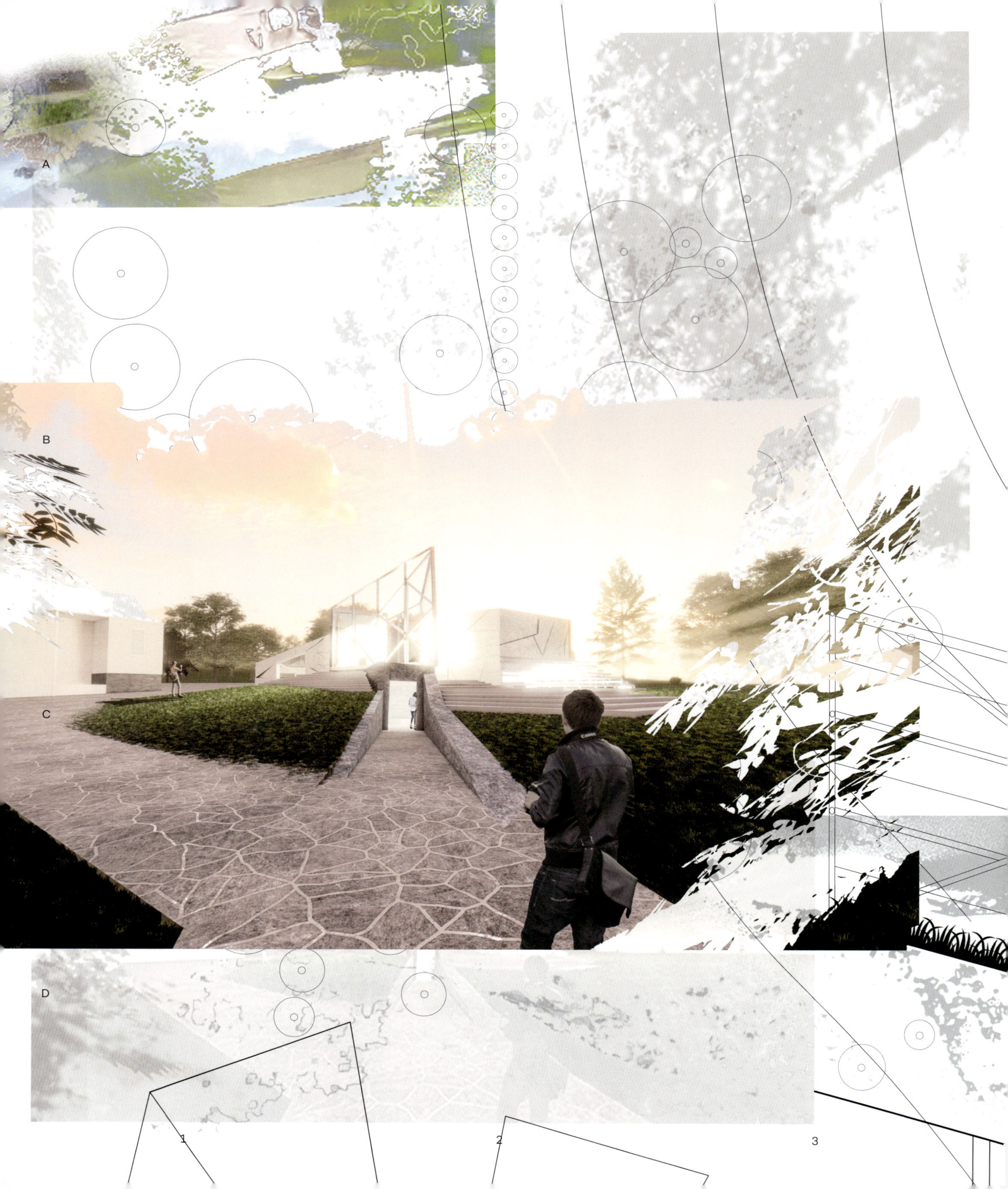
A
B
C
D
1
2
3

Jillian Crandall

C2 Katerina Napoli
B5 Katerina Napoli
D4 Benen Pominville

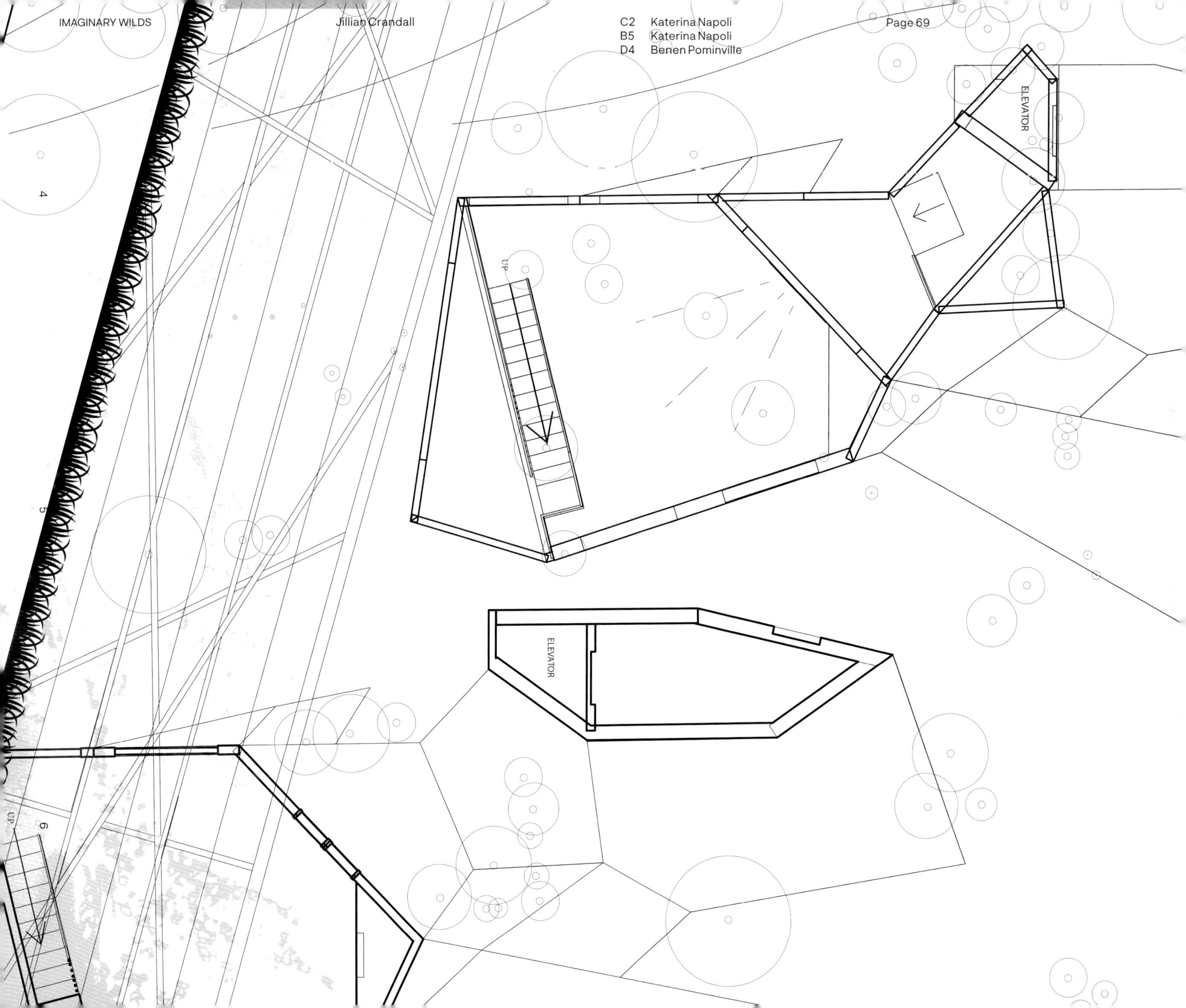

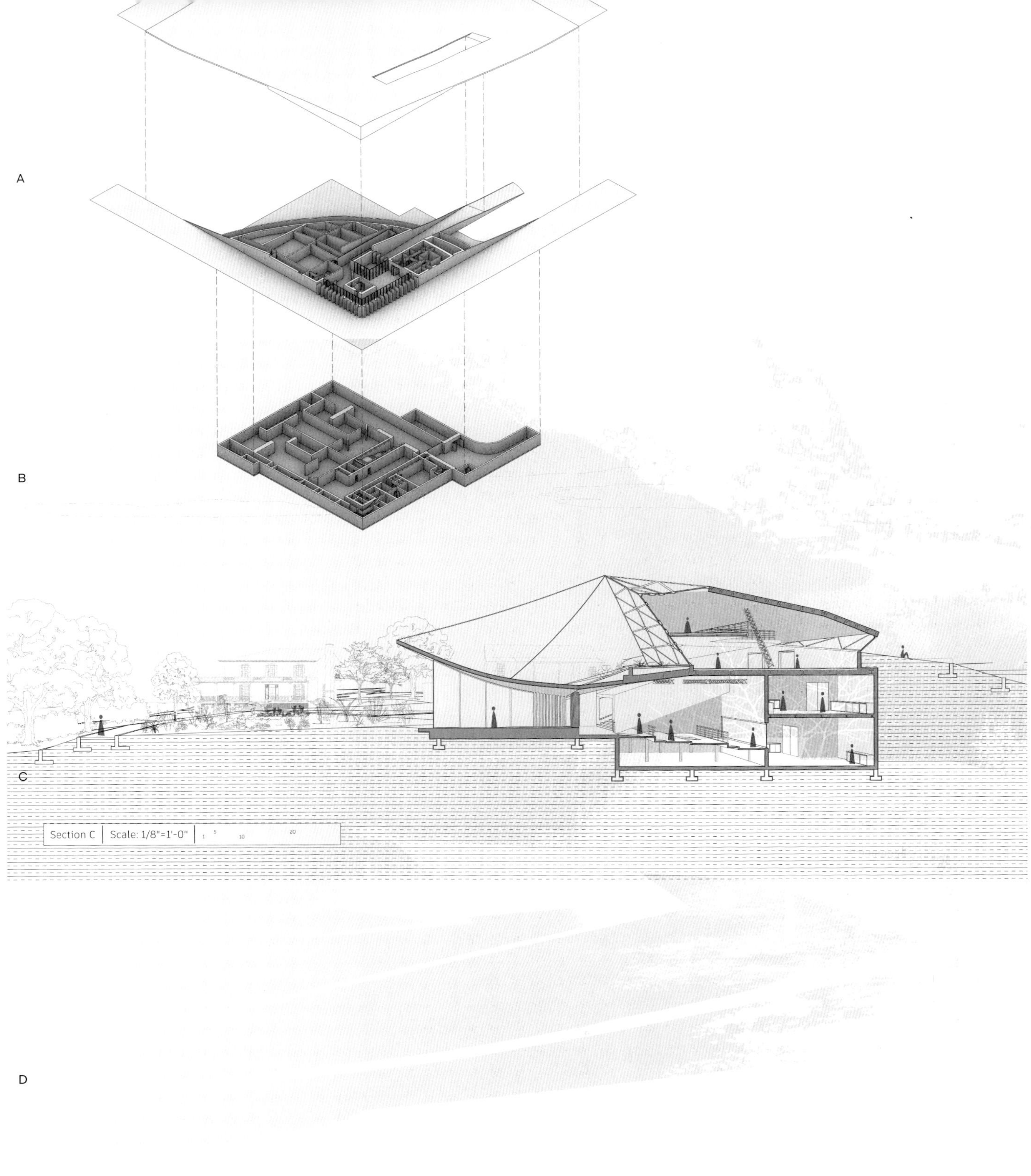
A
B
C
Section C
Scale: 1/8"=1'-0"
1
5
10
20
D
1
2
3

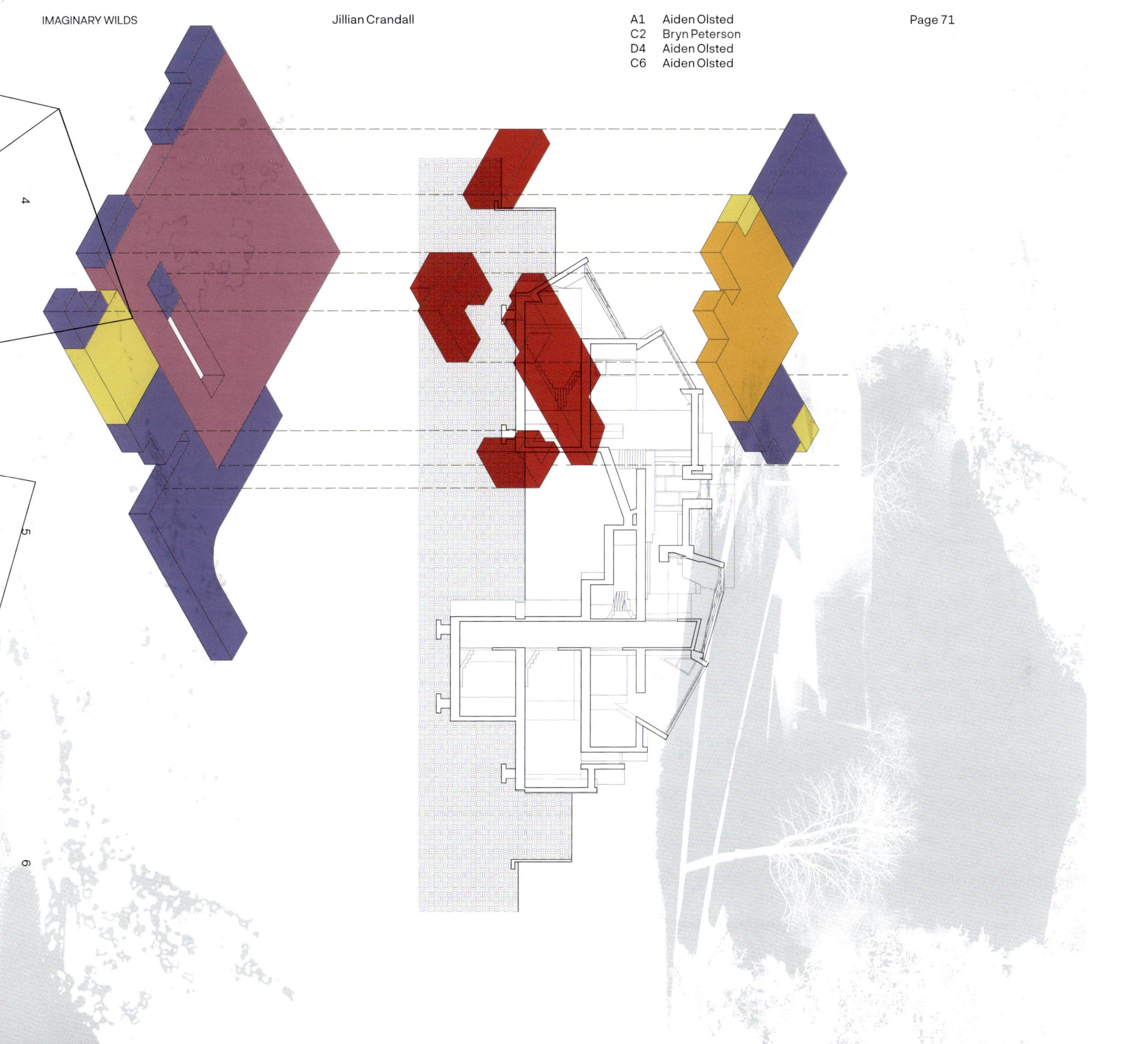
4
5
6

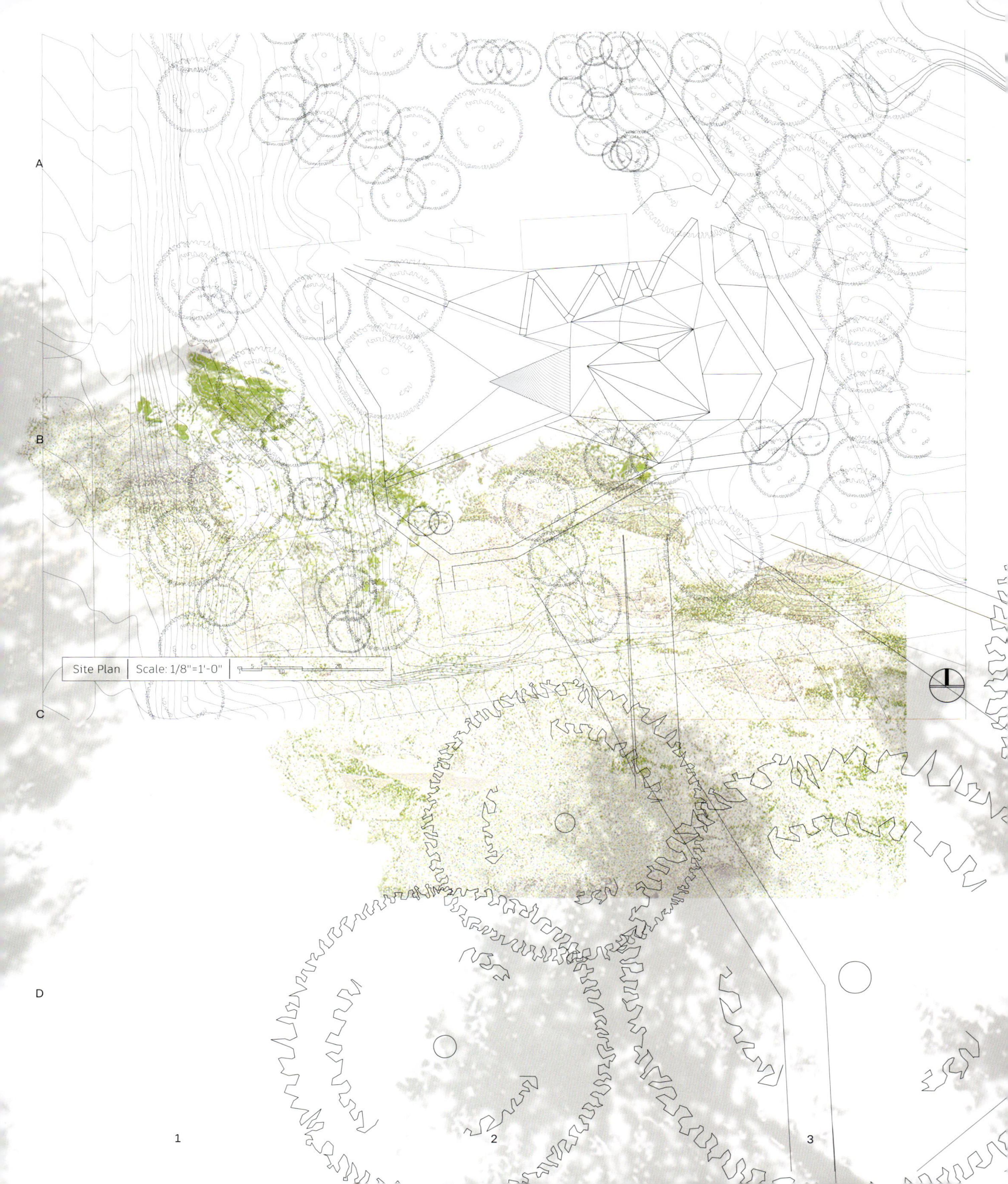
A
B
C
D
1
2
3
Site Plan
Scale: 1/8"=1'-0"

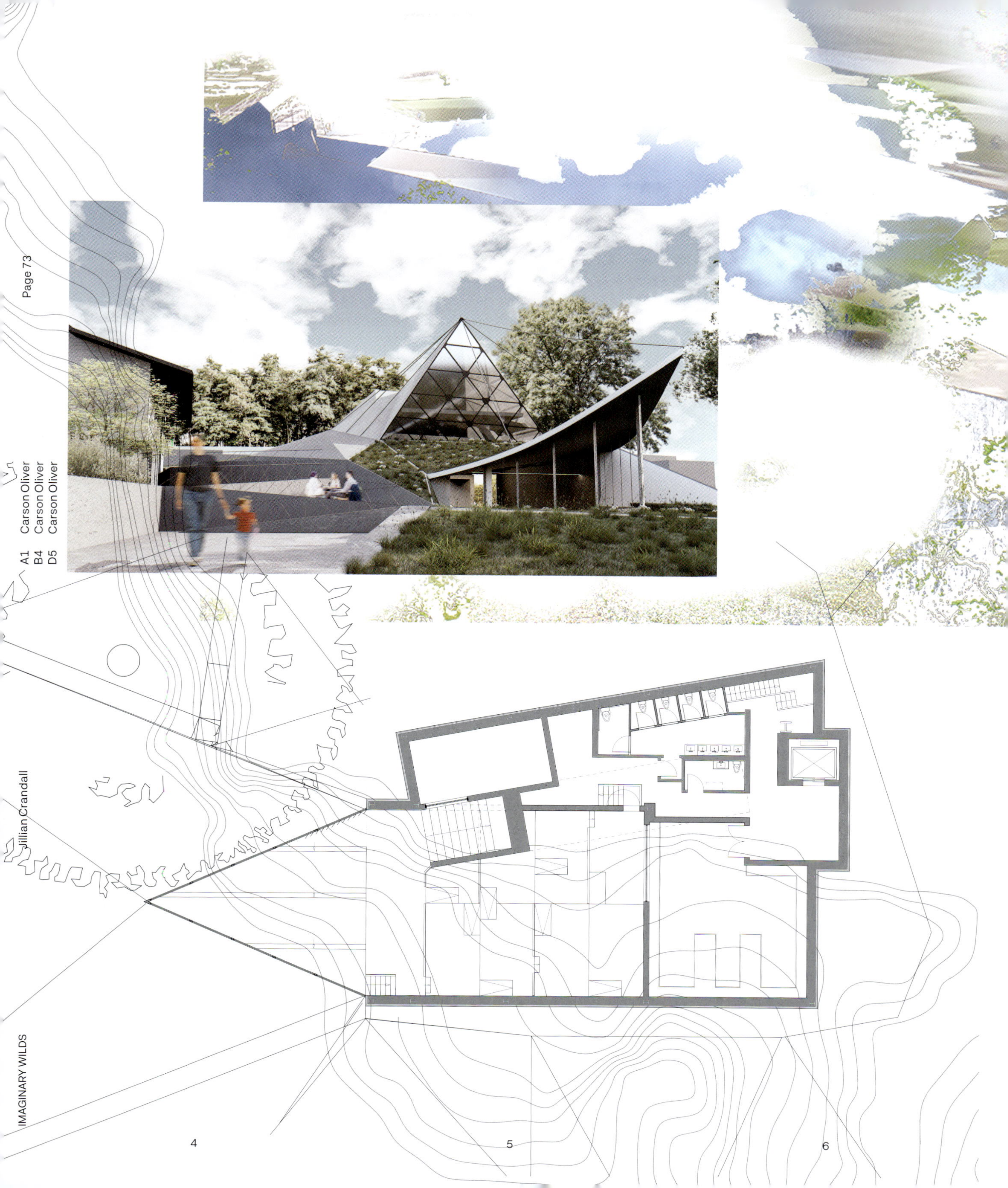

A1 Carson Oliver
B4 Carson Oliver
D5 Carson Oliver

Jillian Crandall

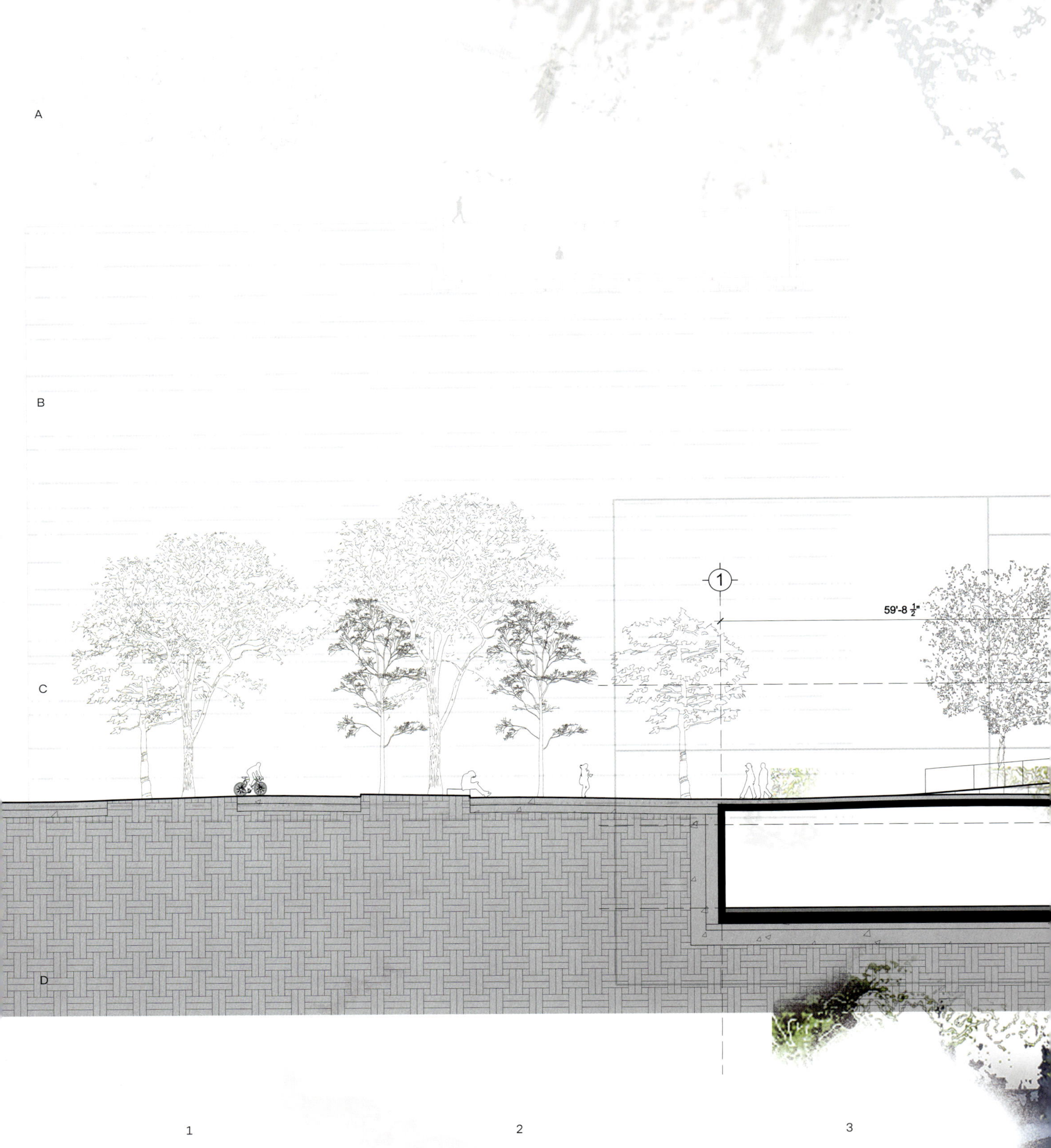

A
B
C
D
1
59'-8 1/2"
1
2
3

A2 Aiden Olsted
C4 Aiden Olsted
A6 Katerina Napoli

Jillian Crandall

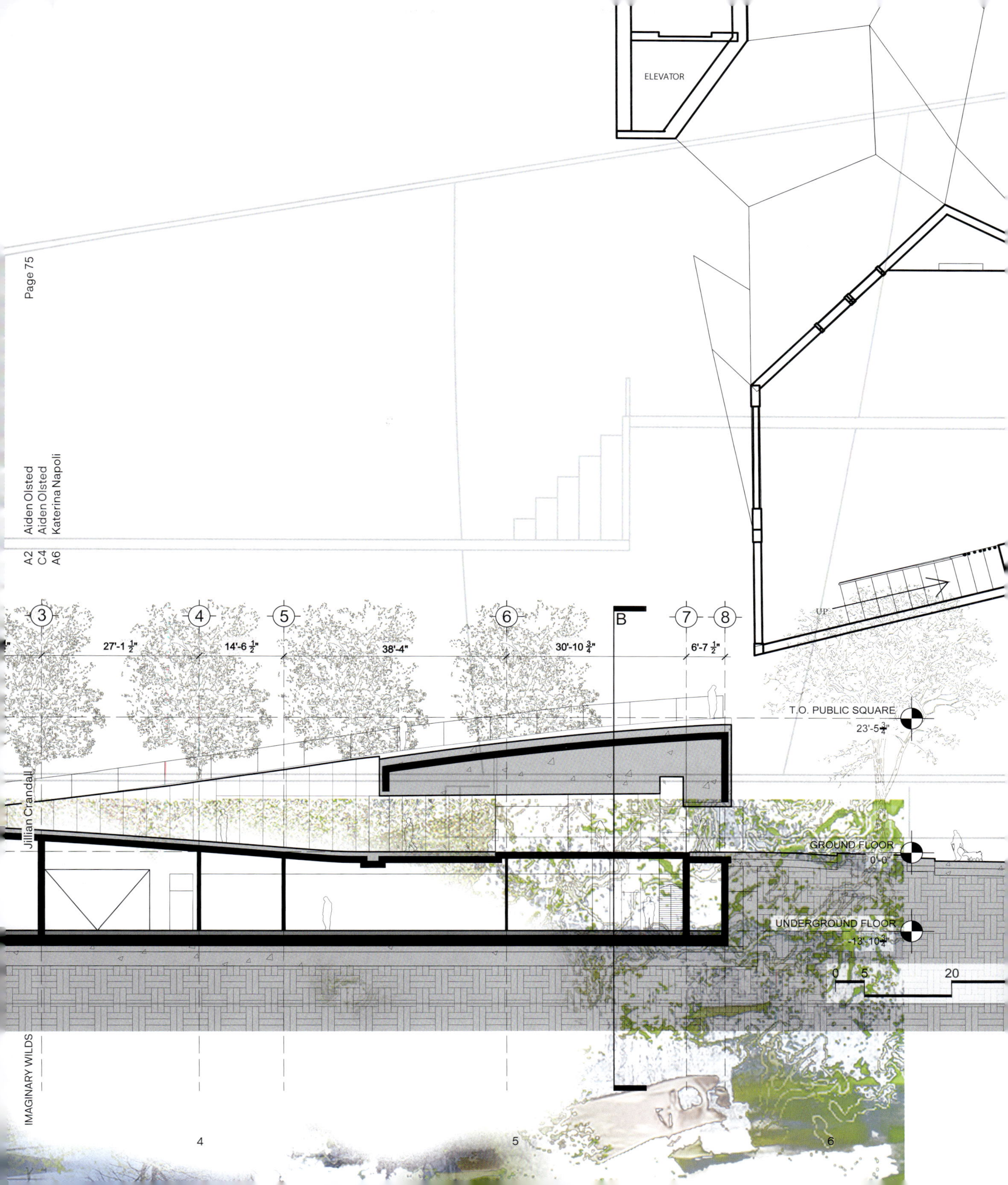

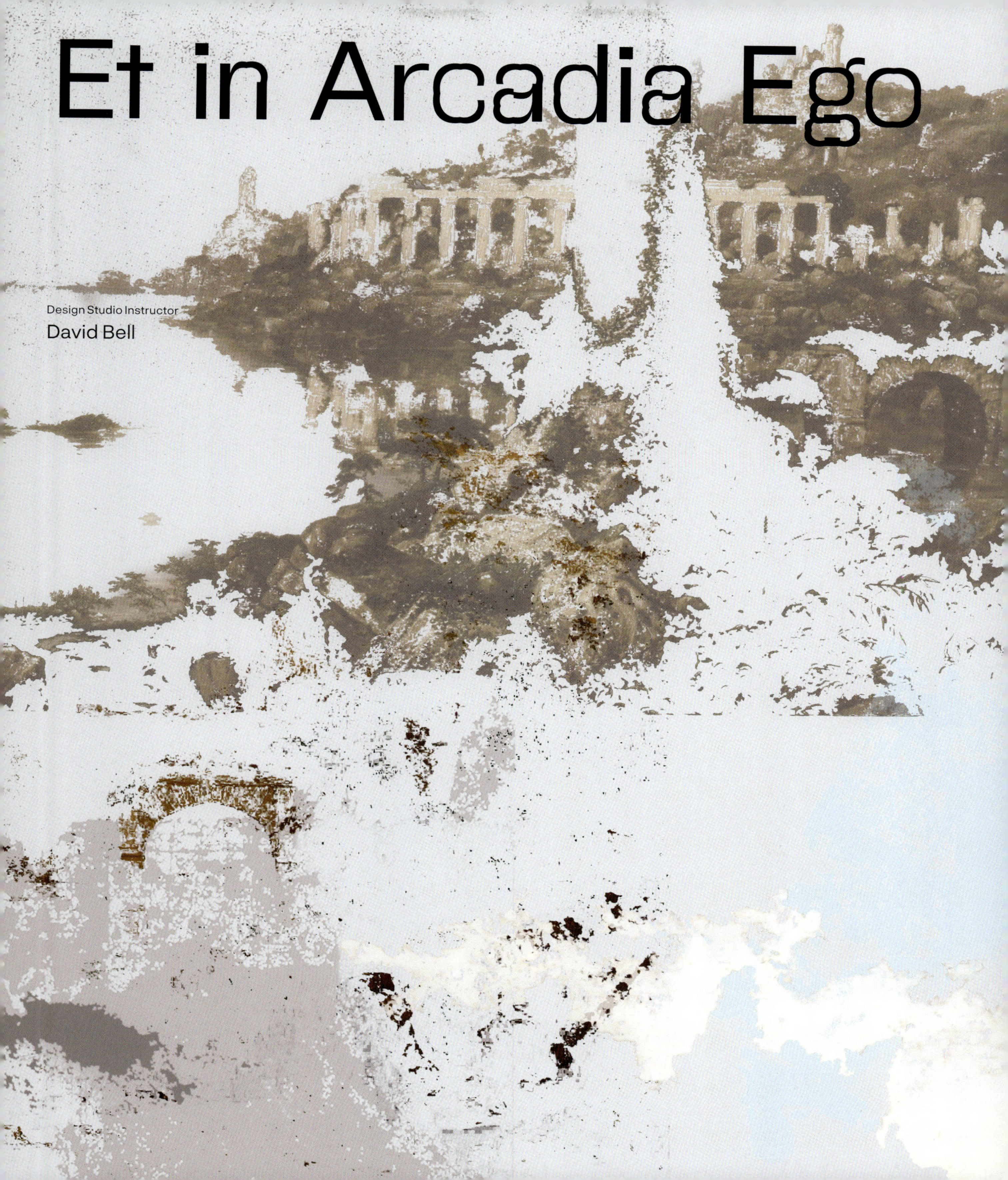
Et in Arcadia Ego
Design Studio Instructor
David Bell

The Thomas Cole National Historic Site presented many opportunities for this semester's project. This particular studio section addressed the site and its program in predominantly realistic terms by assuming that good architecture lives through negotiating constraints. It was left to each student's imagination to interpret these constraints based upon the site's unique characteristics and the program. The program for the building would involve a collection of various exhibition spaces (mostly for paintings and a few three-dimensional pieces), a café, and perhaps a gift shop that could either be an auxiliary to the existing gift shop or its replacement (each student could make such a determination).

The principal constraints involved: (1) entry to the site, (2) avoidance of significant excavation or any radical disturbance to the existing order of the site, its vegetation, and its topography, (3) recognizing the importance of natural light as well as its possible deleterious effect on works of art, (4) the unique nature of circulation in the design of exhibition spaces, (5) an inherent understanding of Thomas Cole's approach to painting, and (6) an awareness that the entire Thomas Cole site is an exhibition space with an established circulation pattern that could or should be modified or augmented and strongly correlated to the design of the new exhibition structure.

Items 3 through 6 are self-explanatory. However, items 1 and 2 require elaboration. The nature of the Thomas Cole site within the town of Catskill strongly precludes a direct vehicular or pedestrian entrance. The preponderance of its visitors arrive by automobile or, in the case of school groups, by bus. Nevertheless, it has no dedicated parking for its visitors and shares its vehicular entry and parking lot with the adjacent Temple Israel. Consequently, once one disembarks from auto or bus, there is no well-defined entry into the site proper. Hence, one criterion for the project was to design a definitive entry statement for the site and to coordinate both that point of entry and the new building as part of a larger sense of circulation on the site. In that respect, students could modify the current site circulation as long as it maintained the principal intent that visitors would conclude their visit at the Main House, which occupies the extreme northwestern end of the site, and which also affords the only long view to the surrounding Catskill landscape. In addition, students were required to respect the topography of the existing landscape by limiting any architectural intervention to the surface, with minimal or preferably no substantial excavation for any belowground spaces.

Within these constraints, students were encouraged to establish their individual, unique approach to the design. Some students attenuated the site circulation, while others created a unique but respectful compound of buildings. Some students conceived of their designs as a naturalistic rock outcropping from the site. One student developed a scheme that was spatially and formally contemporary yet thoroughly respected the scale and modest articulation that characterized the existing buildings on the site.

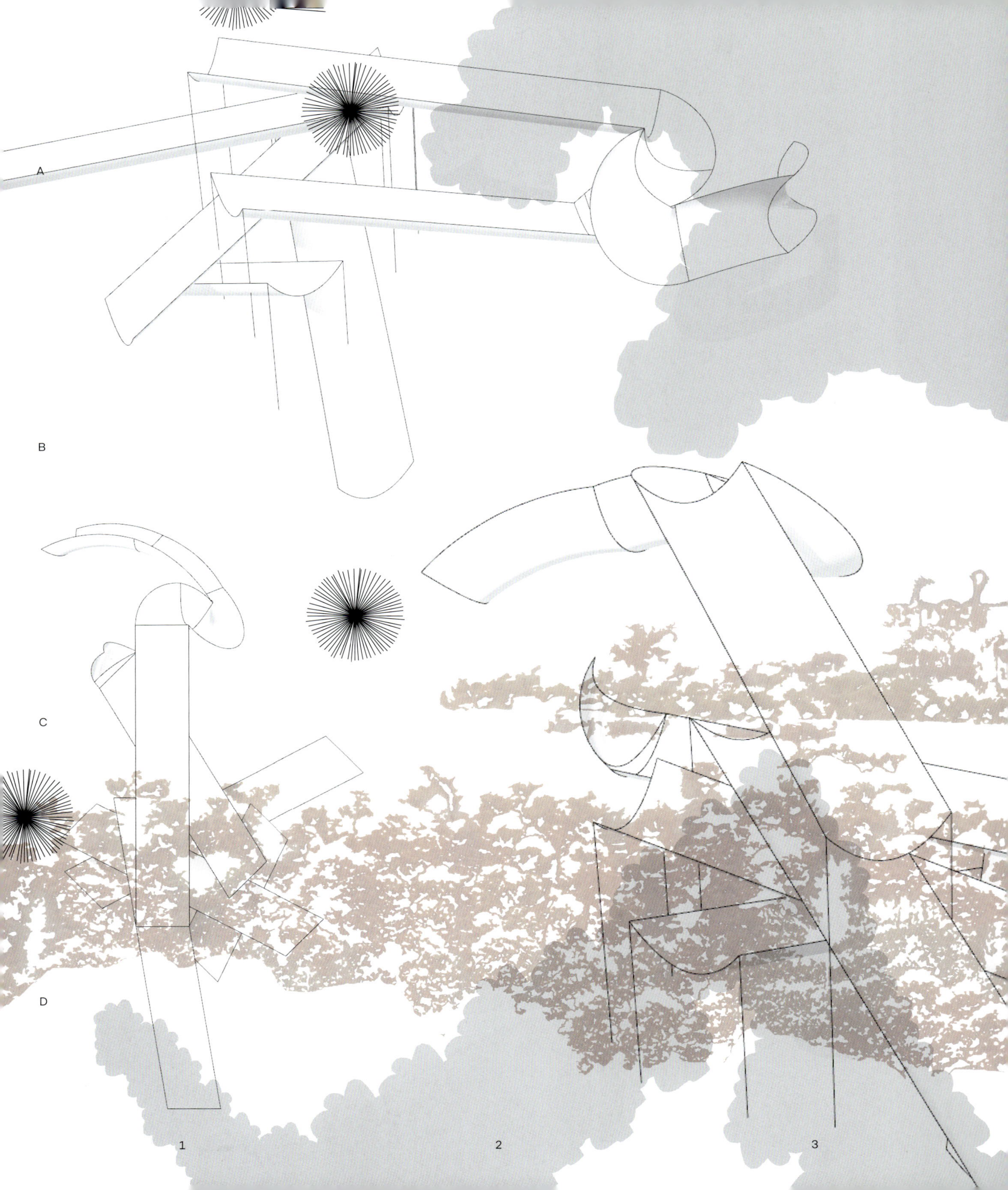
A
B
C
D
1
2
3

A1	Mykala Barrett
C1	Mykala Barrett
A4	Emily Beane
C4	Nicolas Roscioli-Barran
BC5	Shannon Cosgrove

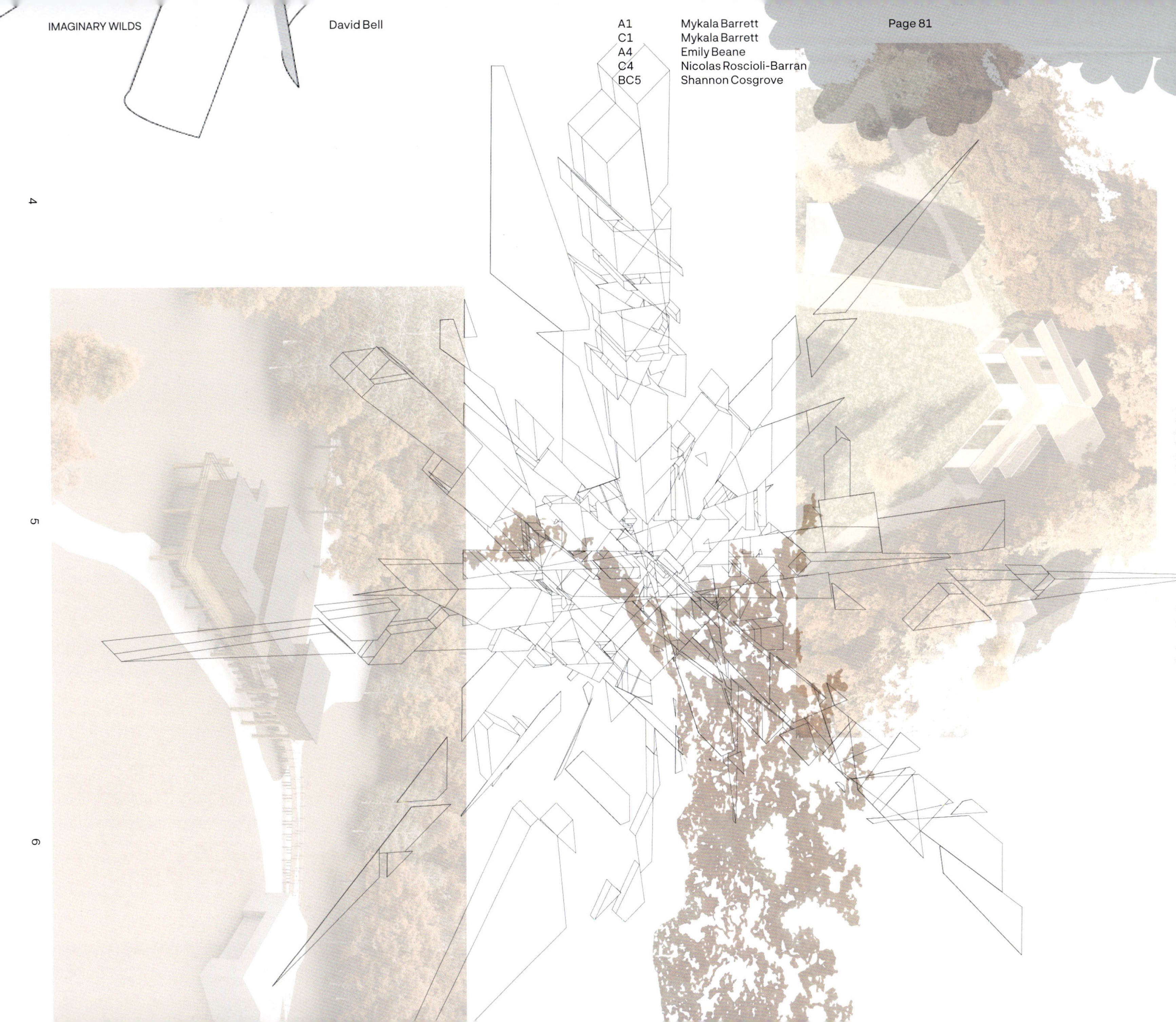

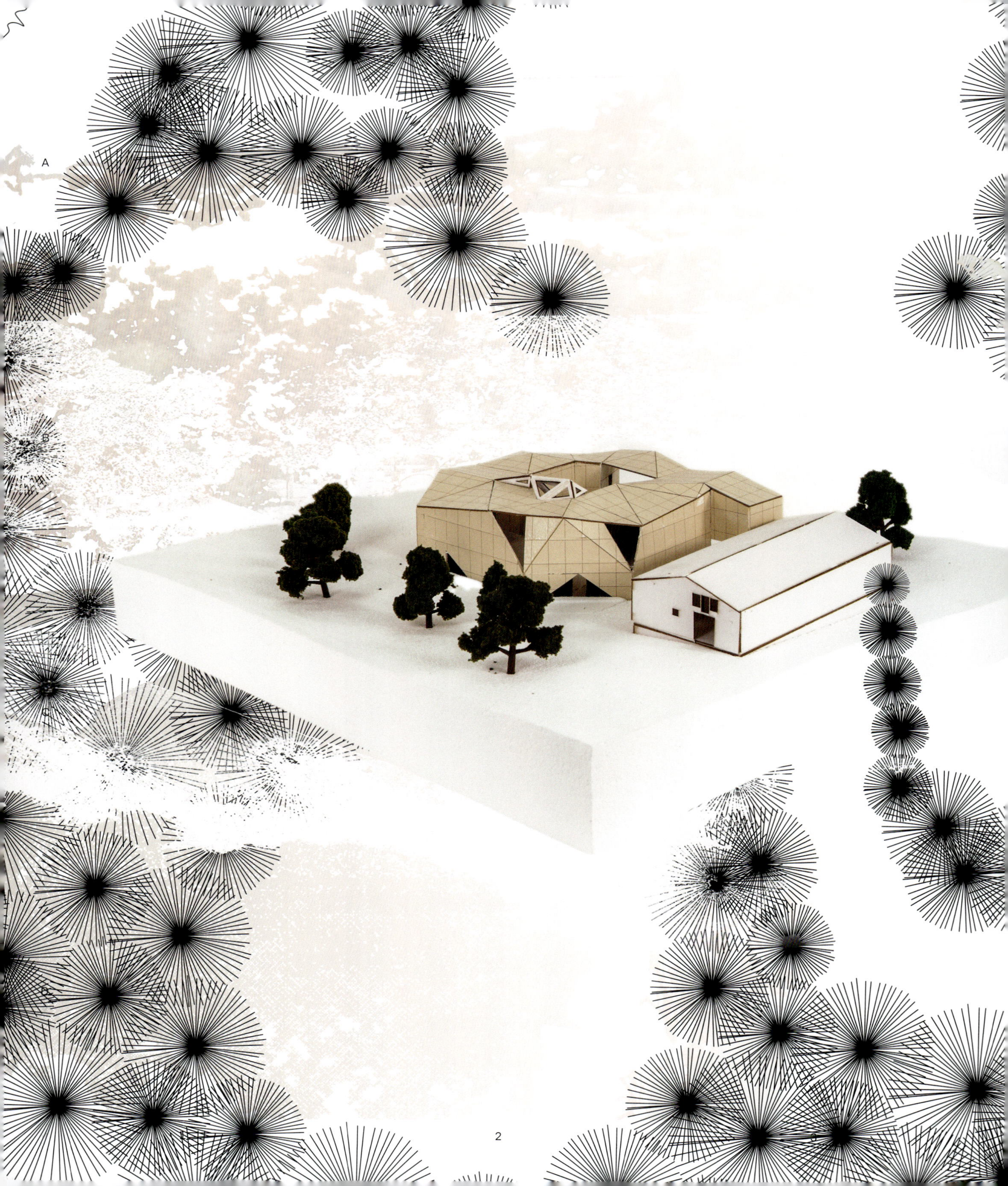
A
2

B1 Stephanie Coraisaca
A4 Emily Beane
D5 Emily Beane
B5 Emily Beane

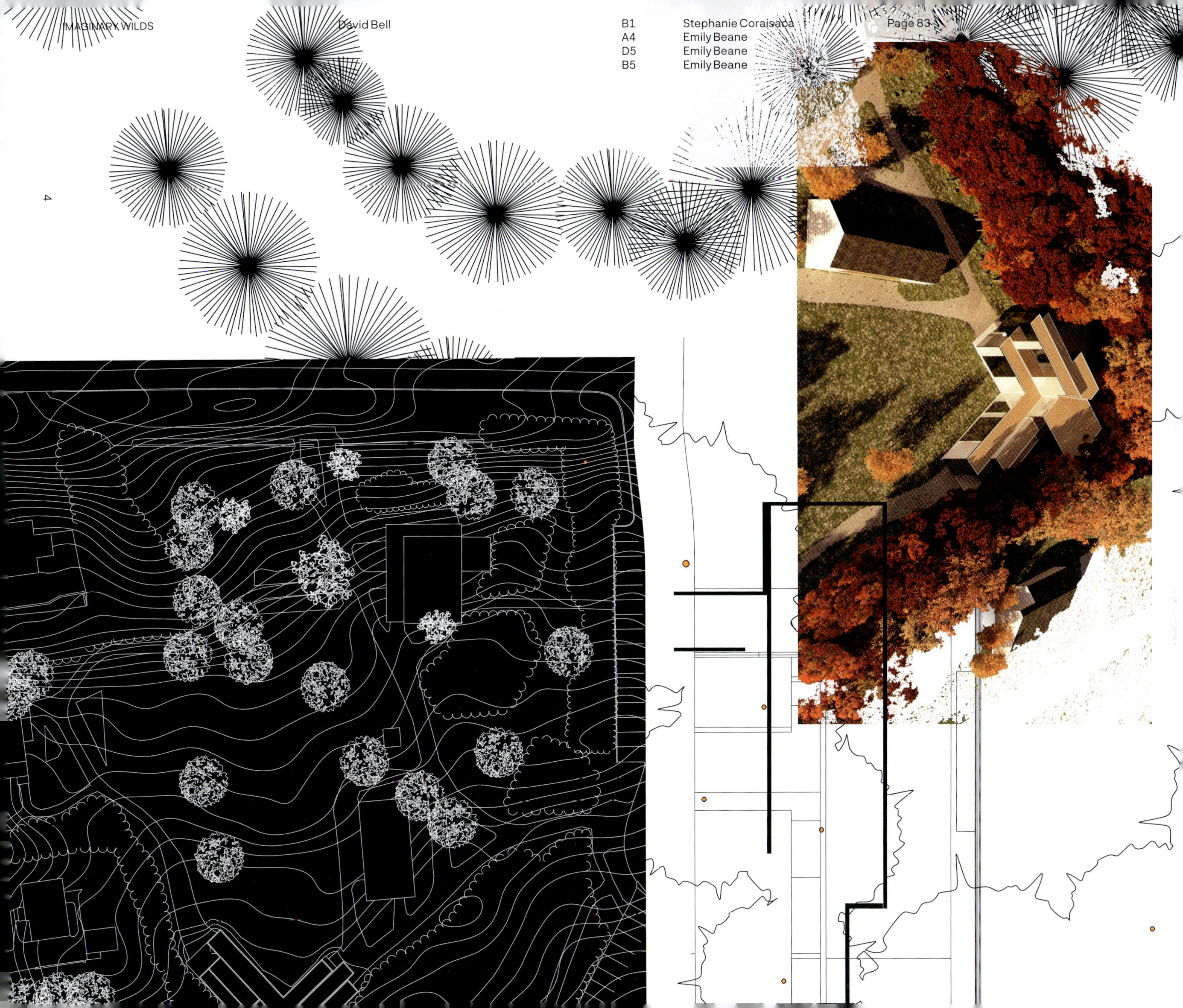

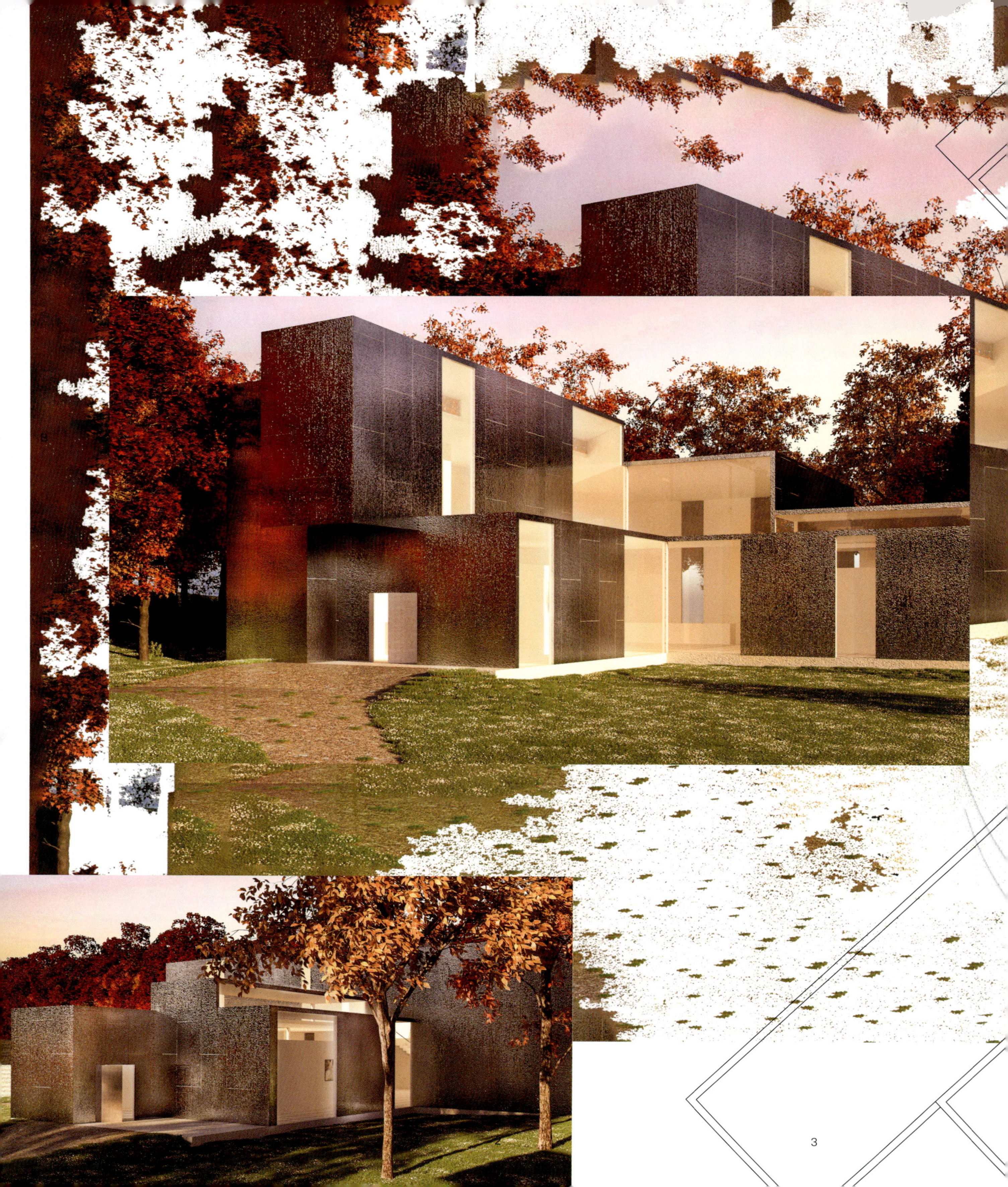
8
3

B2 Emily Beane
D1 Emily Beane
B6 Emily Beane

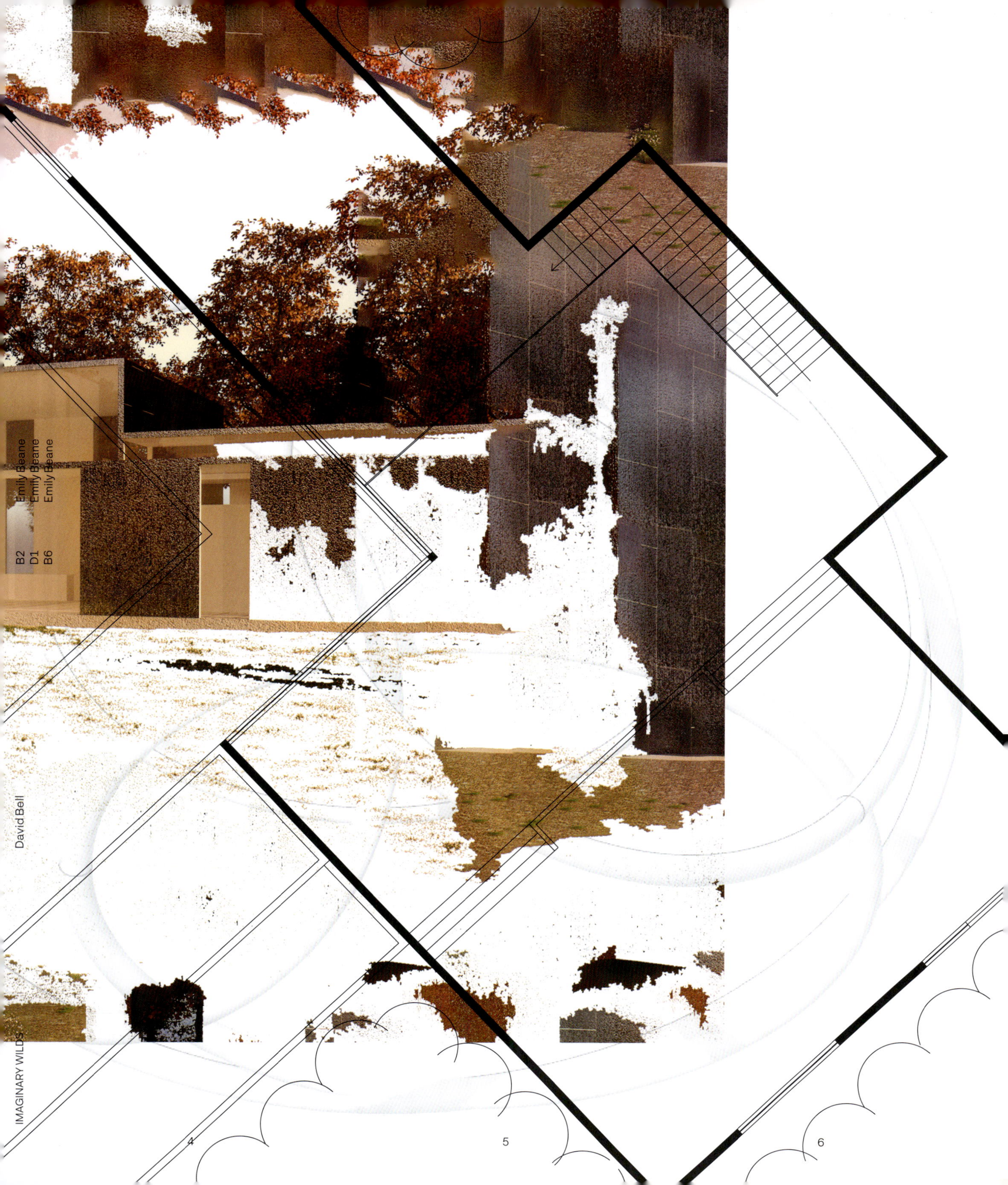

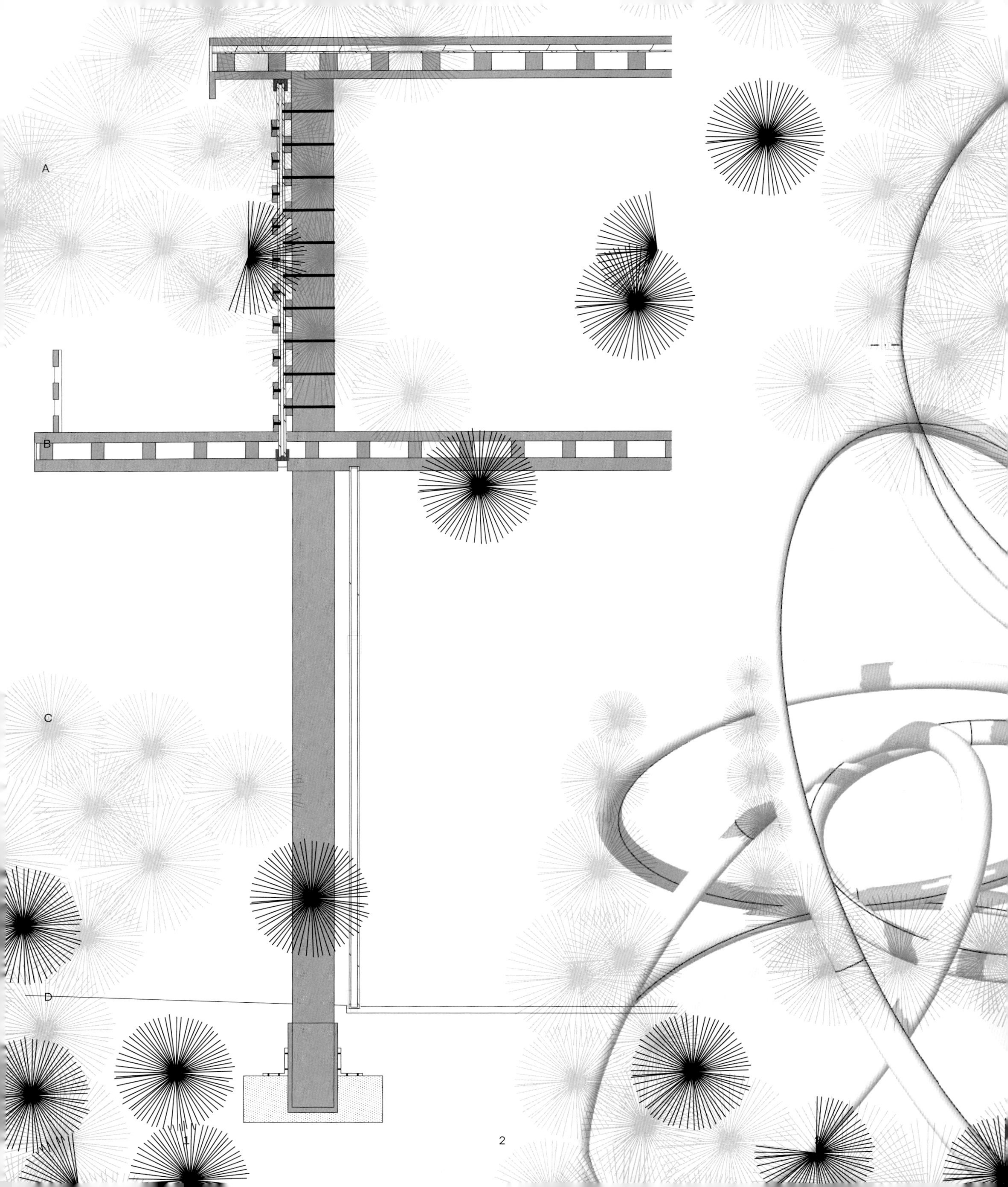
A
B
C
D
1
2
3

A2	Nicolas Roscioli-Barran
C3	Mykala Barrett
A4	Mykala Barrett
C4	Mykala Barrett

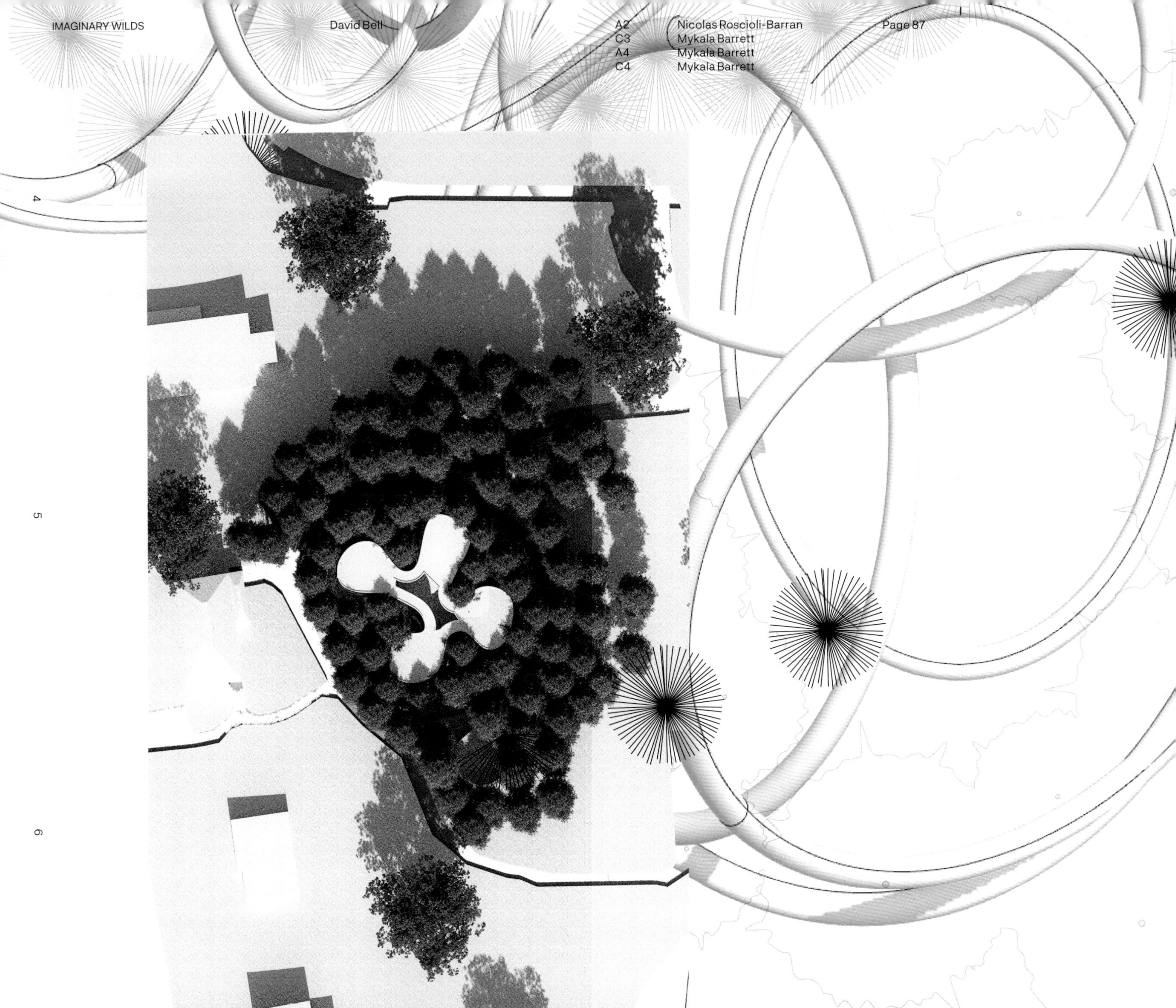

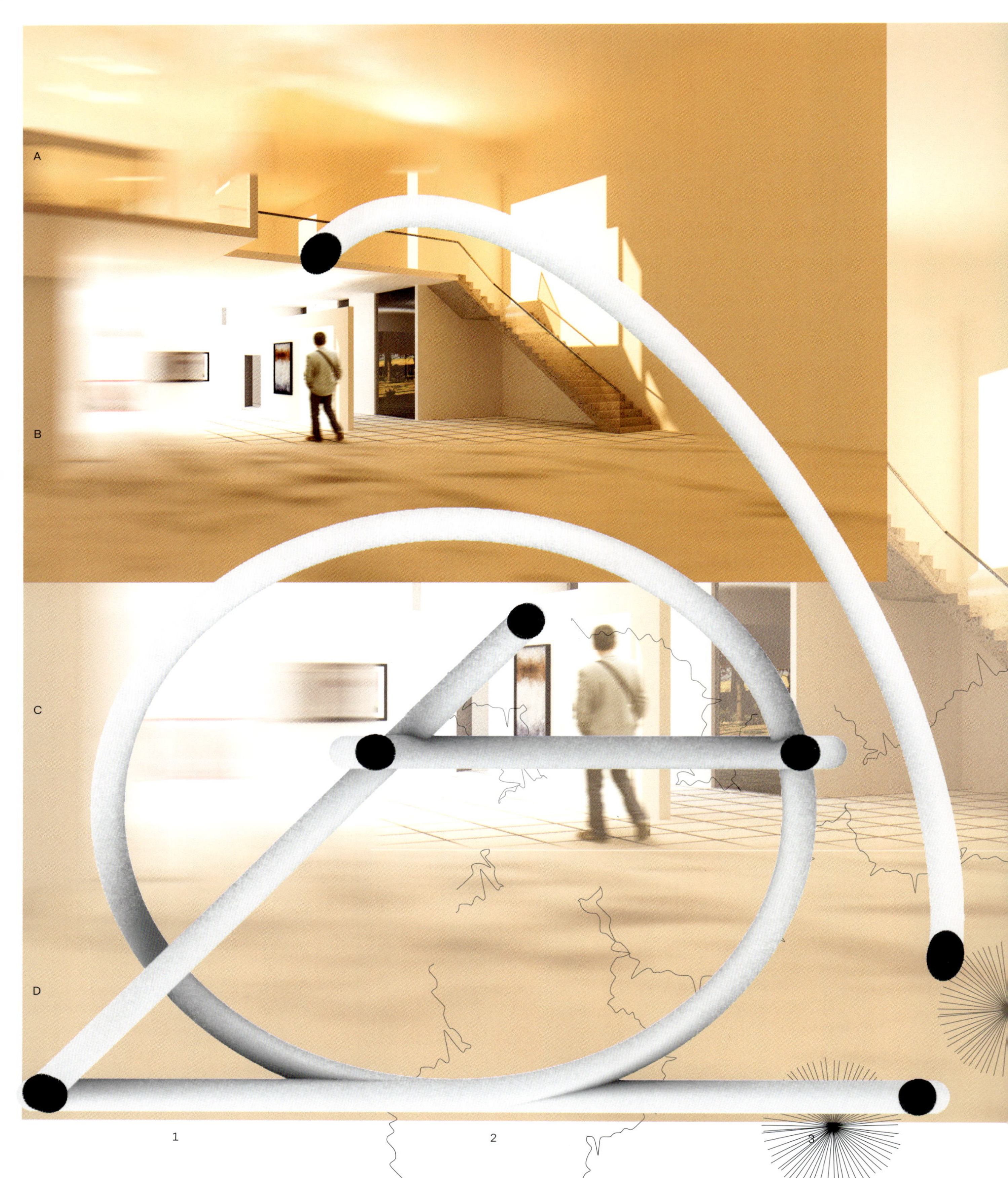
A
B
C
D
1
2
3

A1 Emily Beane
C2 Mykala Barrett
C5 Mykala Barrett
A5 Emily Beane

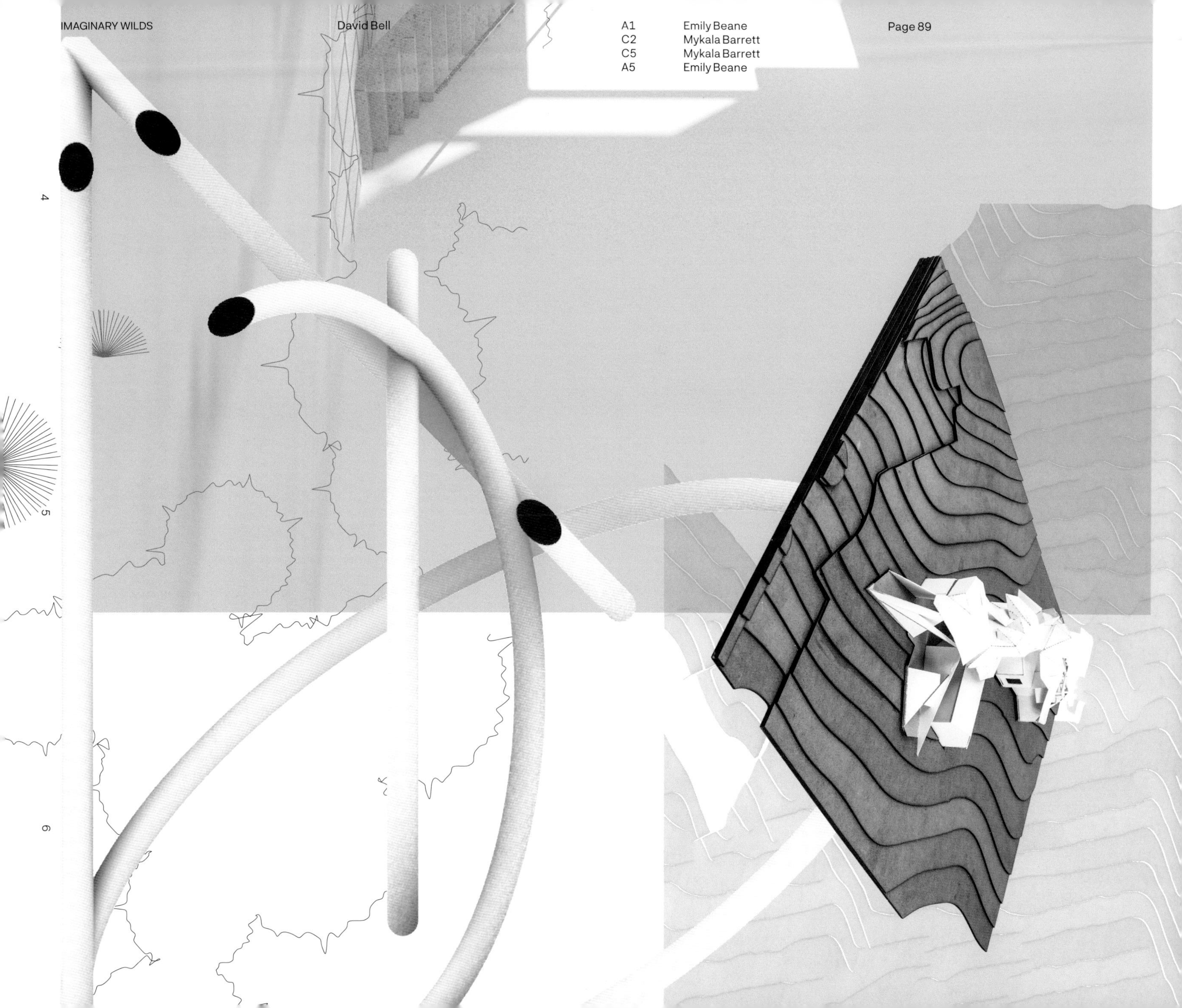

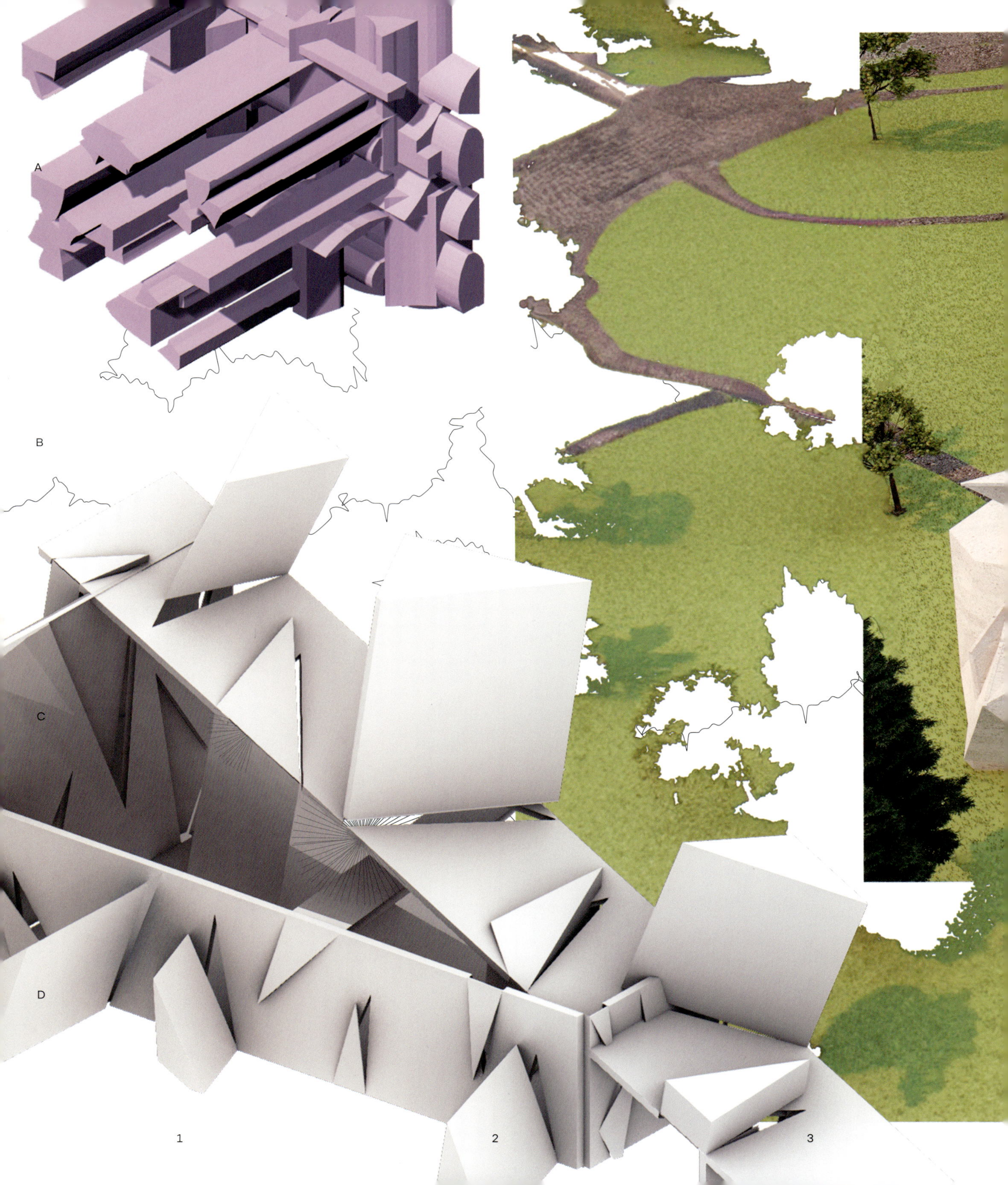
A
B
C
D
1
2
3

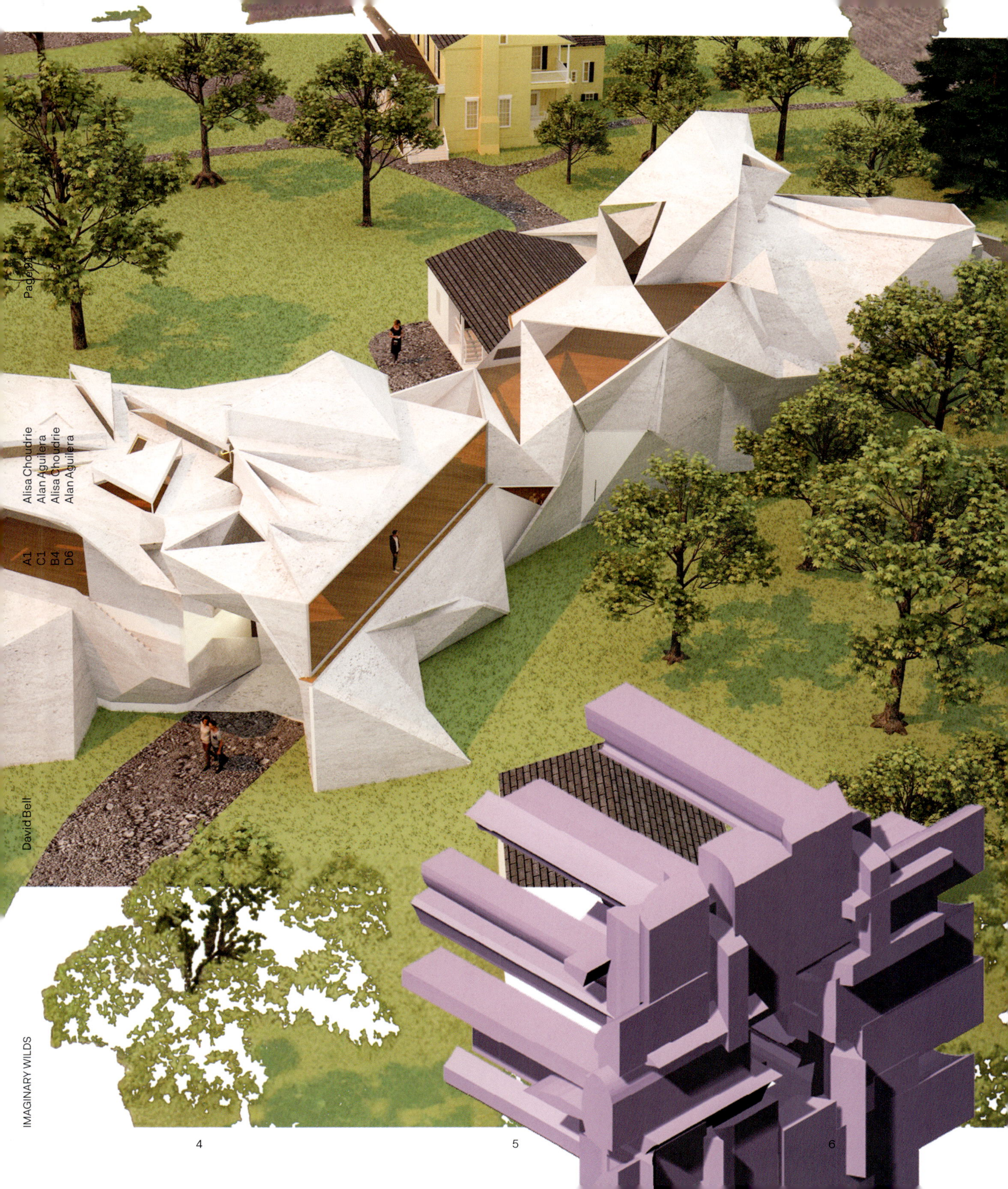

A1 Alisa Choudrie
C1 Alan Aguilera
B4 Alisa Choudrie
D6 Alan Aguilera

David Bell

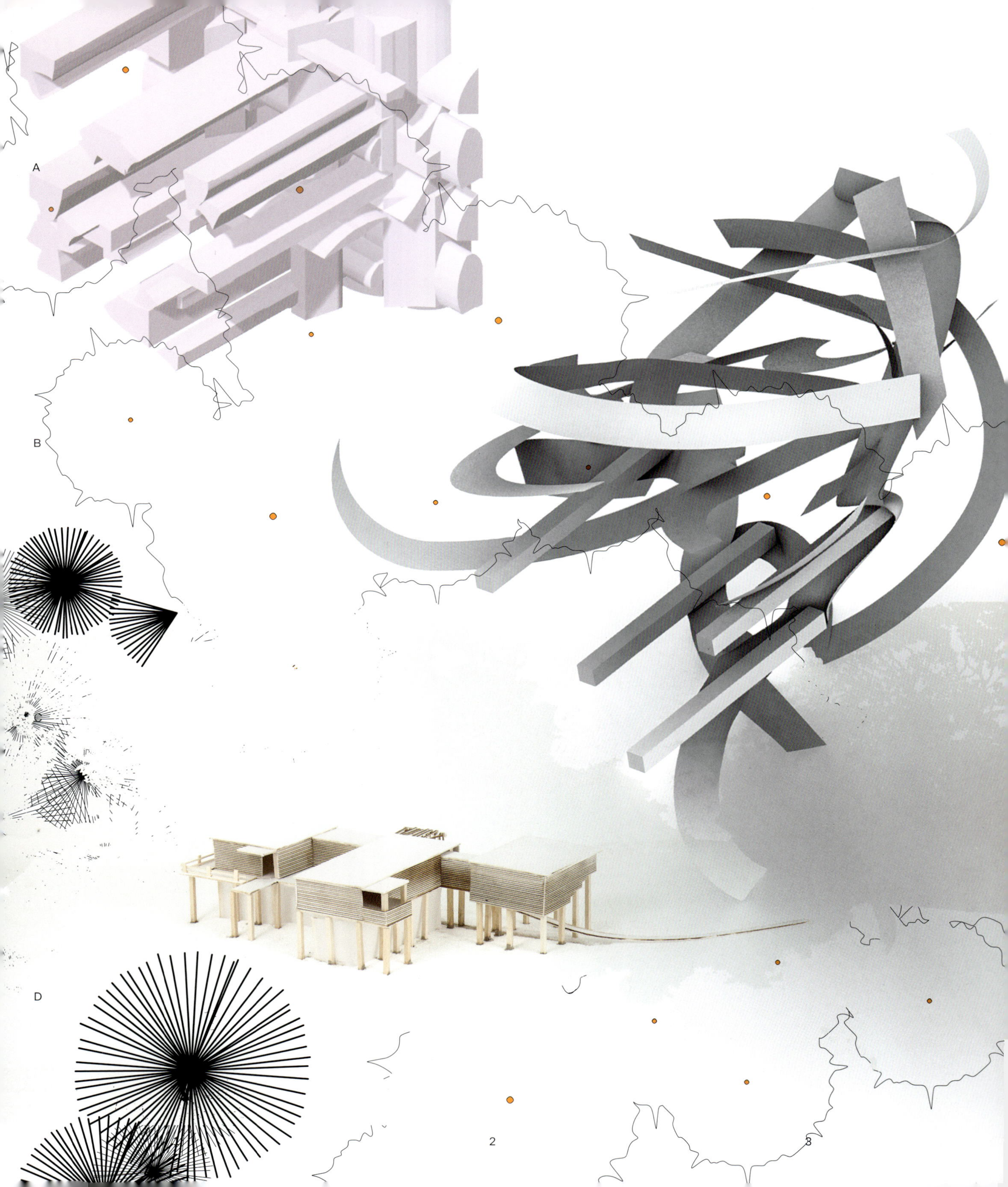
A
B
D
2
3

B3	Nicolas Roscioli-Barran
D1	Nicolas Roscioli-Barran
D5	Stephanie Coraisaca
B4	Stephanie Coraisaca

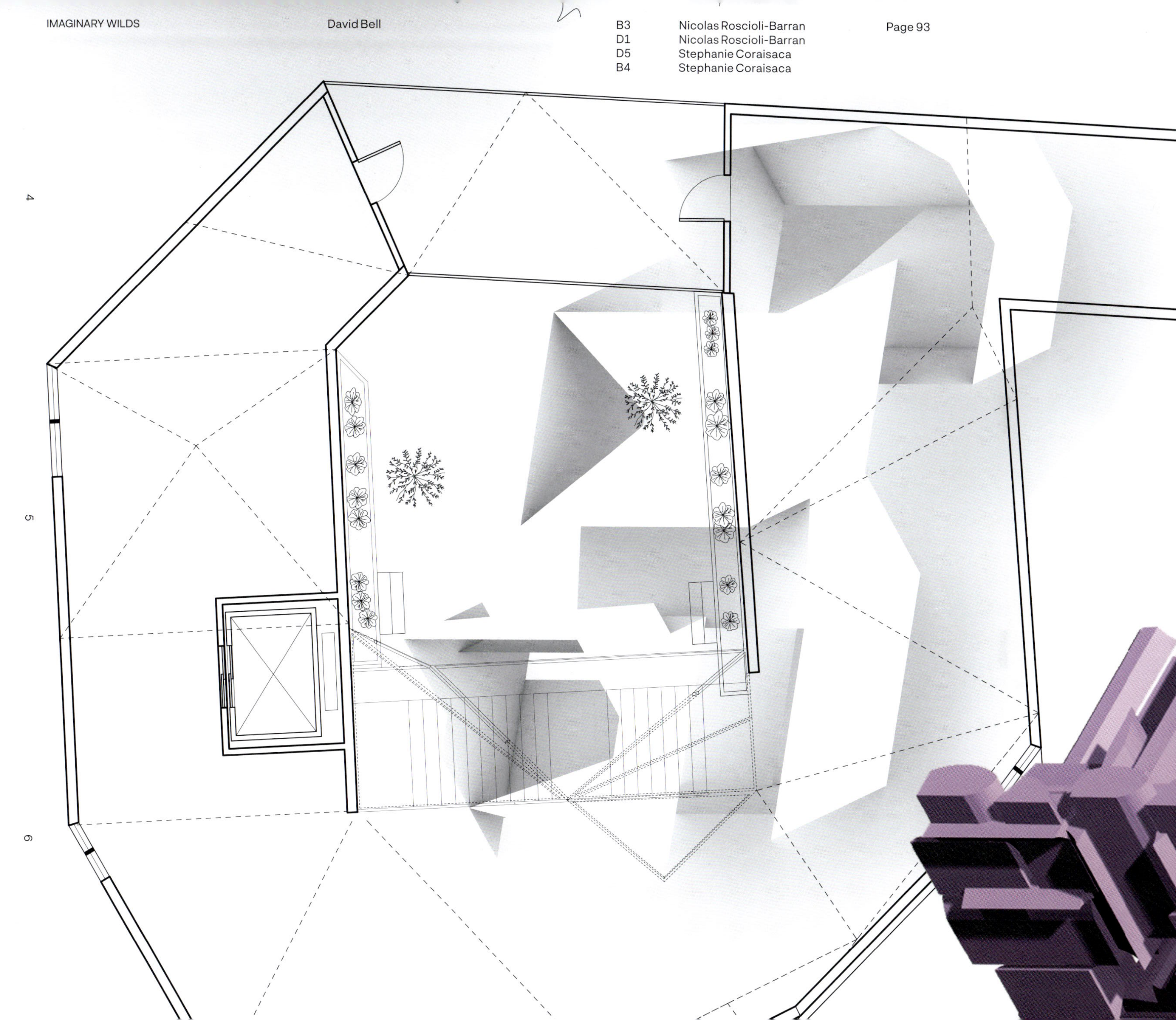

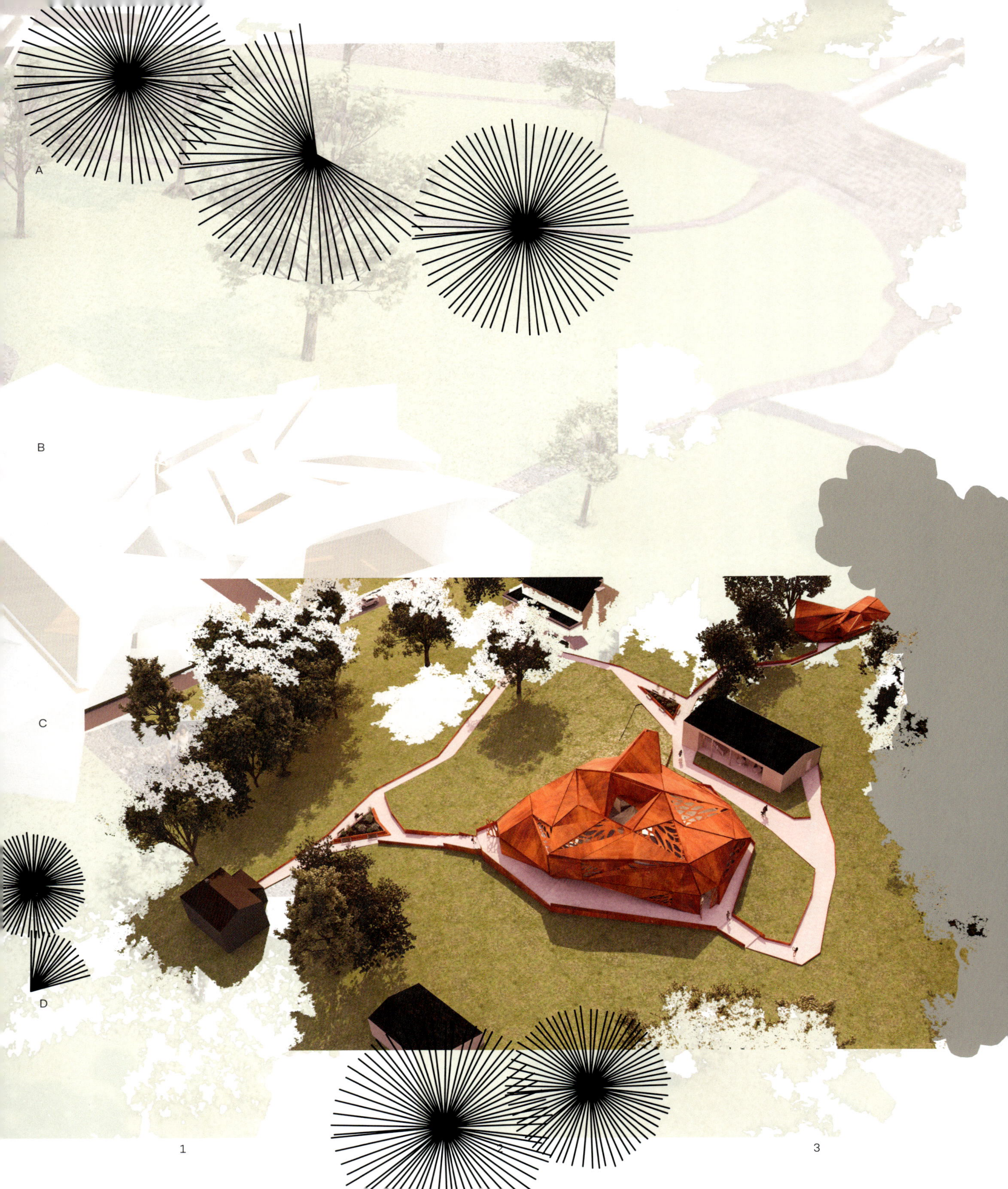
A
B
C
D
1
2
3

B1 Alan Aguilera
C2 Alan Aguilera
B5 Alan Aguilera

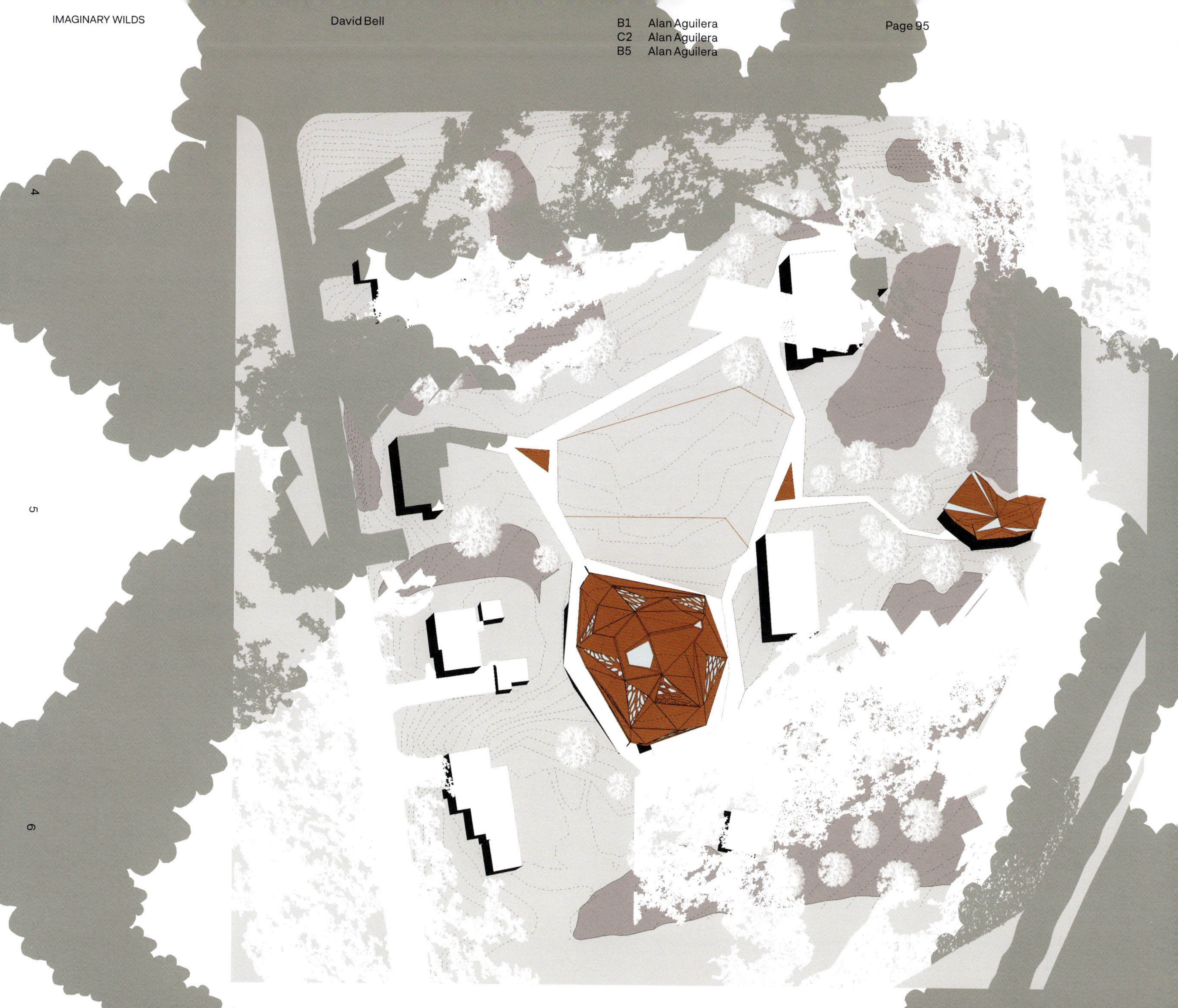

Containers for the Uncontainable

Design Studio Instructor

Adam Dayem

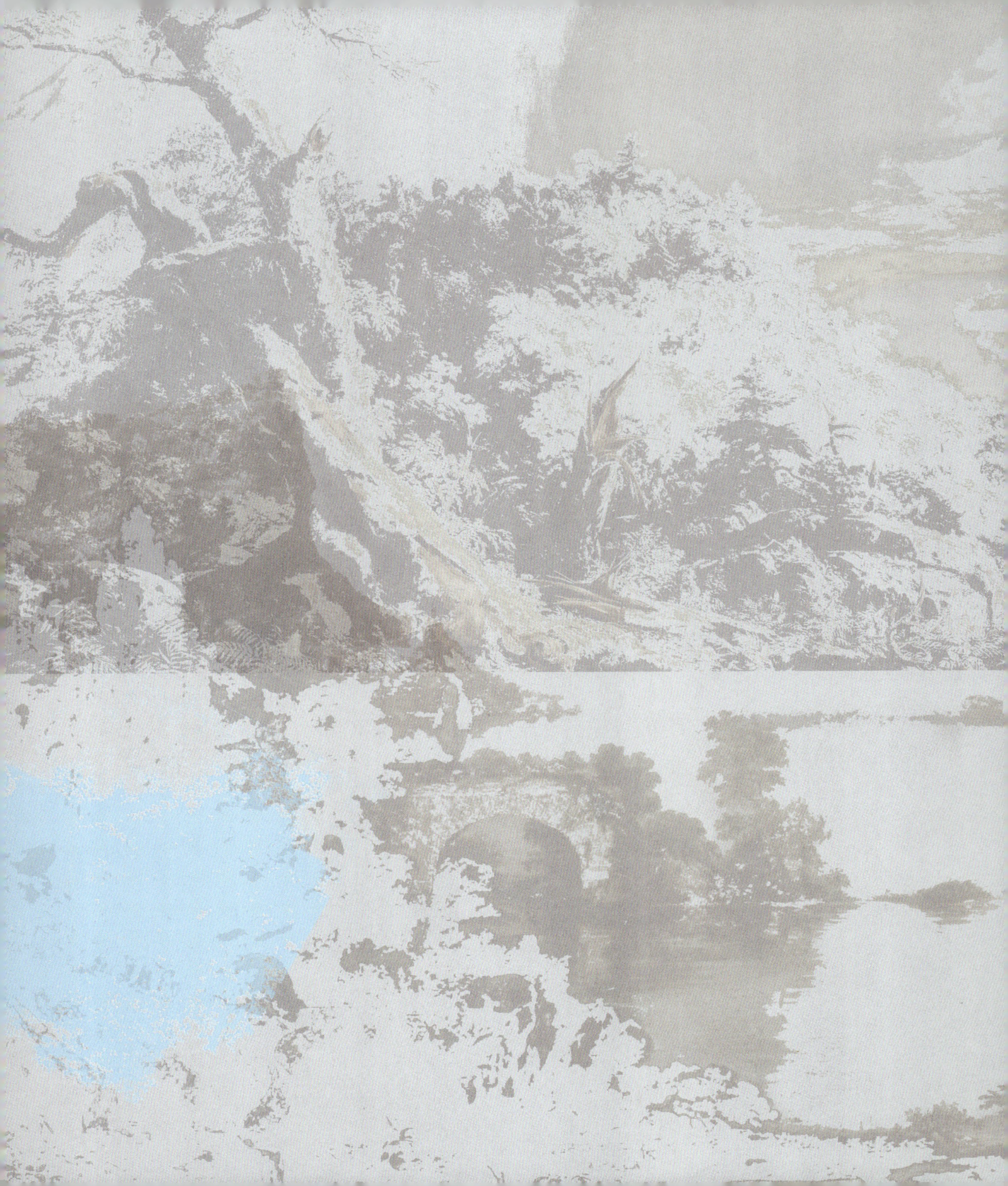

This design studio section started with abstract studies of contained volumes, which explored how one thing can contain another to produce different types of spaces within a single volume and between two volumes. These explorations were informed by Robert Venturi's writing on relationships between the insides and the outsides of buildings, where he notes that the interior and the exterior of a building are always, to a greater or lesser extent, different from each other. This difference must be resolved in a zone existing in between the interior and the exterior, and this in-between is almost always a wall, roof, or ceiling built to the minimum dimensions of construction systems, structural systems, and / or the required thermal properties of a building enclosure. But the in-between can also be given additional thickness in order to contain other elements of architecture, including circulation, program, and indirect lighting systems. The term for this thickened in-between zone in architecture is poché.

Students began by making models composed of two cubic or rectilinear volumes, one being the "container" and the other being the "contained." Each of the two volumes was composed of "inside," or negative geometry, and "outside," or positive geometry. Independent manipulation of the inside and outside geometries allowed the amount of poché between the inside and the outside to be adjusted. Students were then asked to consider the poché as space for circulation, service, and natural lighting, and the spaces contained within and between the container and contained volumes as housing the public programs of a small freestanding gallery building.

These abstract studies were then placed into dialogue with landscapes—both the real landscape of the Thomas Cole National Historic Site and the imaginary landscapes of Cole's paintings. In terms of the real landscape, students were asked to consider how a new freestanding gallery building would relate to the context of the existing buildings and landscape of the site, while keeping in mind that architectural sites are always physical and cultural constructs, regardless of how built-up or natural they may seem to be. As such, students were encouraged to either remake the existing site to contain or be contained by their building proposals, or to imagine their building proposals as integrated elements of the landscape that sensitively redesign the site. In terms of imaginary landscapes, students were asked to consider Cole's conception of America from a contemporary view. The mission of the Thomas Cole National Historic Site was instructive in this regard, as the institution acknowledges cultural evolution both in exhibits of contemporary artists dealing with contemporary ideas of nature, landscape, and its inhabitants, and in re-presentations of Thomas Cole's world from different perspectives. These exhibits can be inherently critical of Cole's thinking, and the students were asked to take a similarly critical view of Cole in designing their gallery buildings.

Explorations of real and imaginary landscapes encouraged students to acknowledge that architecture must be able to engage both material and ideal worlds, and that neither of these worlds can fully contain or be contained by architecture.

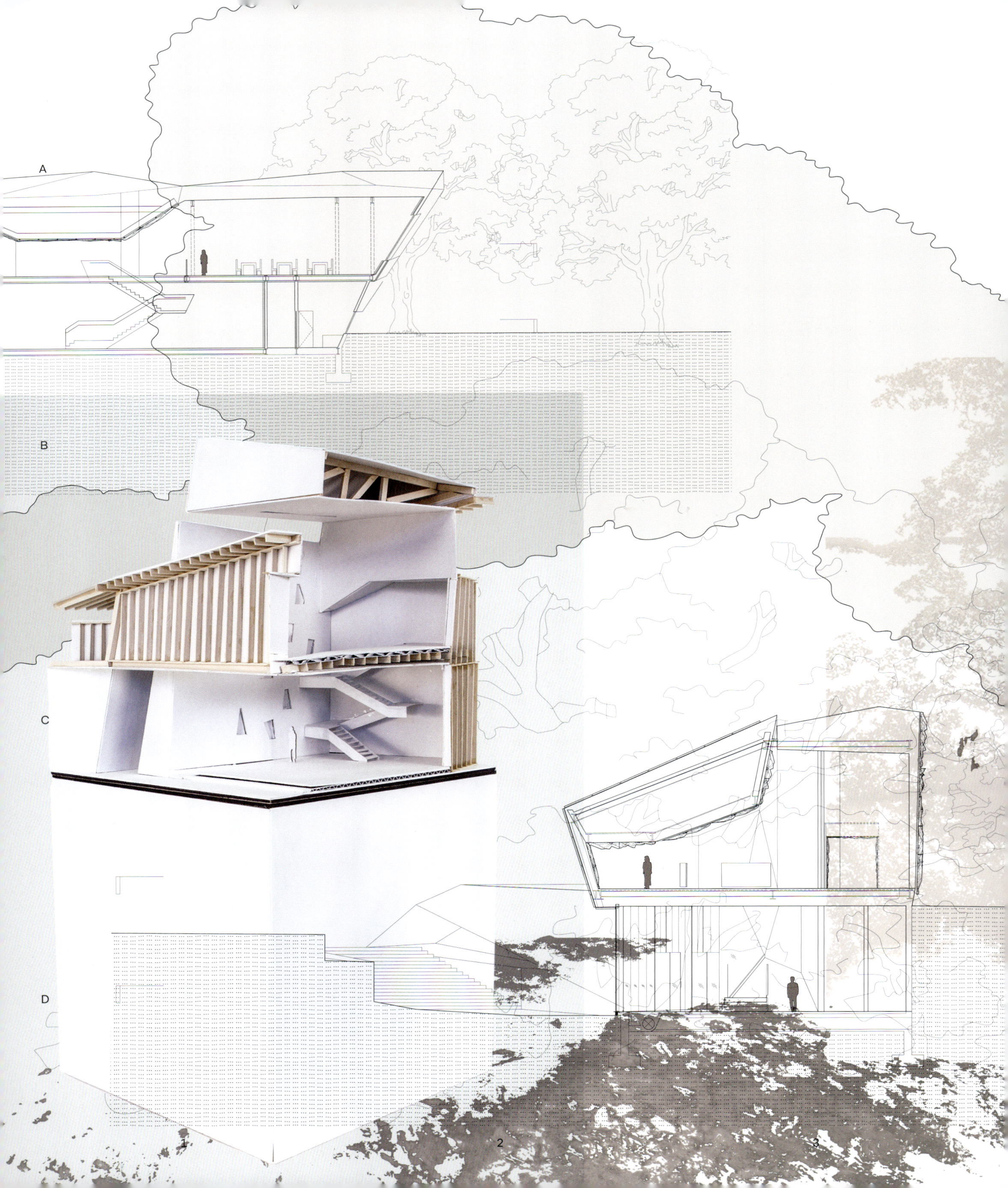

A
B
C
D
1
2
3

A1 Moe Kawakami
C1 William Felcone
D3 Michael Degennaro
A5 Moe Kawakami
D6 Moe Kawakami

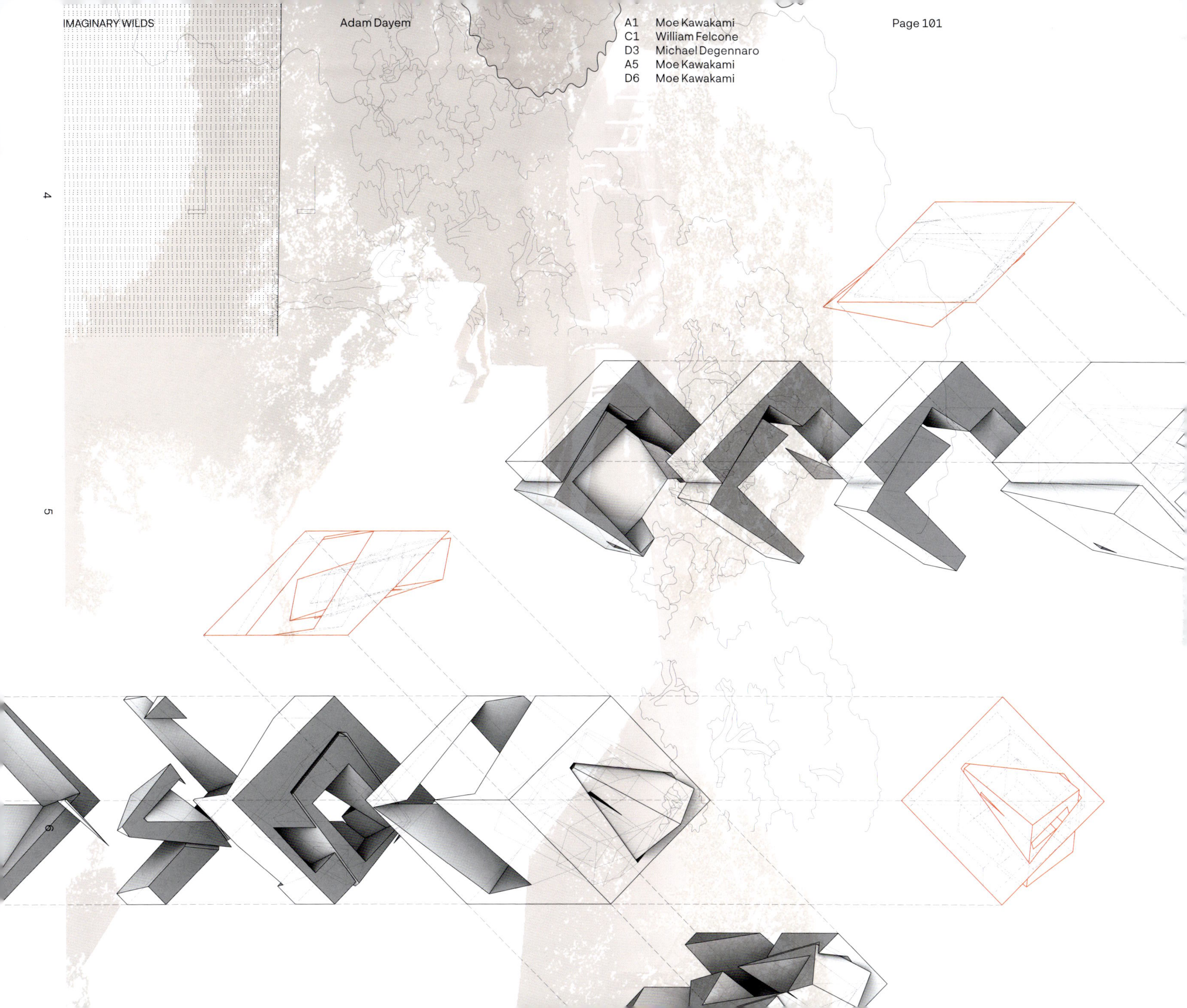

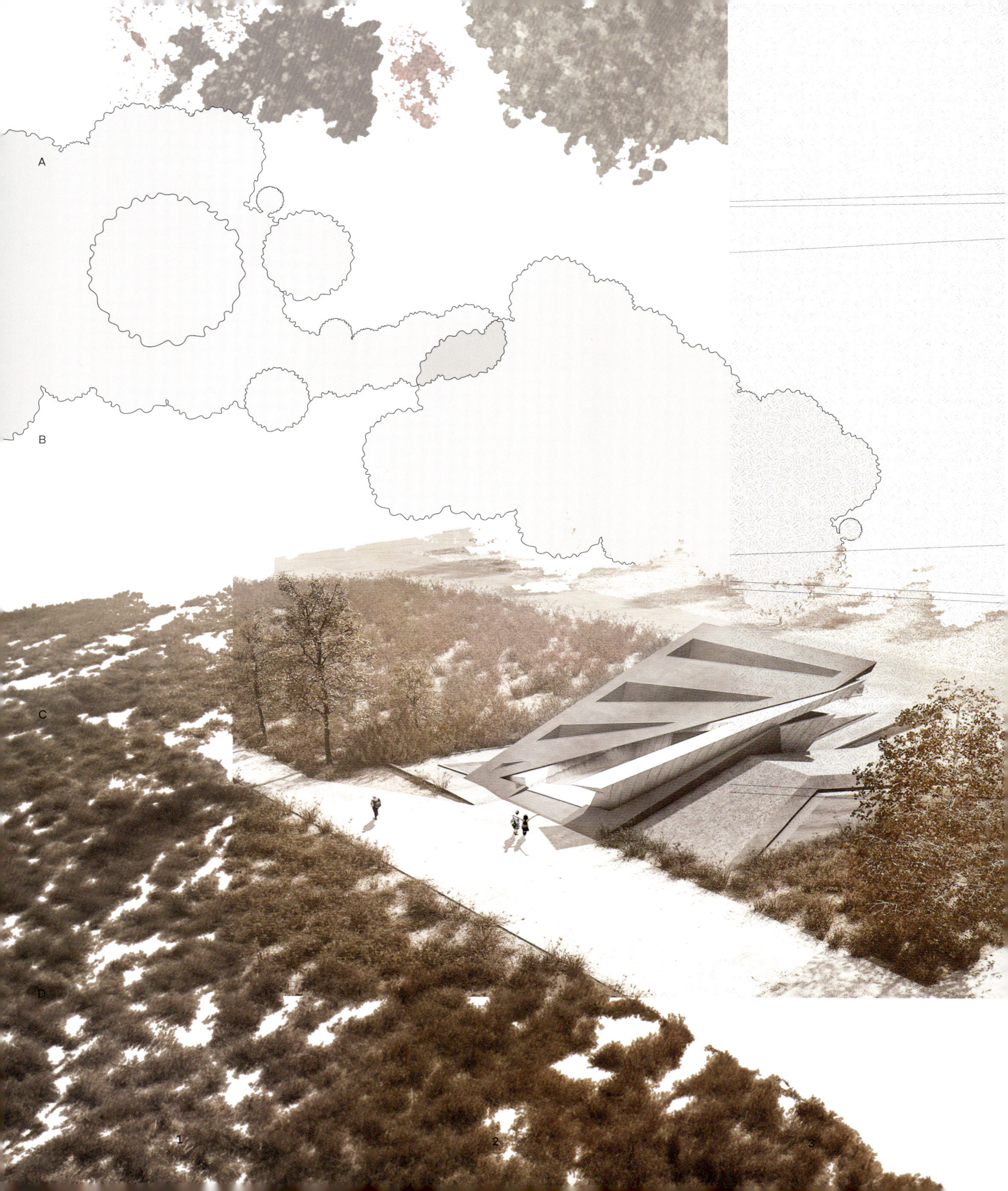
A
B
C
D
1
2
3

Adam Dayem

C3 Sarah Ishida
B6 Sarah Ishida
D5 Sarah Ishida

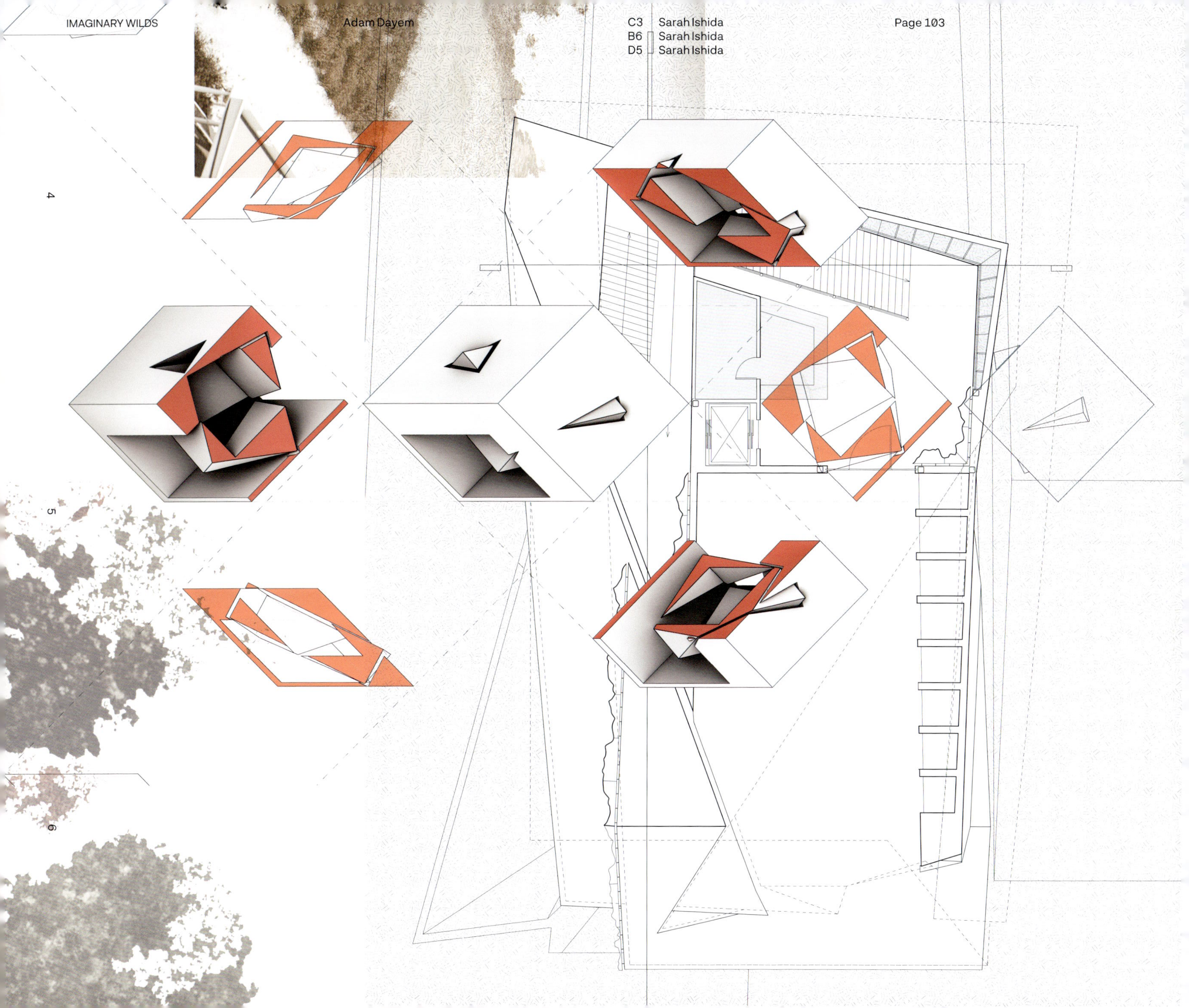

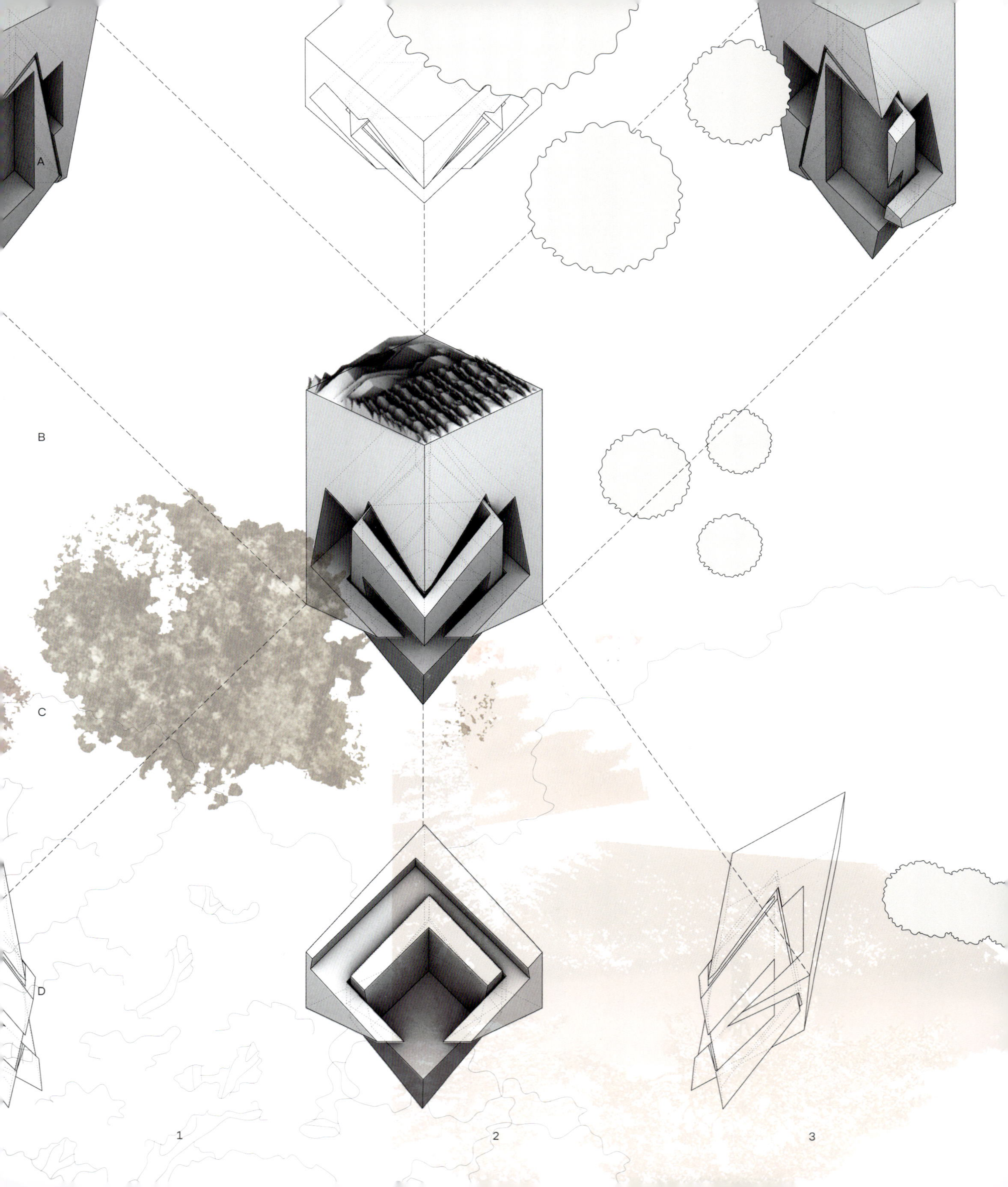
A
B
C
D
1
2
3

B2 Ethan Kang
B4 Michael Degennaro
D5 Ethan Kang

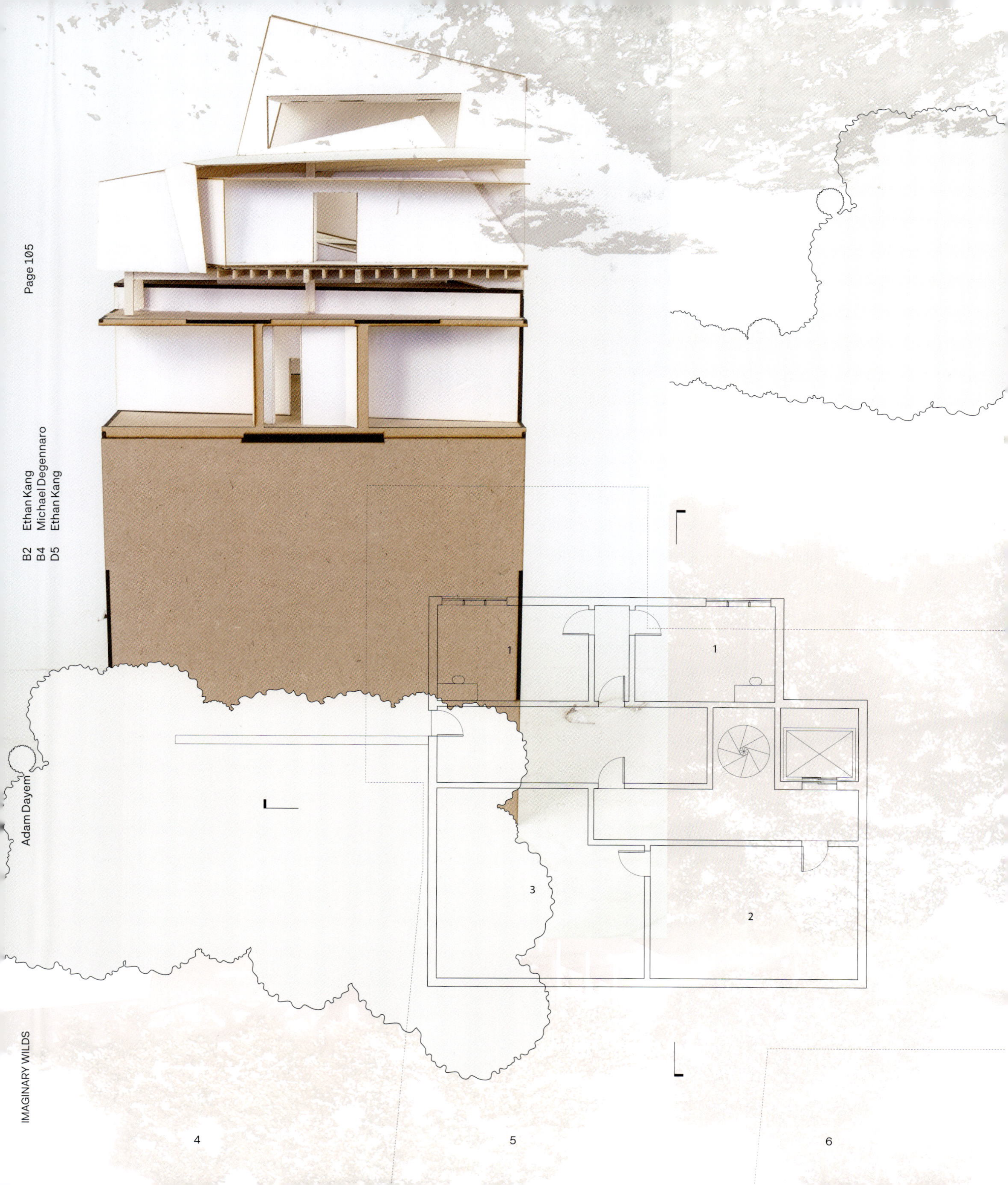

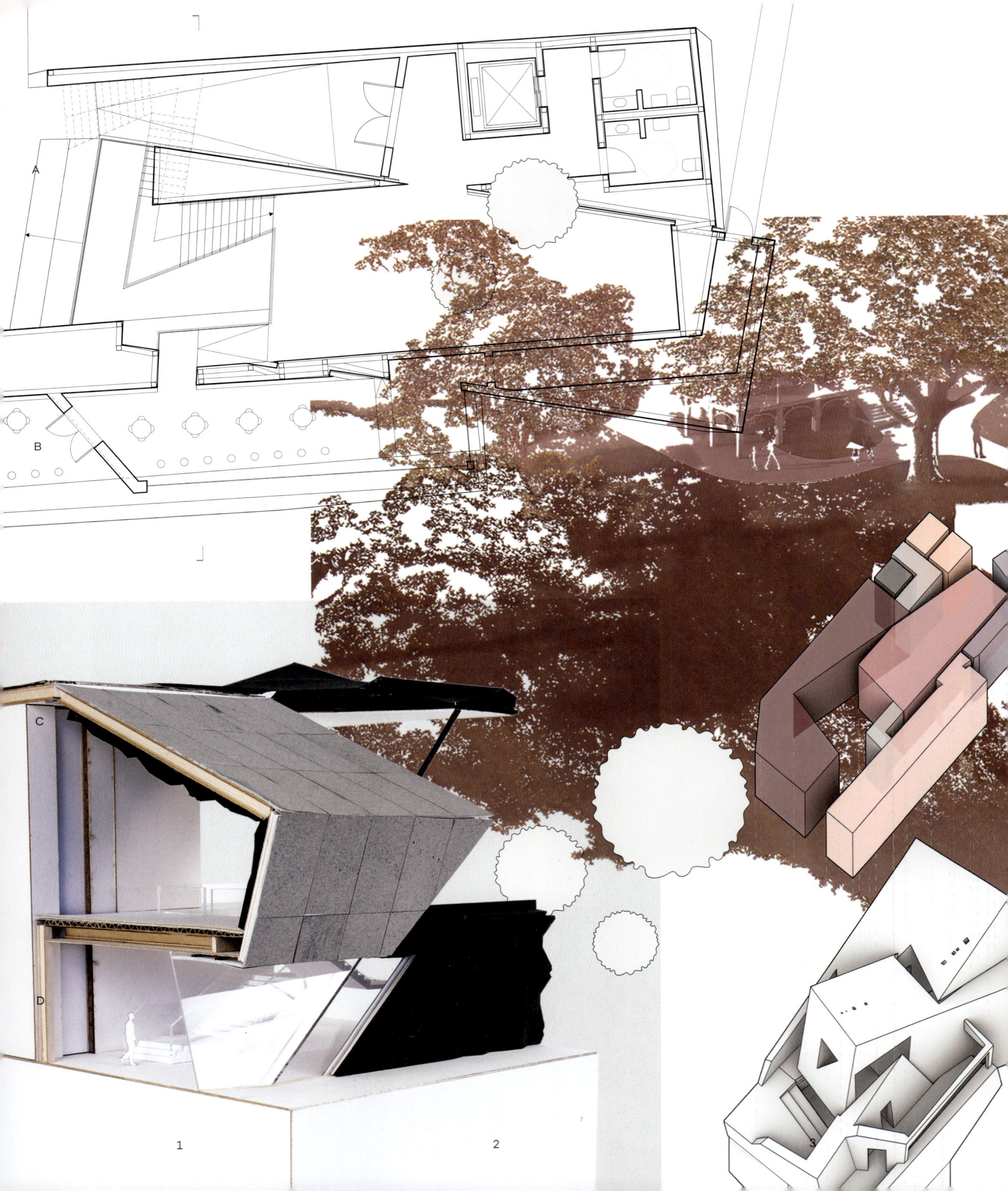
A
B
C
D
1
2
3

A1 Michael Degennaro
D1 Moe Kawakami
D3 Michael Degennaro
A6 Michael Degennaro
C5 Michael Degennaro

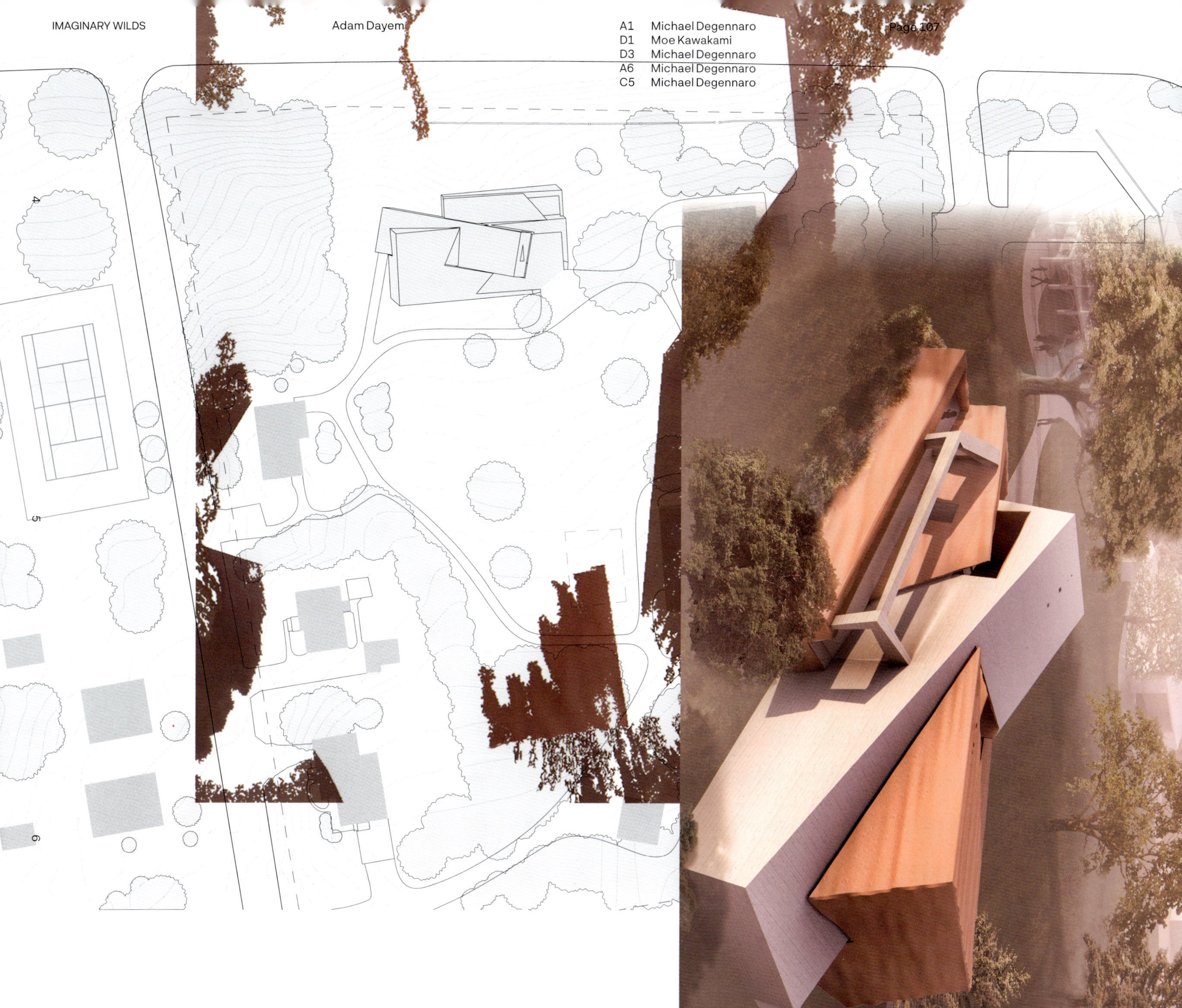

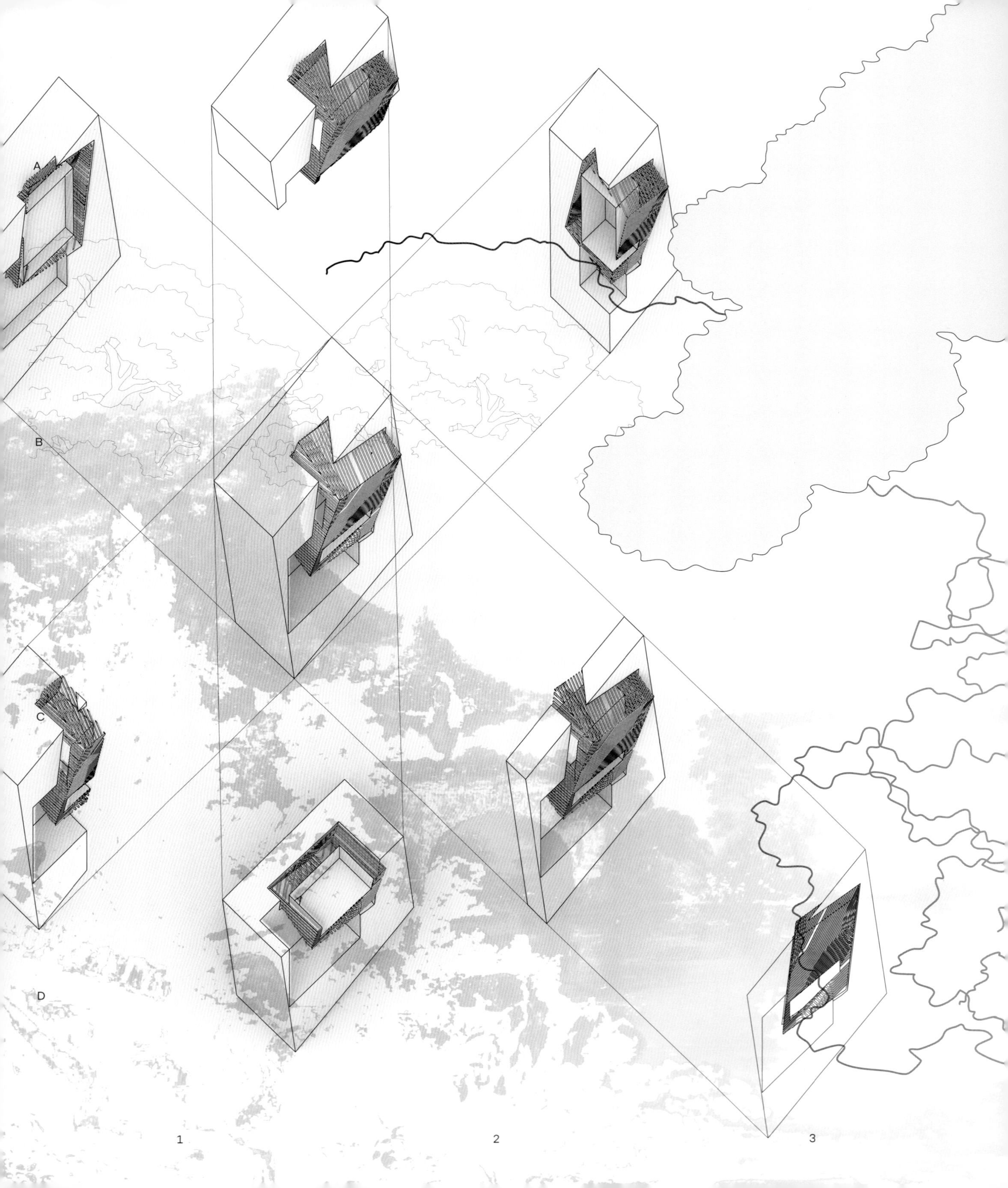
A
B
C
D
1
2
3

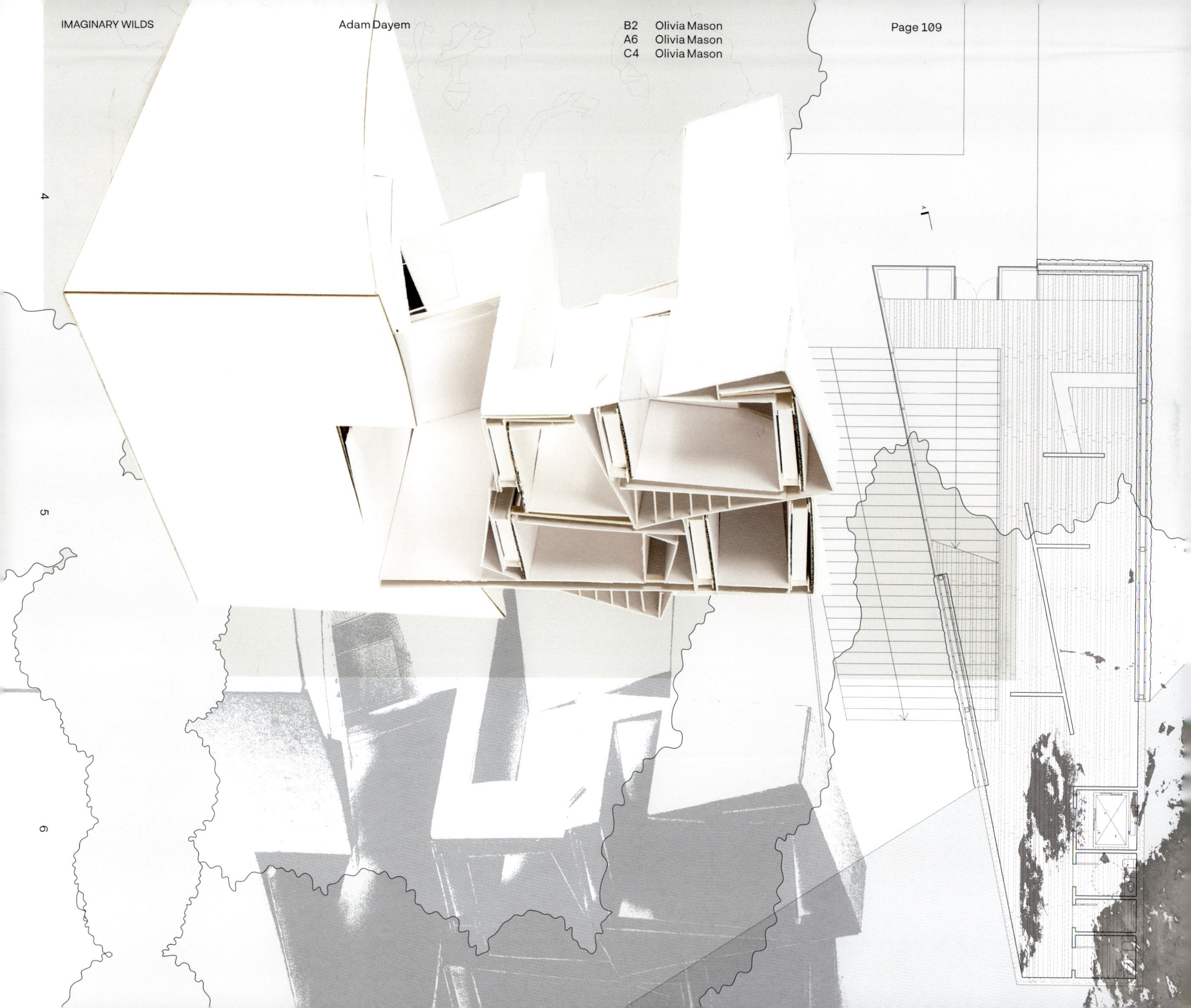
4
5
6

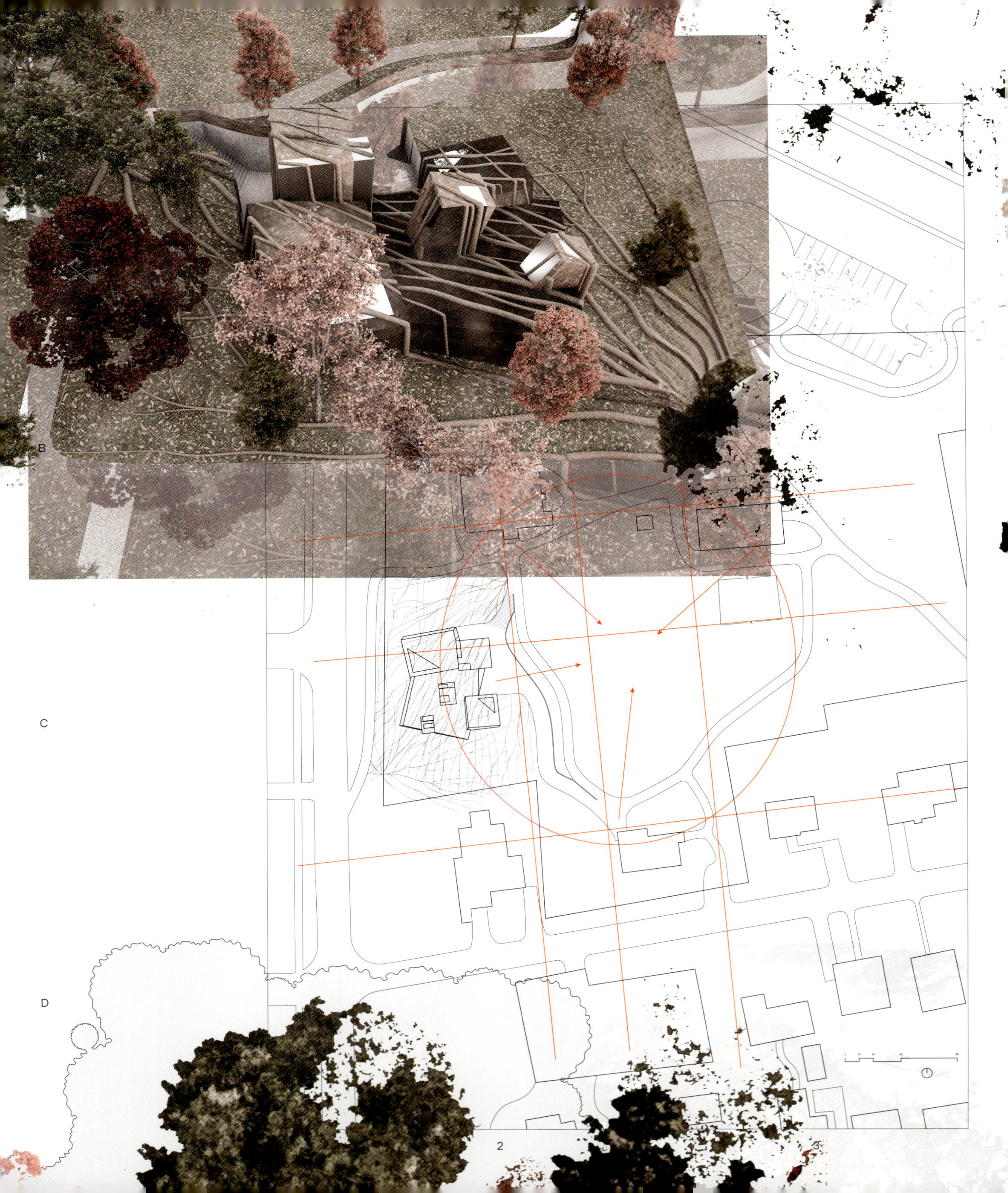
B
C
D
2
3

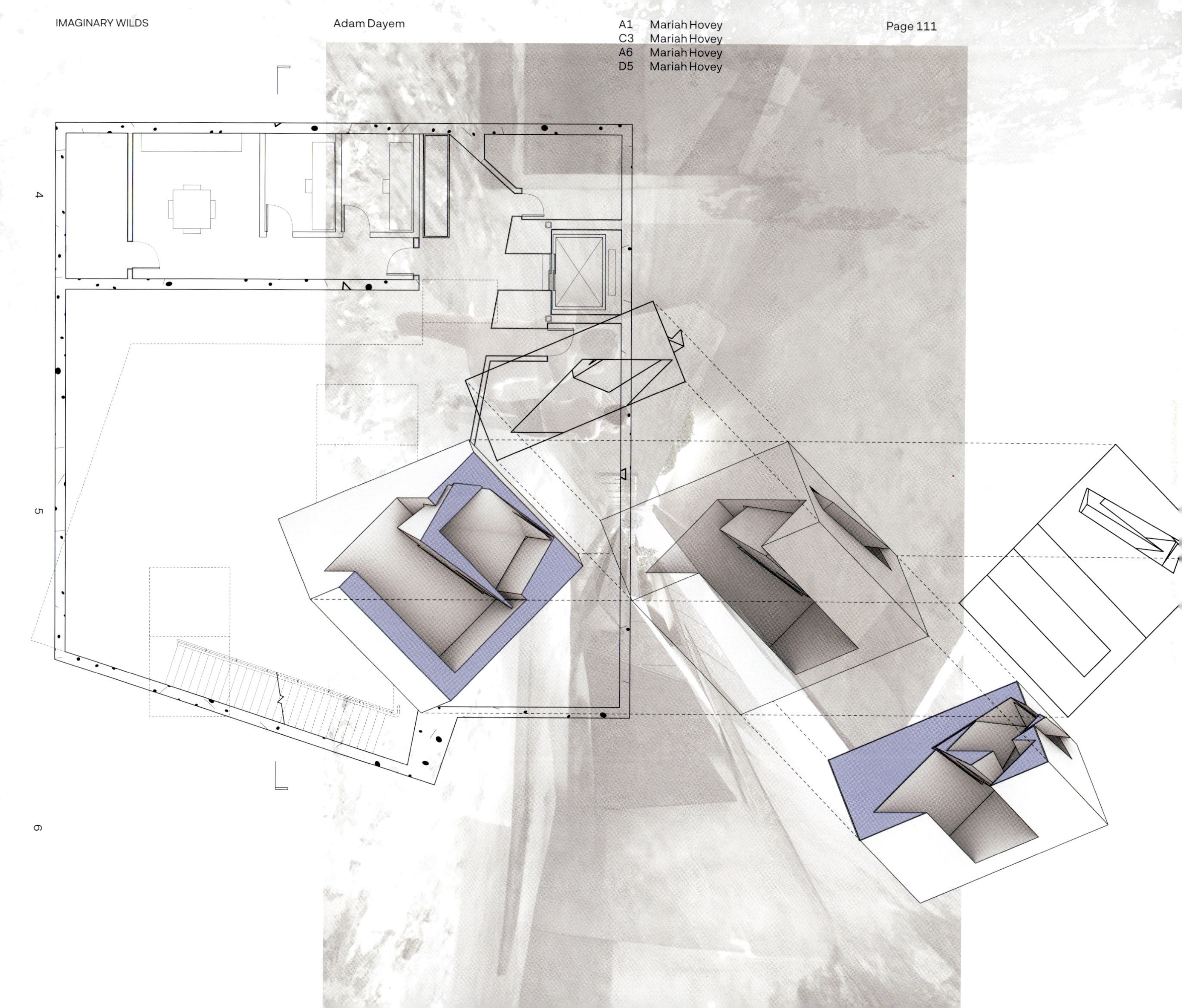
4
5
6

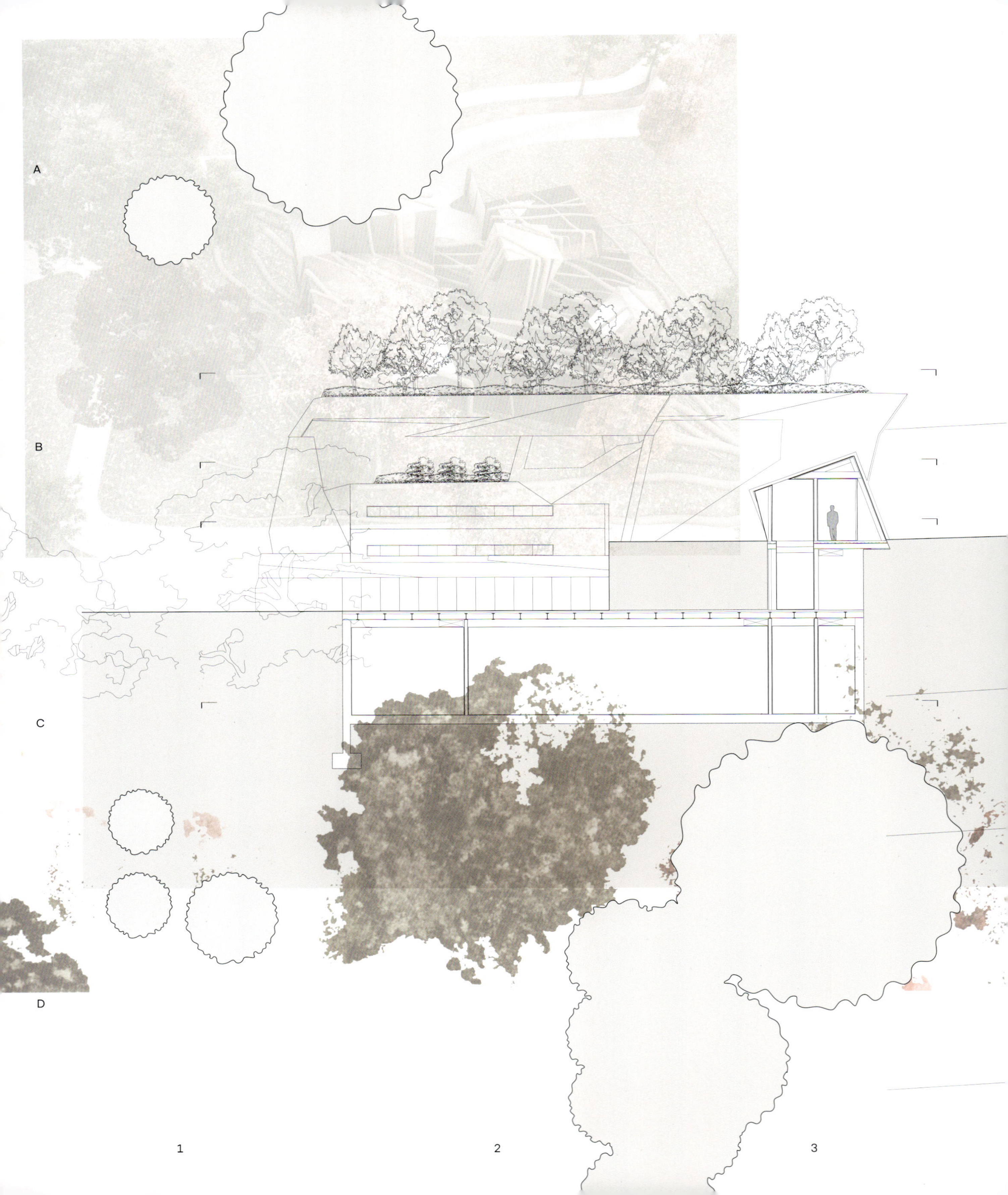
A
B
C
D
1
2
3

B2 Kyra Gregoire
B5 Kyra Gregoire
D5 Kyra Gregoire

Adam Dayem

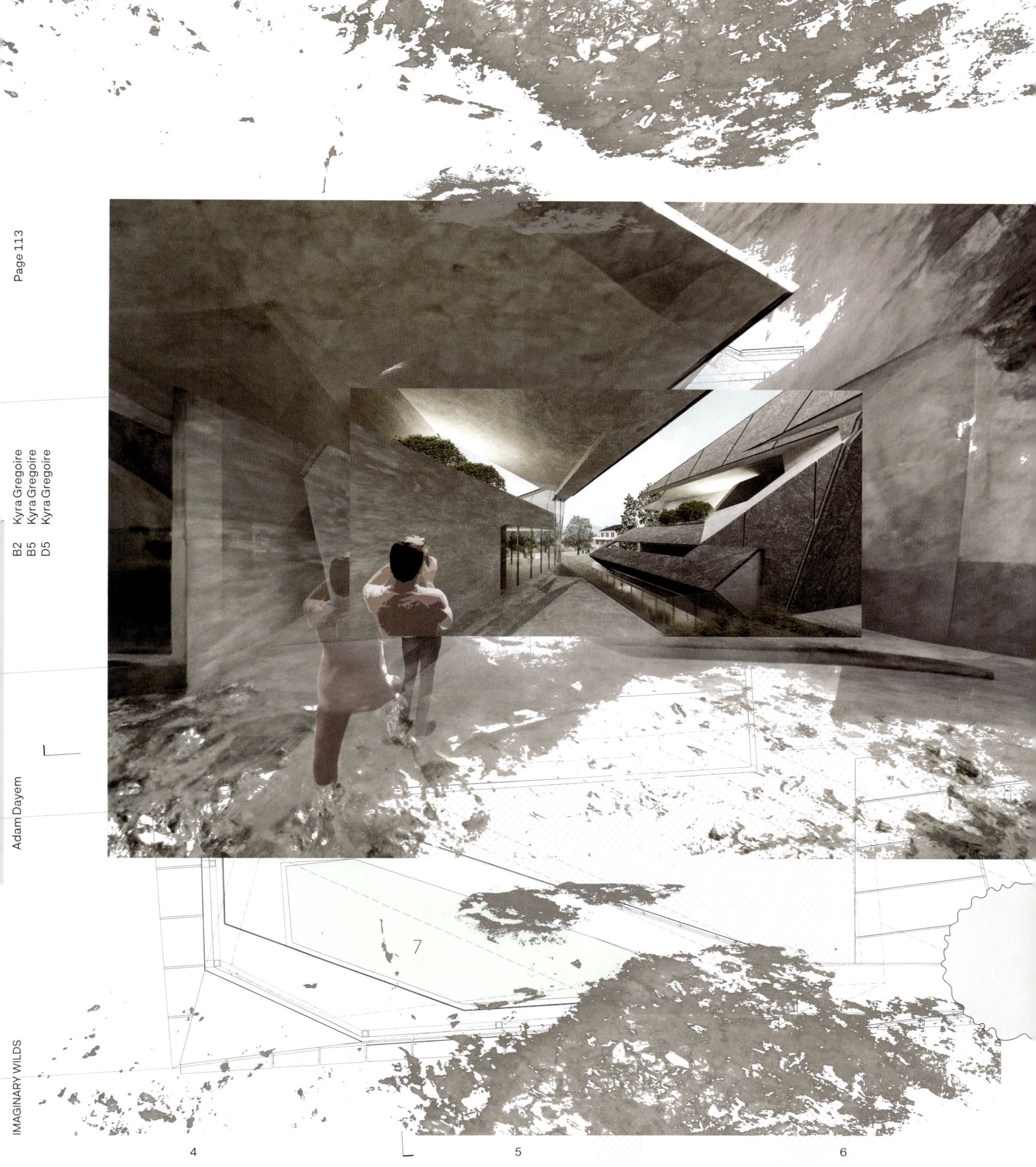

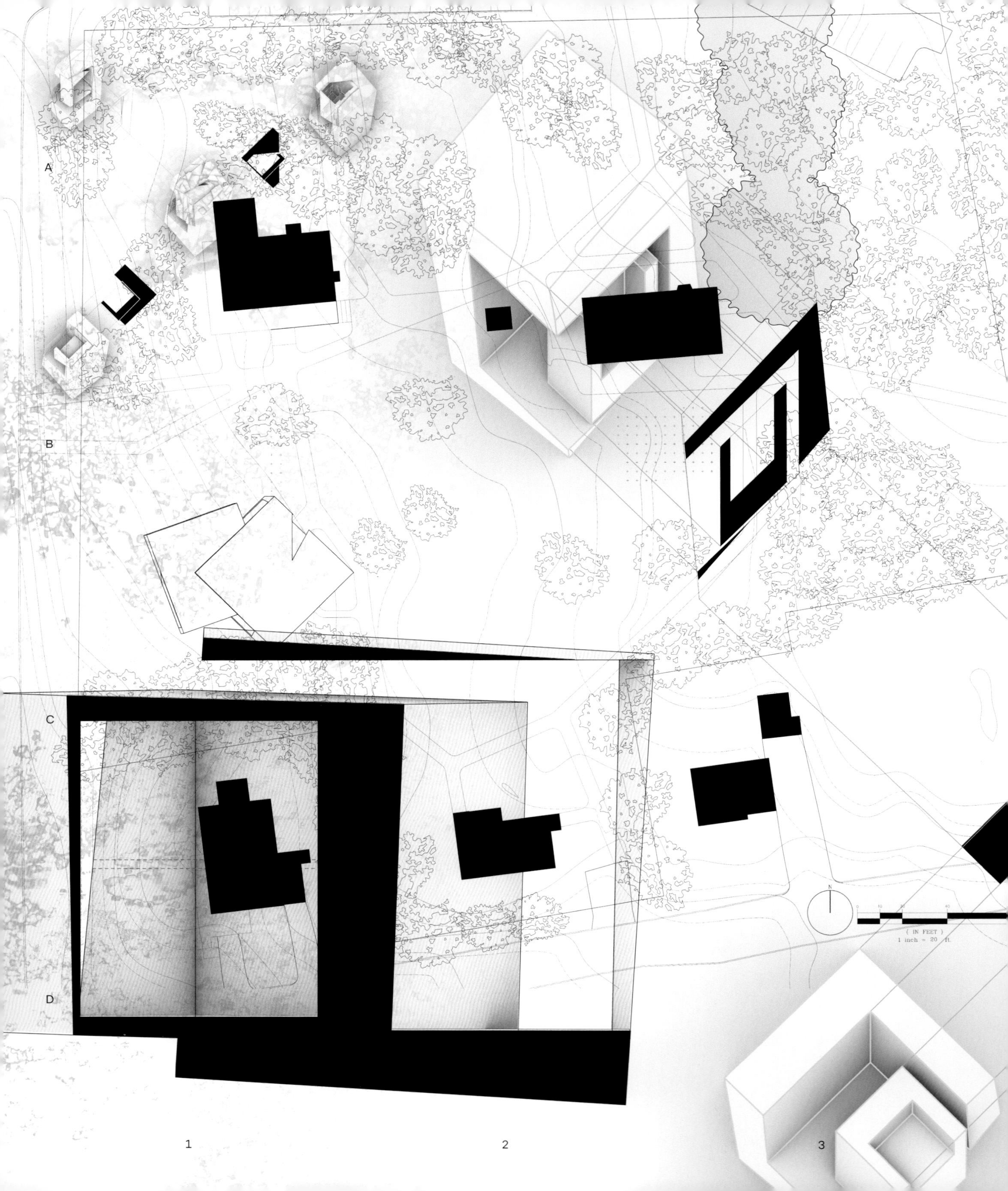
A
B
C
D
N
0
10
20
40
(IN FEET)
1 inch = 20 ft.
1
2
3

A3 Connor Henry
A2 Connor Henry
D1 Connor Henry
D6 Connor Henry

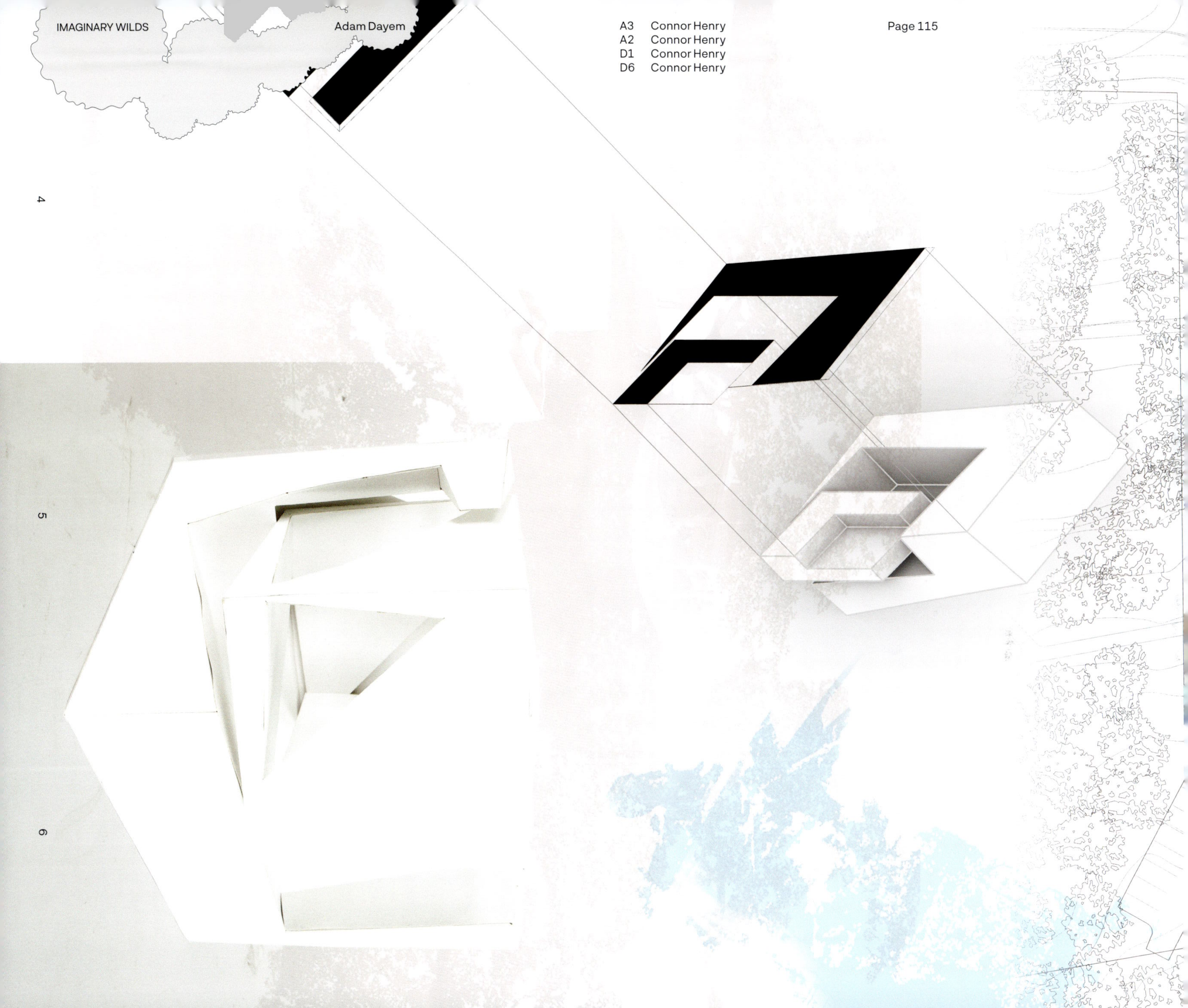

4

5

6

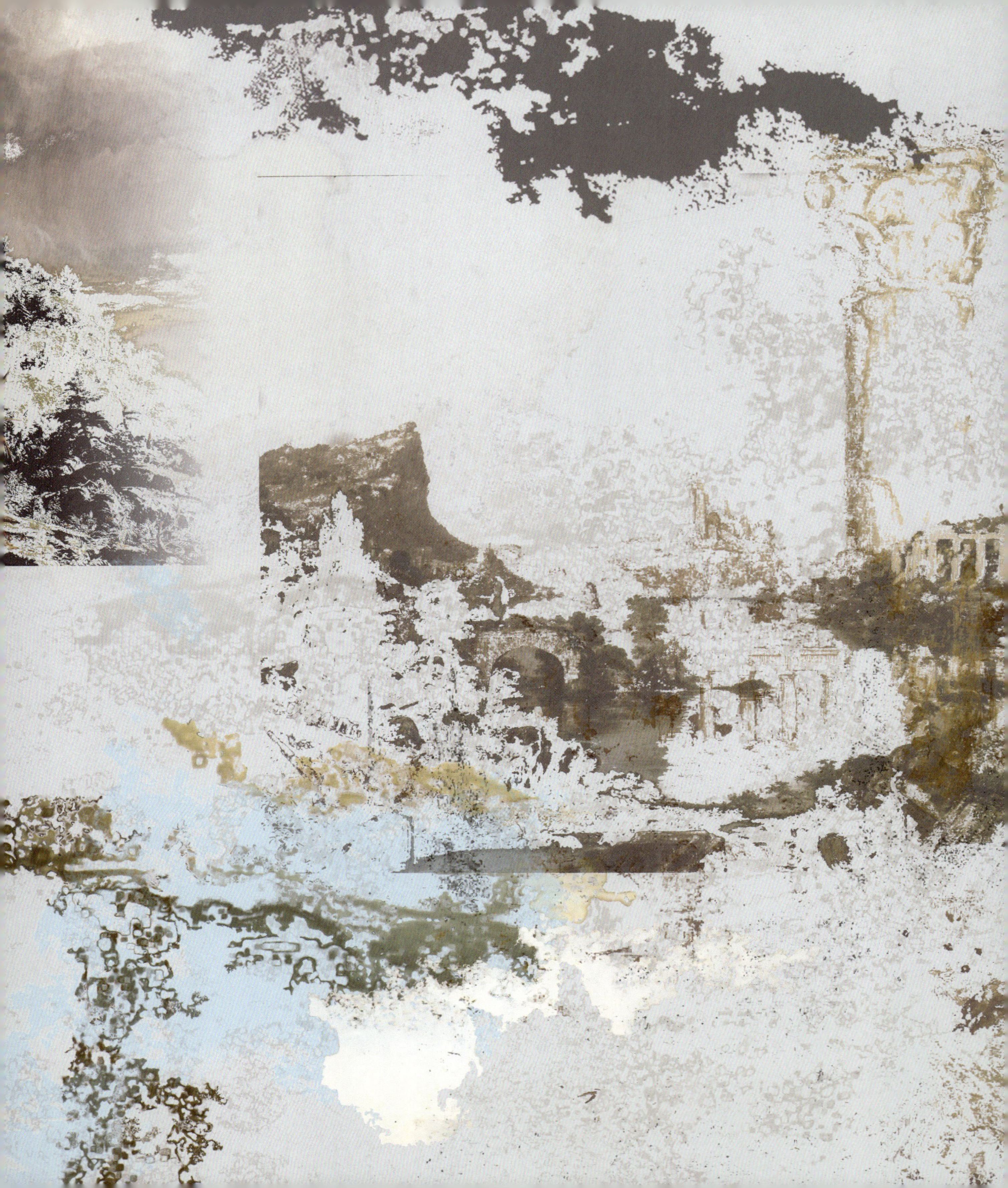

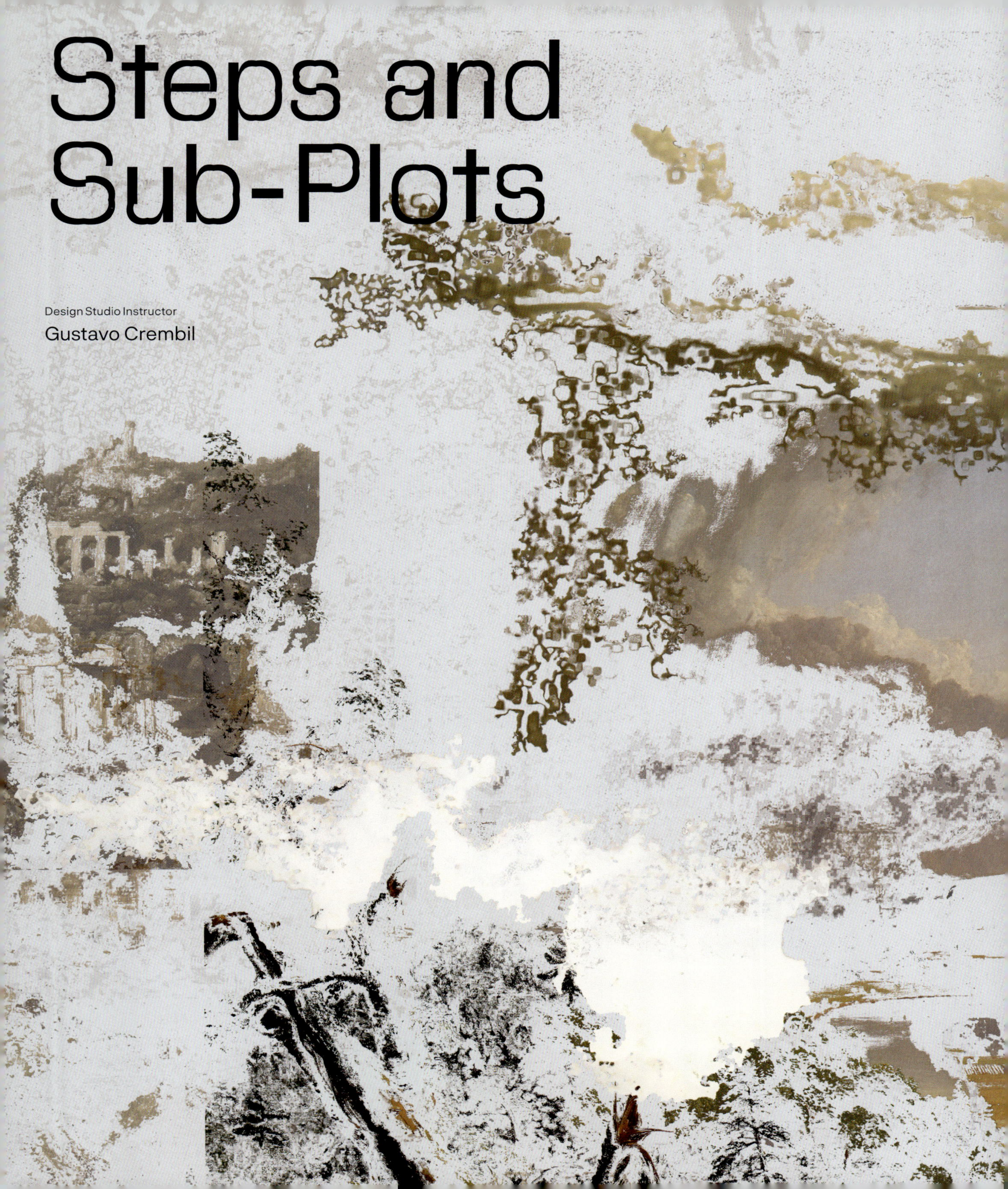

Steps and Sub-Plots

Design Studio Instructor

Gustavo Crembil

Students began the studio work by gaining a preliminary understanding of the topic through the analytical study of an existing museum / art gallery building. Different cases were grouped under a taxonomic theme (land, box, umbrella, aggregate) that were crossed, defining mixed research clusters. Even though they were responsible for their individual projects, students were required to acquire a comprehensive knowledge of the other projects assigned to their cluster teammates. Students were asked to decode how programmatic and site requirements relate to a strong design agenda.

A series of generative studies based on the precedent studies followed, aiming to seed the basis for an architectural language that could later inform the design. Students were asked to develop a series of abstract studies based on architectural concepts they may have highlighted. Such concepts could be specific (a particular roof form, a volumetric arrangement, a grid system, etc.) or more abstract (a light atmosphere, spatial compression / decompression, etc.). These preliminary speculations were scaleless and without programmatic requirements, except for enclosing/capturing space and a path sequence.

Upon visiting the museum and its grounds and conducting their own research on Thomas Cole (and the Hudson River School of painting), students were guided to articulate an introductory assessment of how the existing buildings and site work and/or do not work in terms of the museum's stated mission. At this stage, speculating on potential areas of location for a new building in relation to the detected general system of the site was critical. As well, an understanding of the natural topographic conditions and their technical representation was emphasized.

The studio brief called for the design of a "small freestanding building at the Thomas Cole National Historic Site with a precise tectonic language, highly considered and resolved interior spaces, and a clear daylighting strategy." It was to be a 5,000-square-foot freestanding building containing two main programmatic zones: (1) exhibition (spaces where art is shown), and (2) public areas (non-exhibit spaces that all museumgoers can access), plus corresponding ancillary areas.

A reductionist vision may consider that buildings are the sole result of the confluence of uses, circulation, and structure. Students were asked to attempt a critical position vis-a-vis the complex network of activities/uses, labeled as "program." Architects design buildings as much as the complex of activities to be hosted in them and their response (and impact) to site demands.

Tectonics (the preliminary understanding of relations between structure, skin/enclosure, and topography) were placed in the forefront by requiring students to propose clear structural *partii* that both acknowledged and related to the ground. Historian Kenneth Frampton notes that "the primary principle of architectural autonomy resides in the *tectonic* rather than in the *scenographic*: that is to say, this autonomy is embodied in the revealed ligaments of the construction and in the way in which the syntactical form of the structure explicitly resists the action of gravity."

Final emphasis was placed on the presentation of students' 2D drawings, in both their communication quality and technical precision, as well as the exploration of narrative-driven (so-called hyperrealistic) 3D imagery.

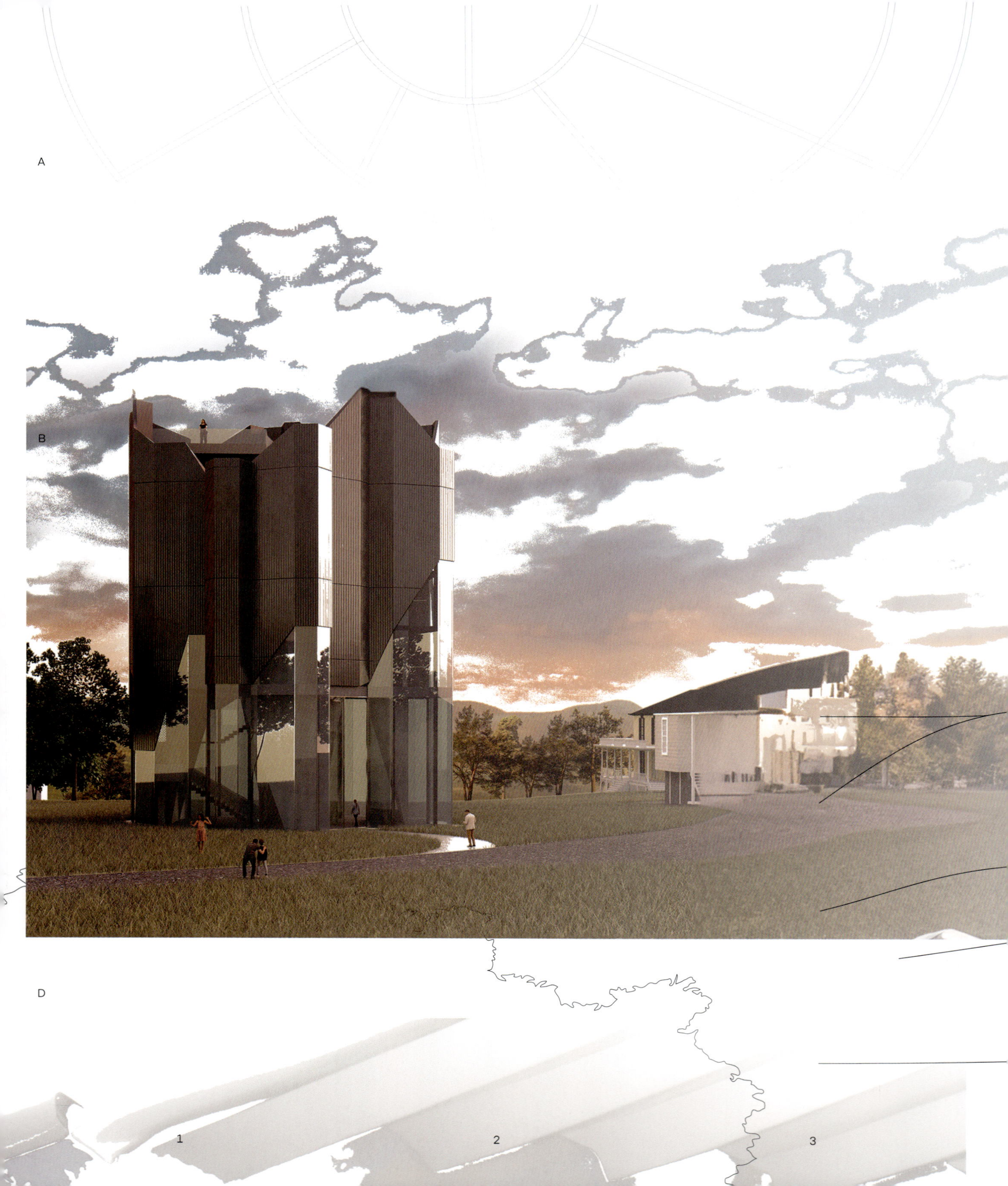

A
B
D
1
2
3

Gustavo Crembil

A2 Bryanna Ricks
B1 Helly Rana
A5 Helly Rana
C6 Helly Rana

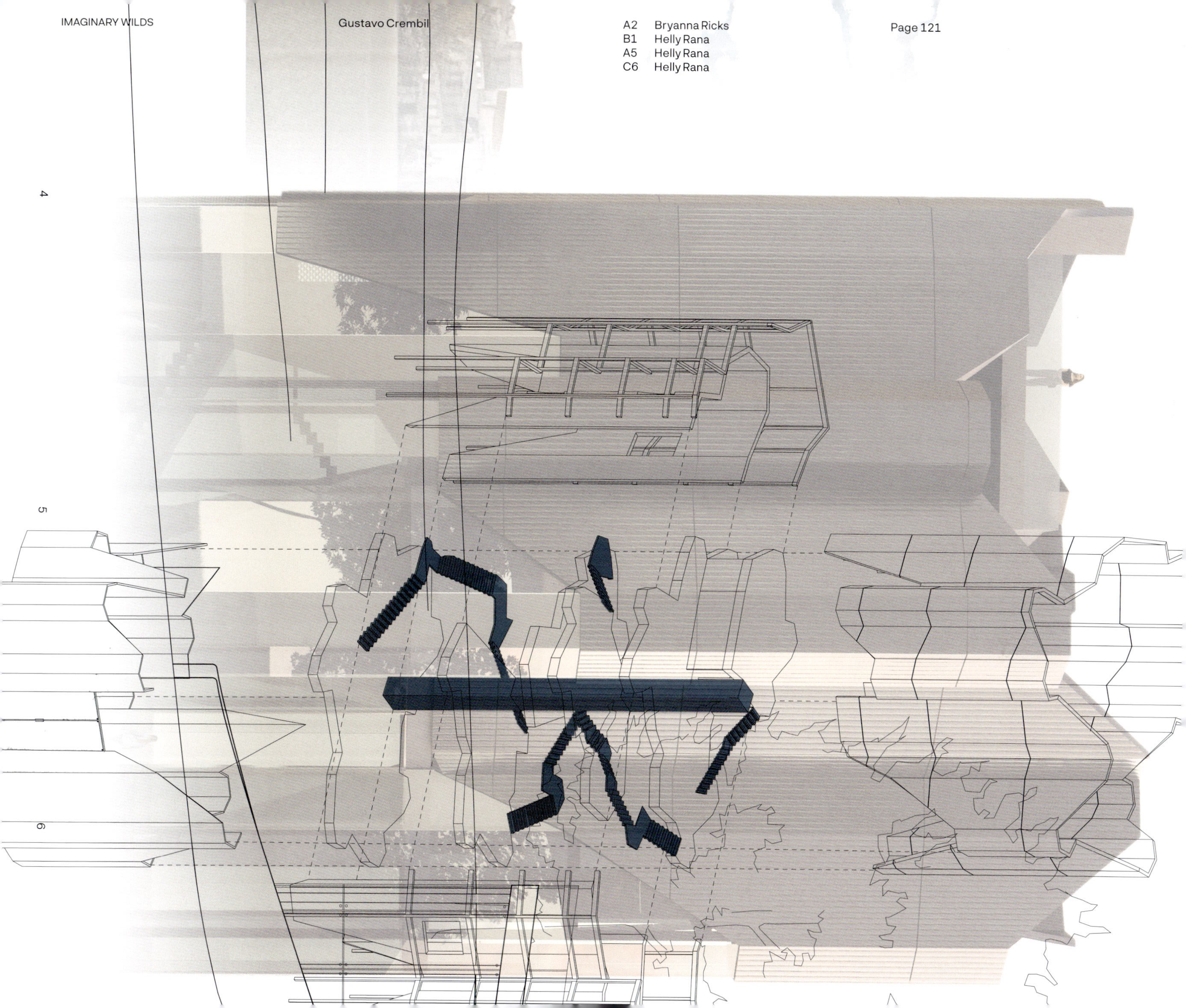

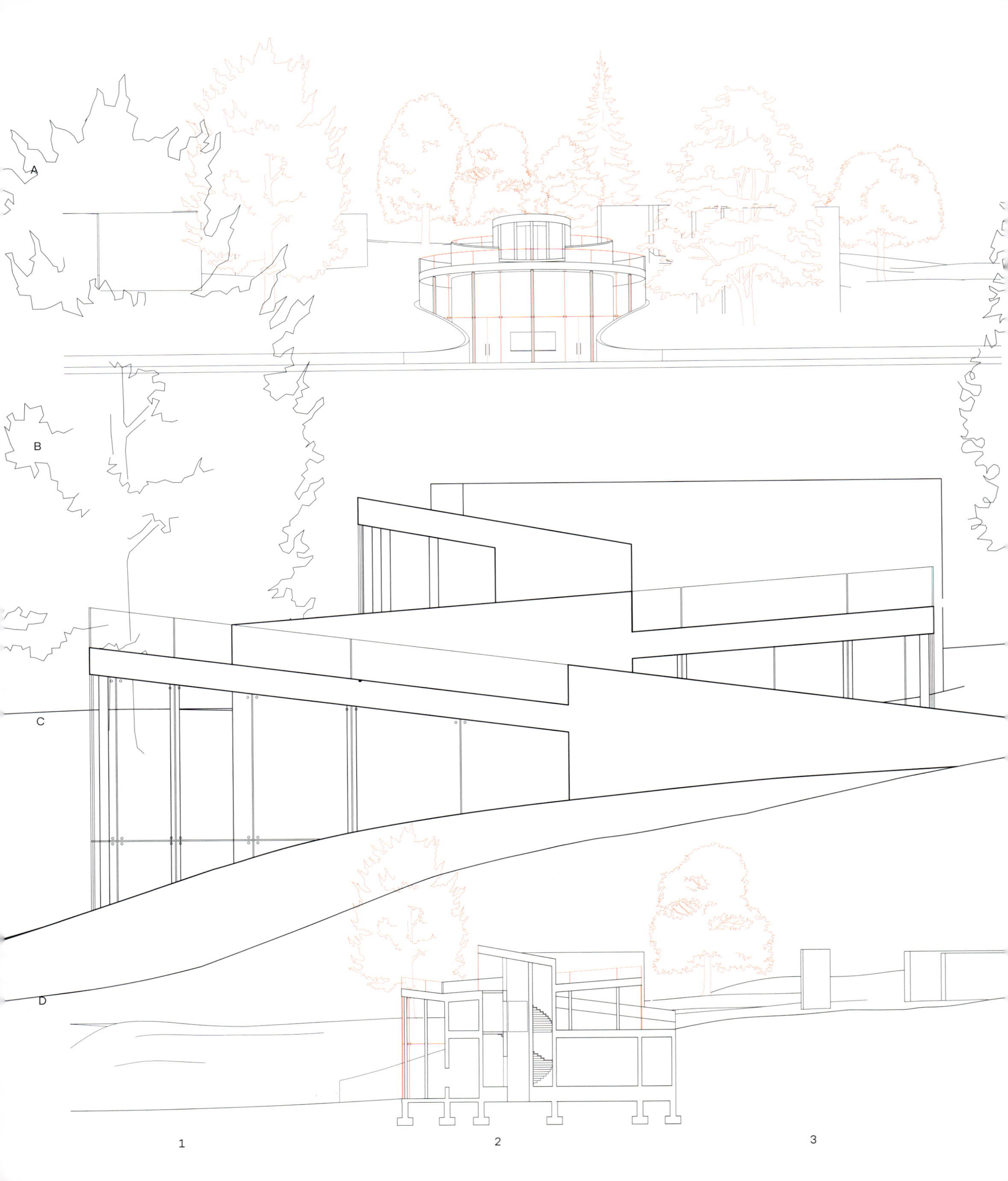
A
B
C
D
1
2
3

A2 Bryanna Ricks
C2 Bryanna Ricks
D2 Bryanna Ricks
C5 Bryanna Ricks

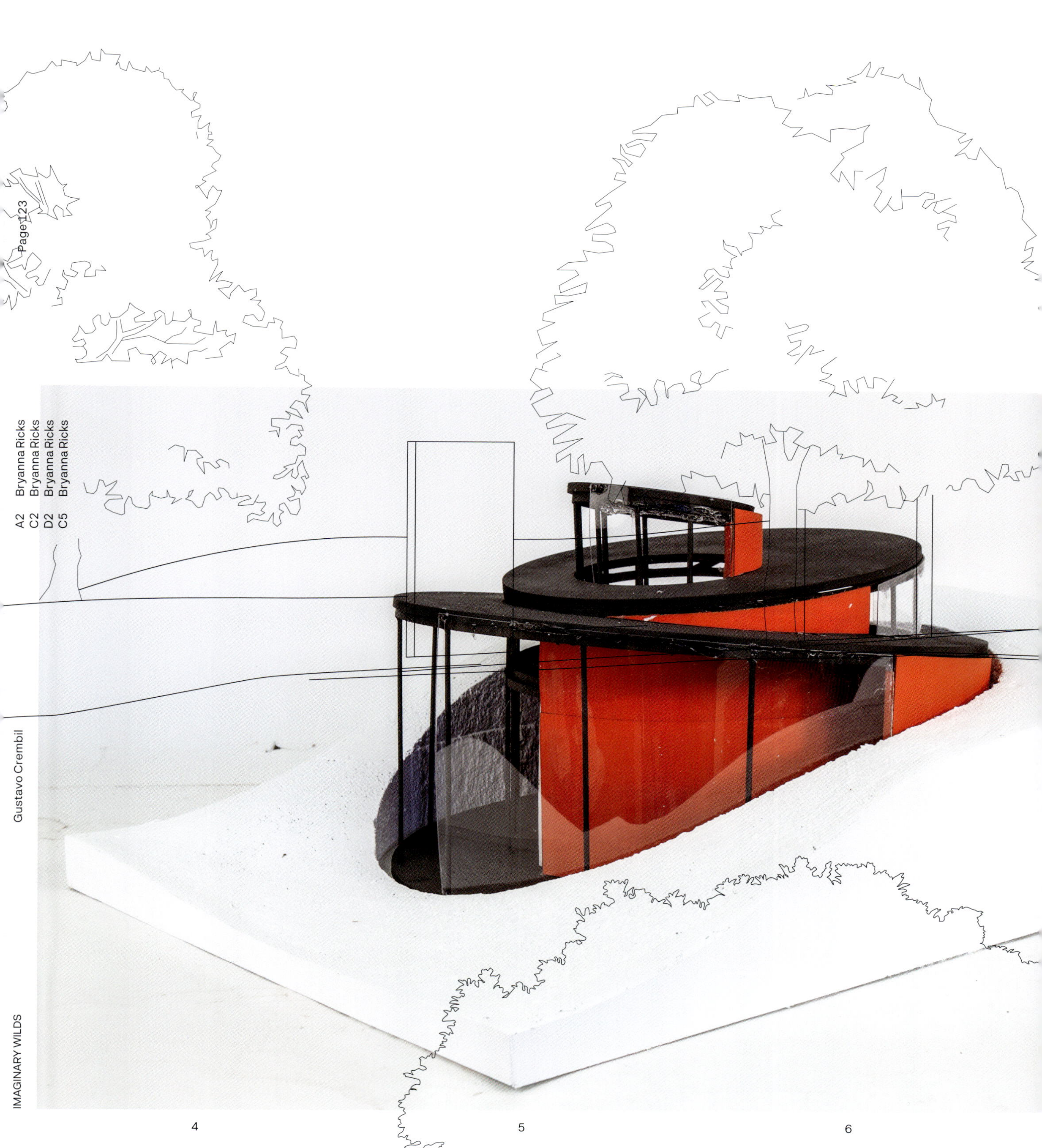

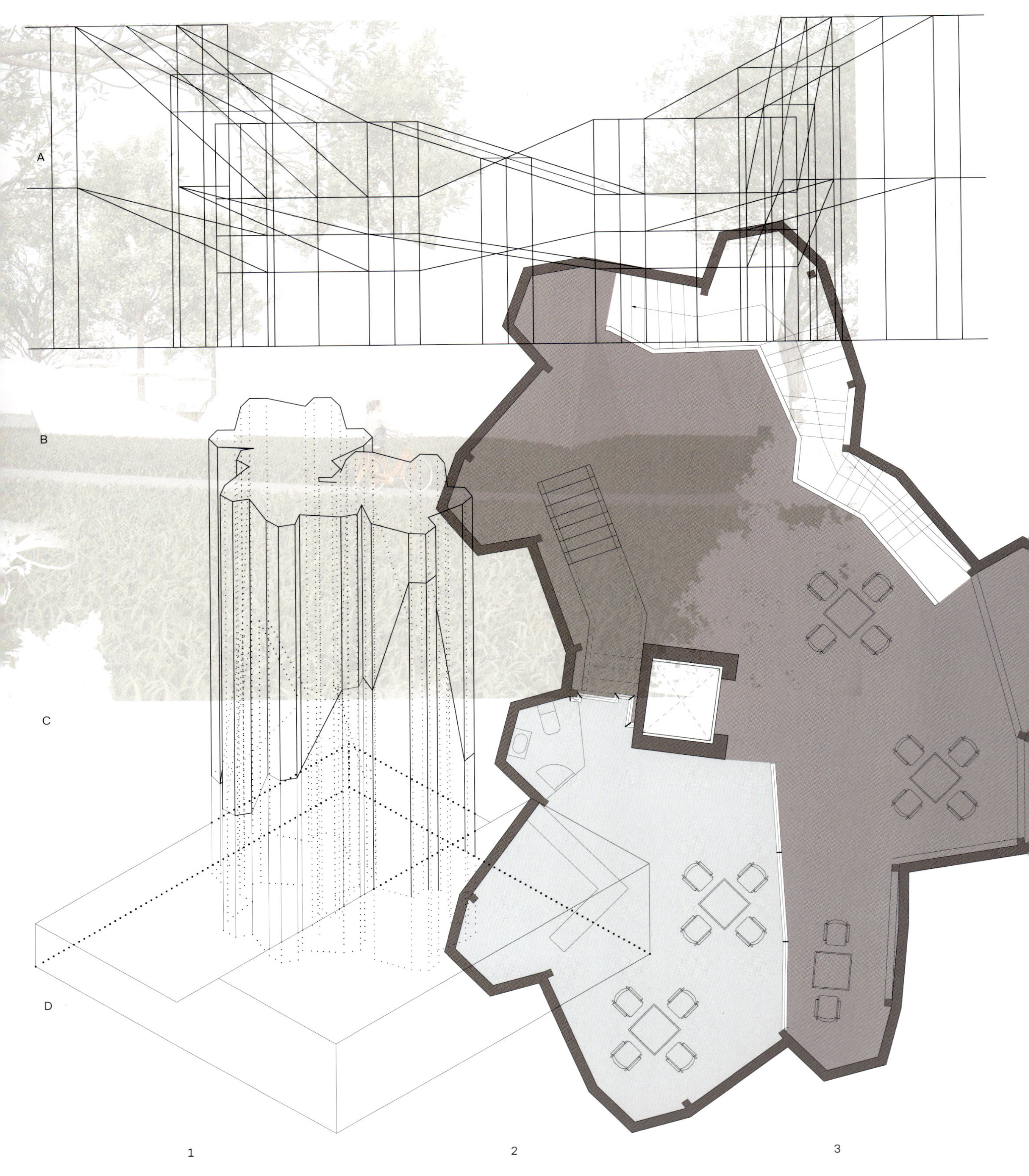
A
B
C
D
1
2
3

A2 Helly Rana
D1 Helly Rana
C3 Helly Rana
A5 Sean Shannon
B5 Sean Shannon

4

5

6

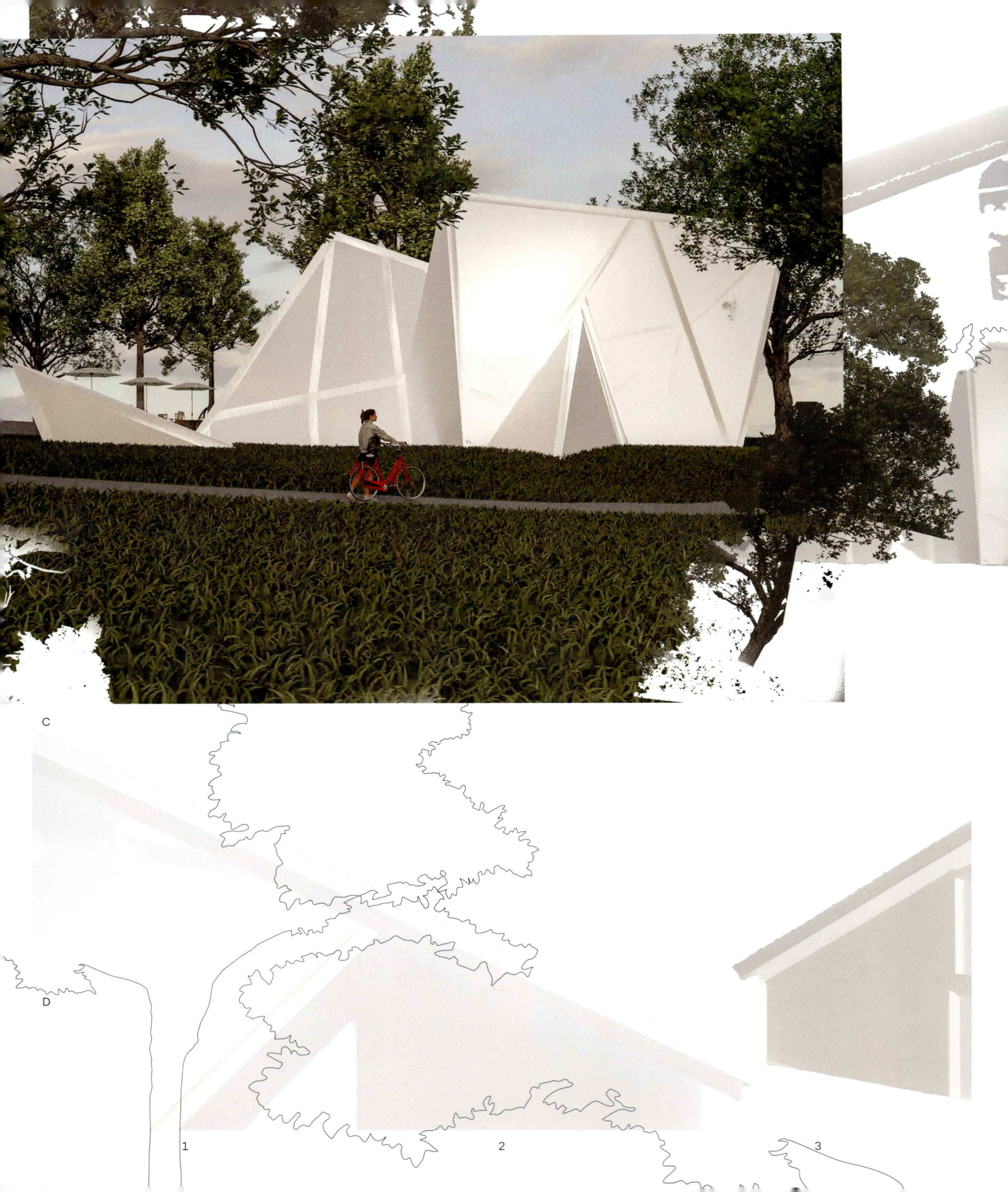
C
D
1
2
3

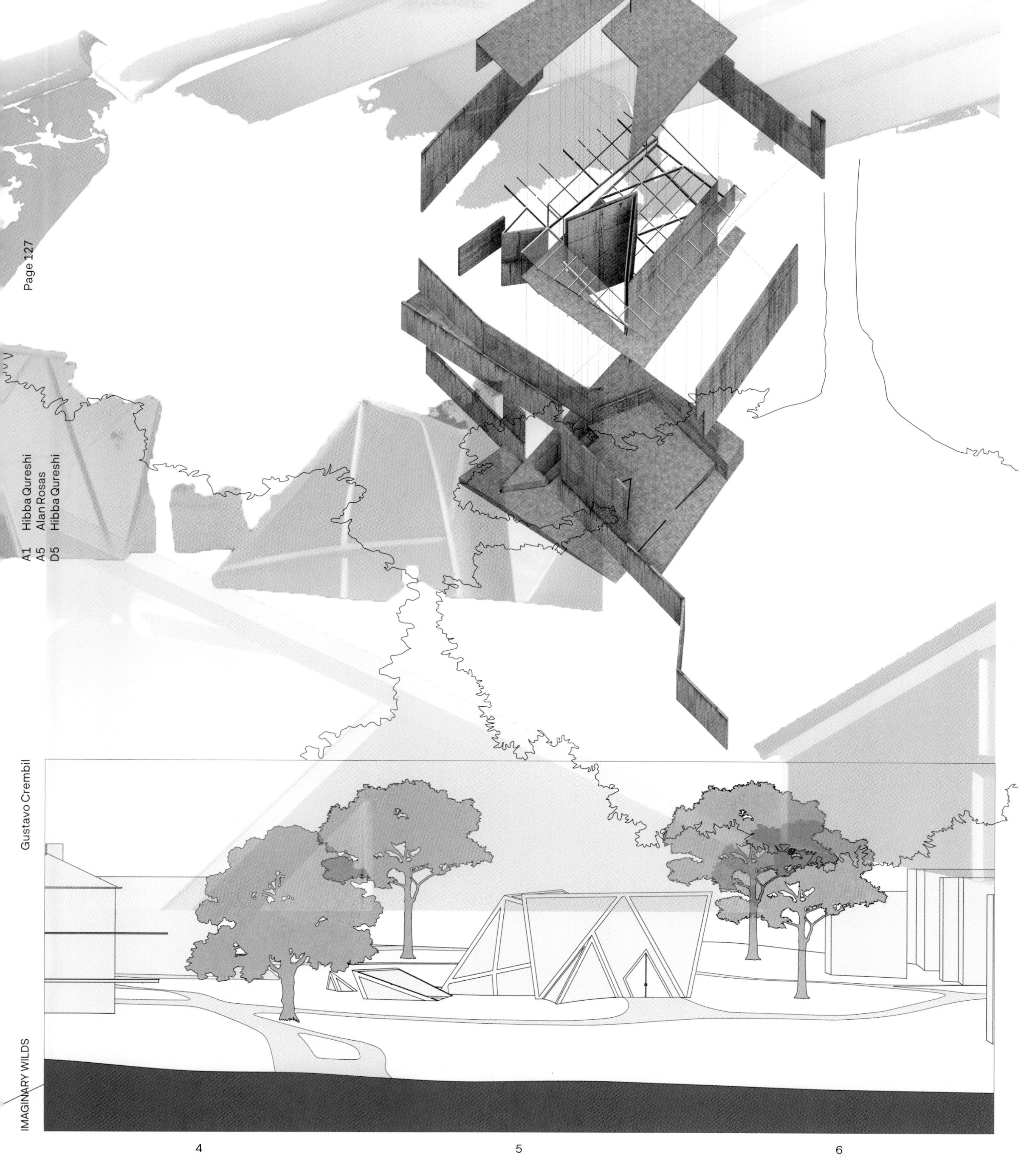

A1 Hibba Qureshi
A5 Alan Rosas
D5 Hibba Qureshi

Gustavo Crembil

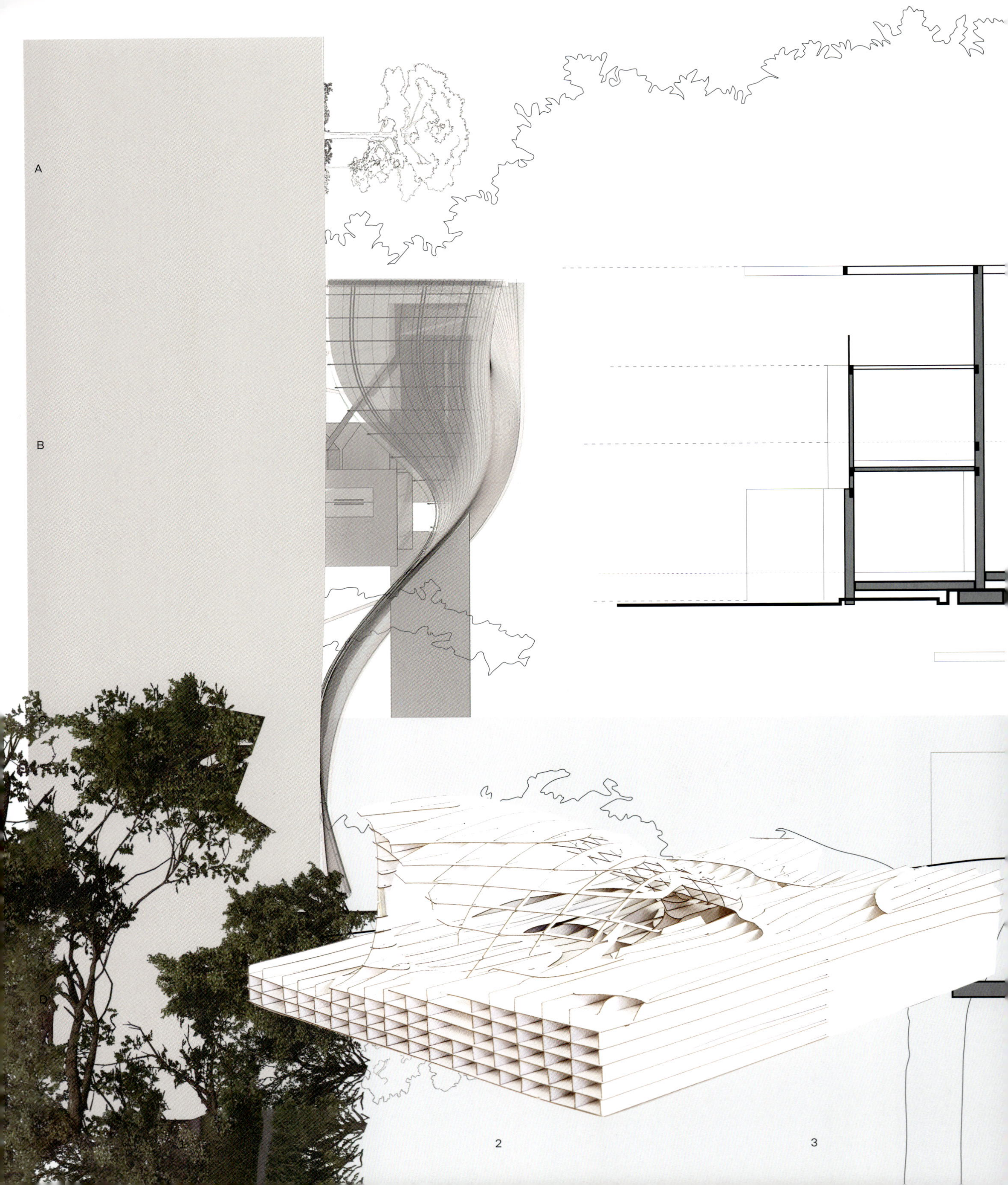
A
B
C
D
1
2
3

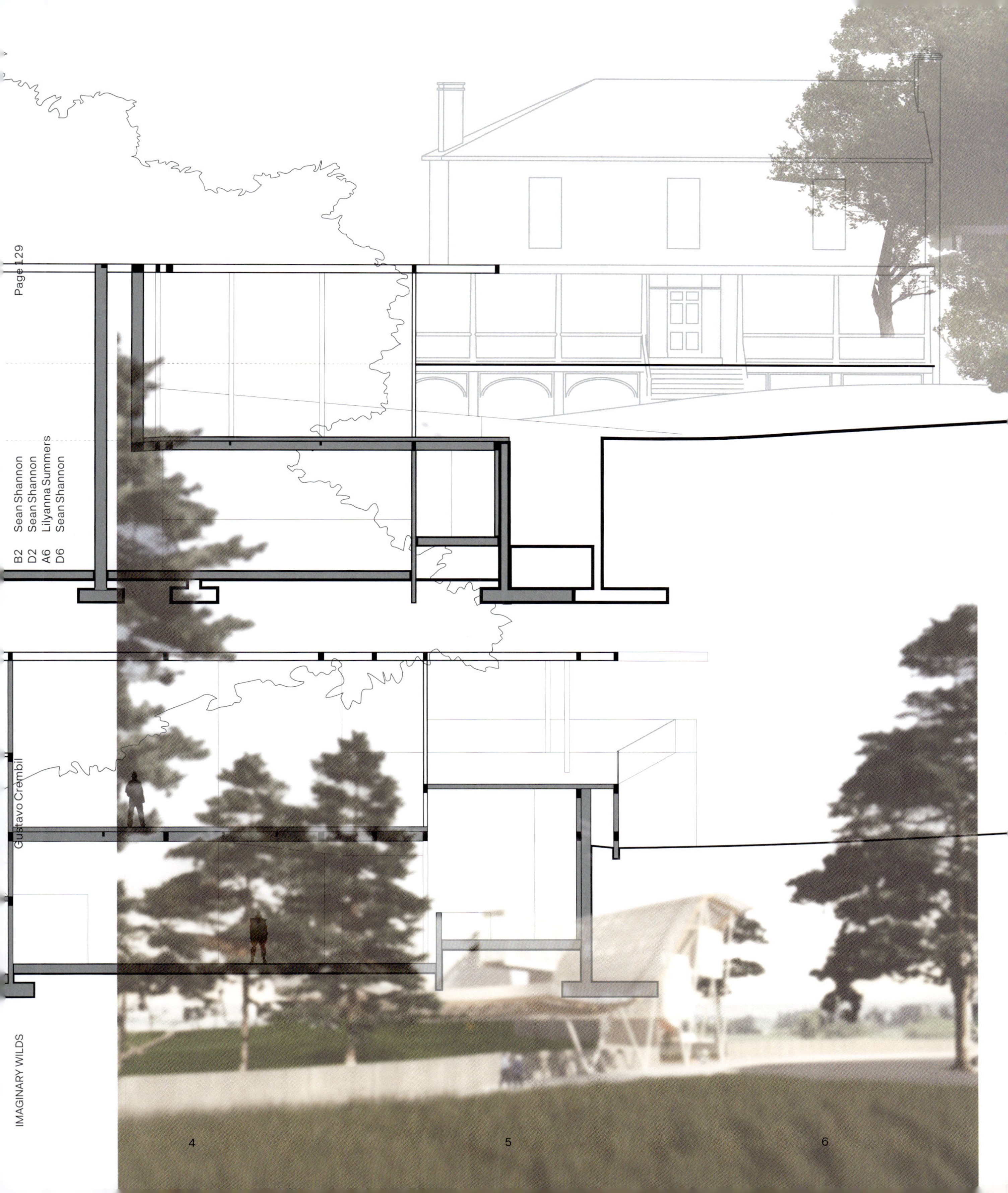
B2 Sean Shannon
D2 Sean Shannon
A6 Lilyanna Summers
D6 Sean Shannon
Gustavo Crembil
4
5
6

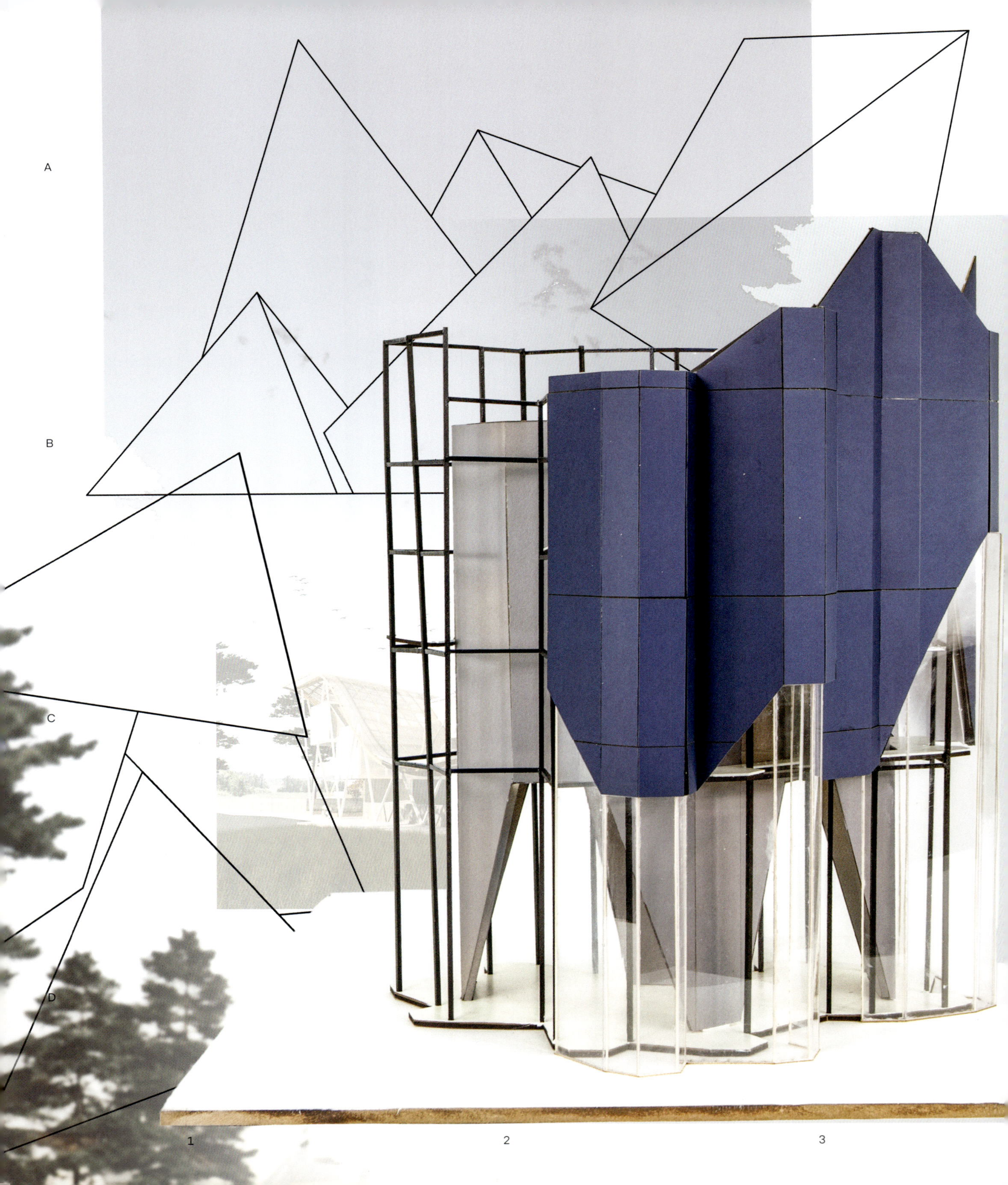
A
B
C
D
1
2
3

A2 Hibba Qureshi
C3 Helly Rana
A5 Hibba Qureshi
C5 Hibba Qureshi
D6 Ayush Singh

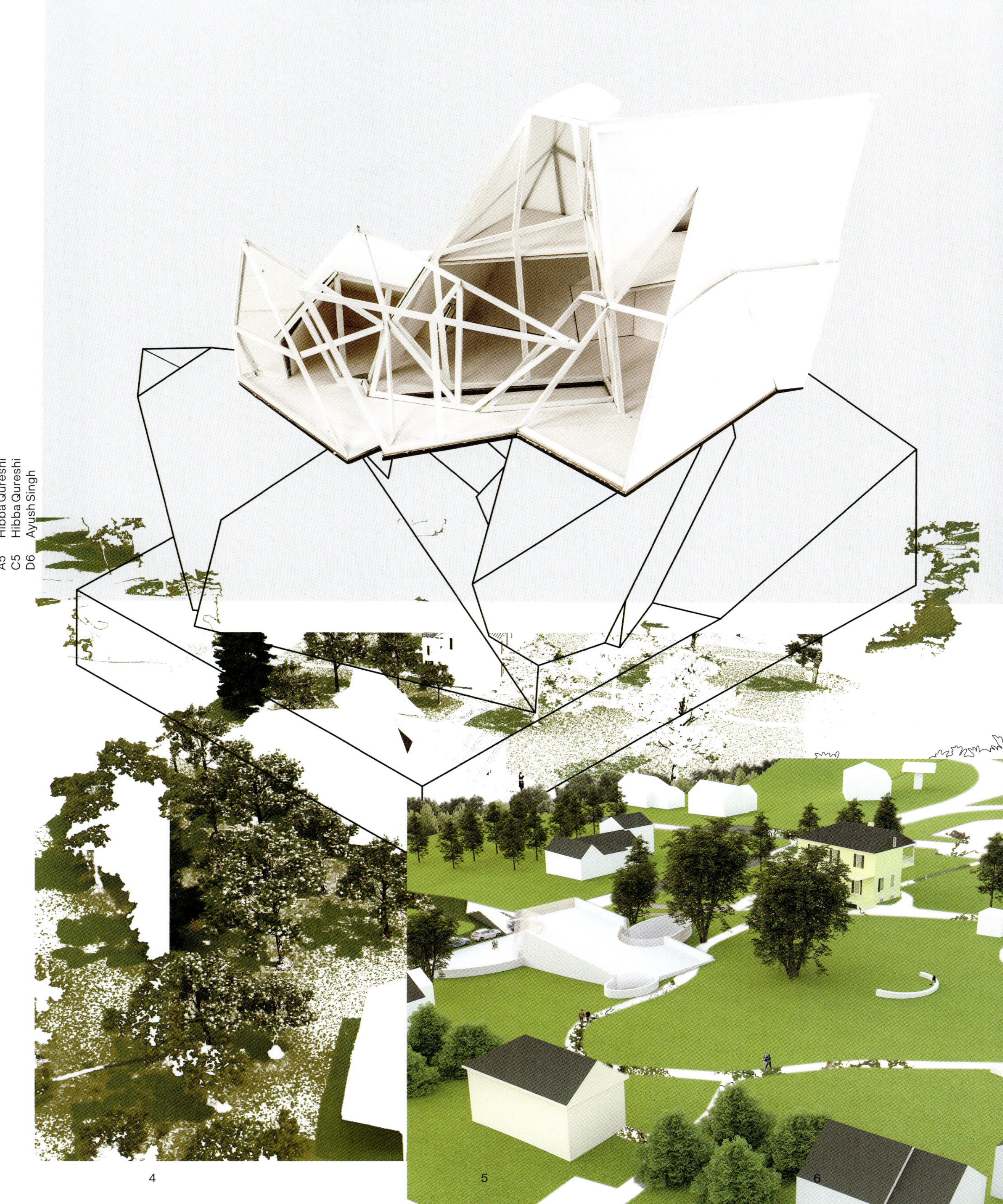

4

5

6

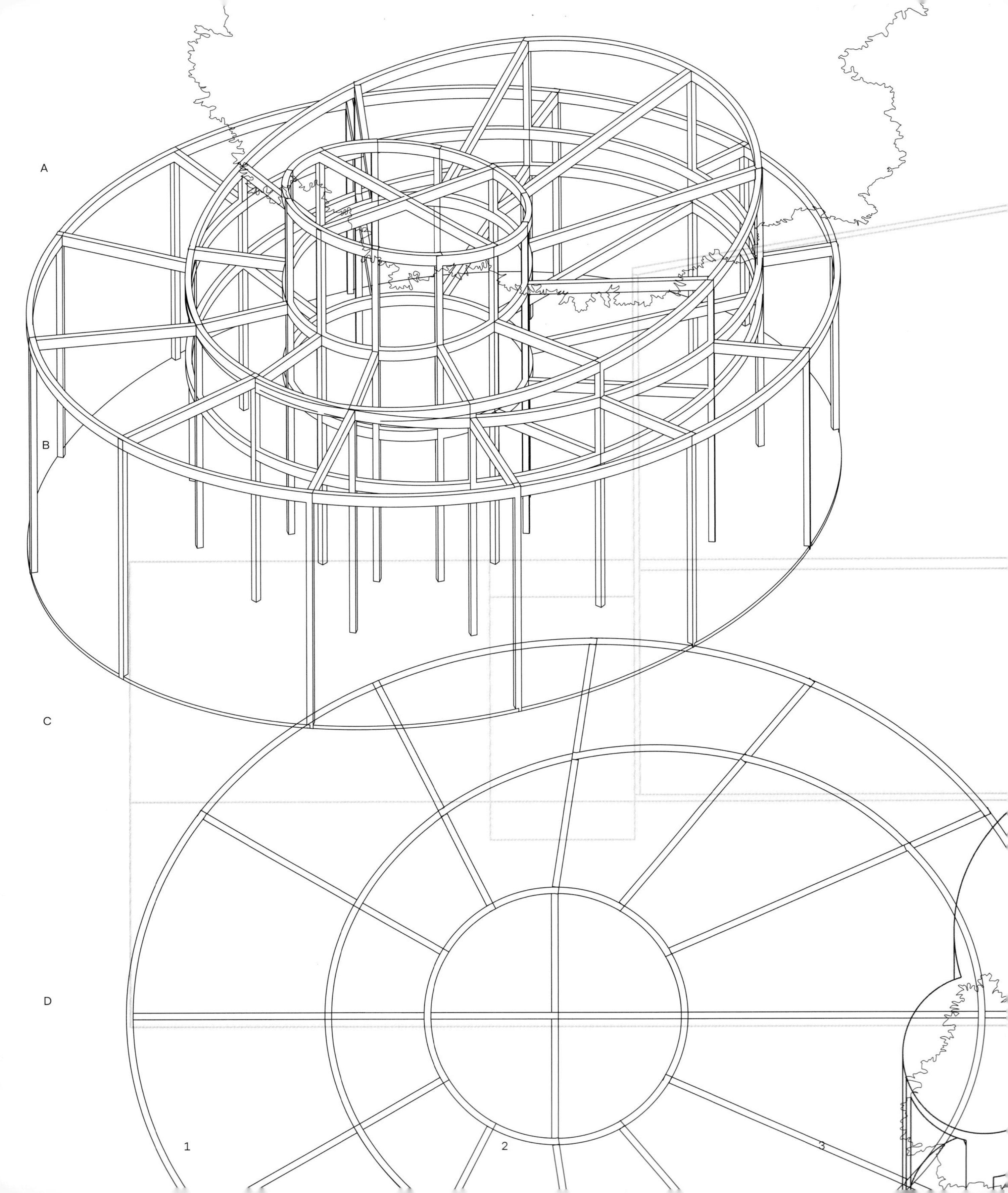
A
B
C
D
1
2
3

B2 Bryanna Ricks
D2 Bryanna Ricks
B6 Olivia Rouge
D5 Olivia Rouge

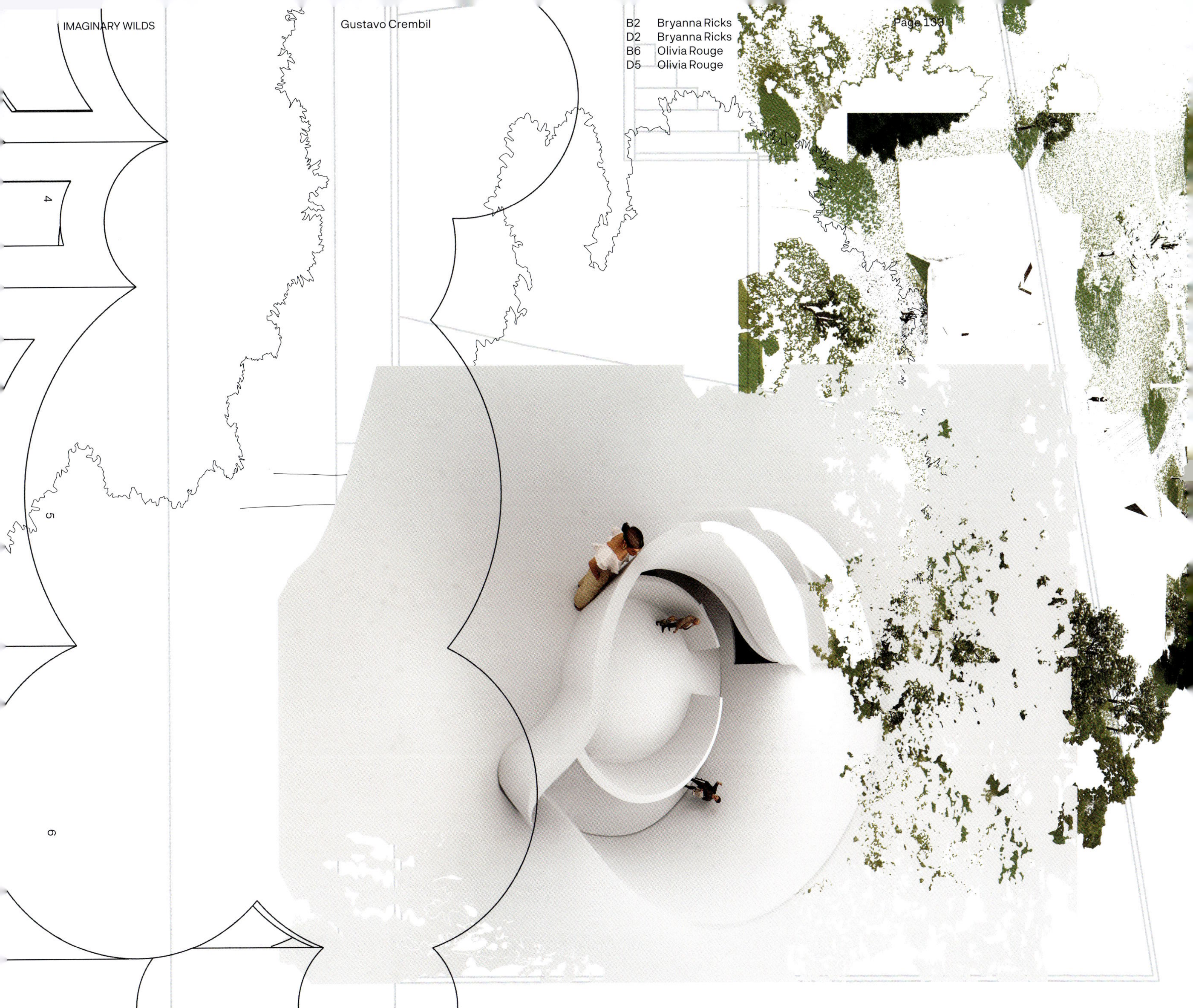

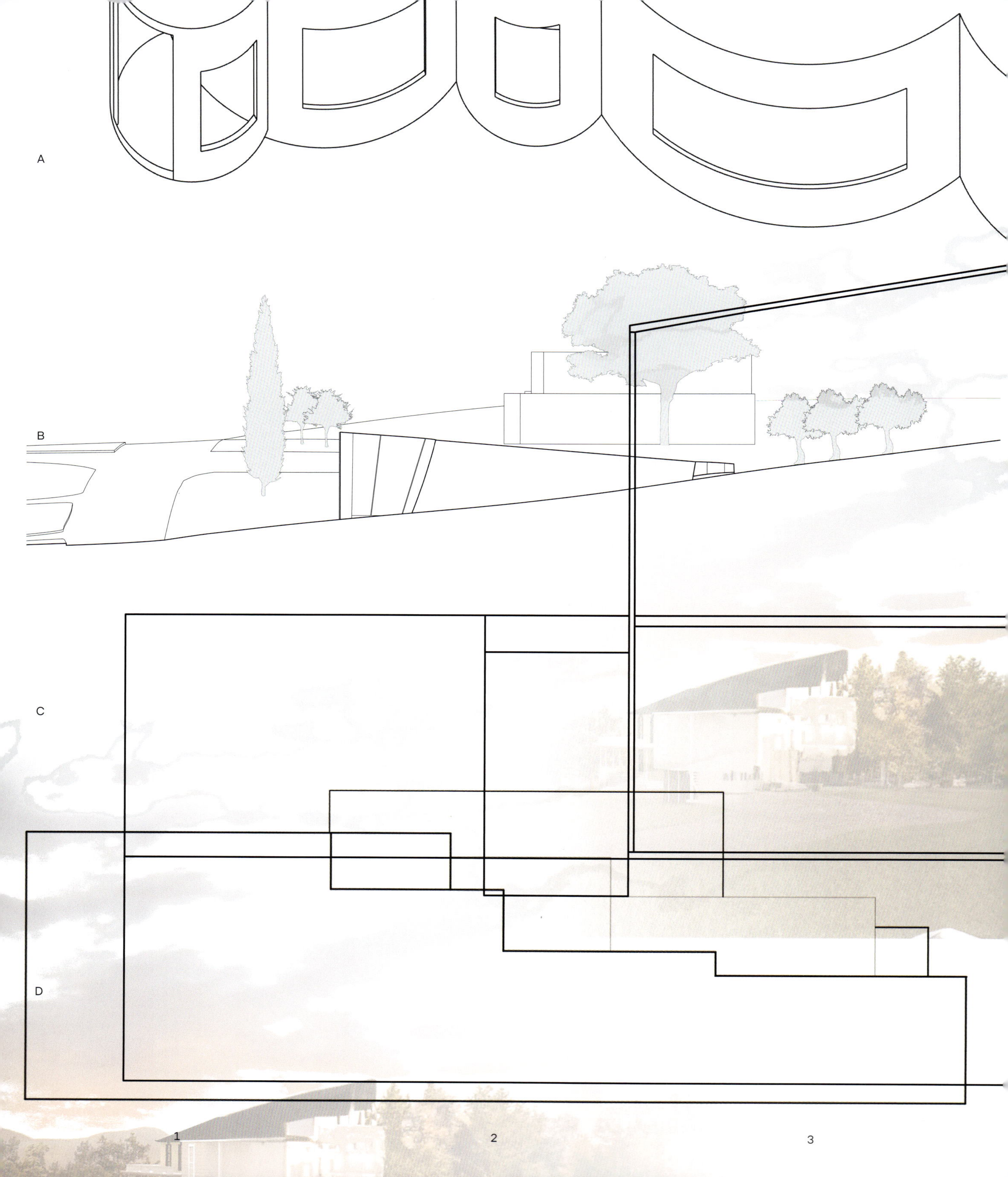
A
B
C
D
1
2
3

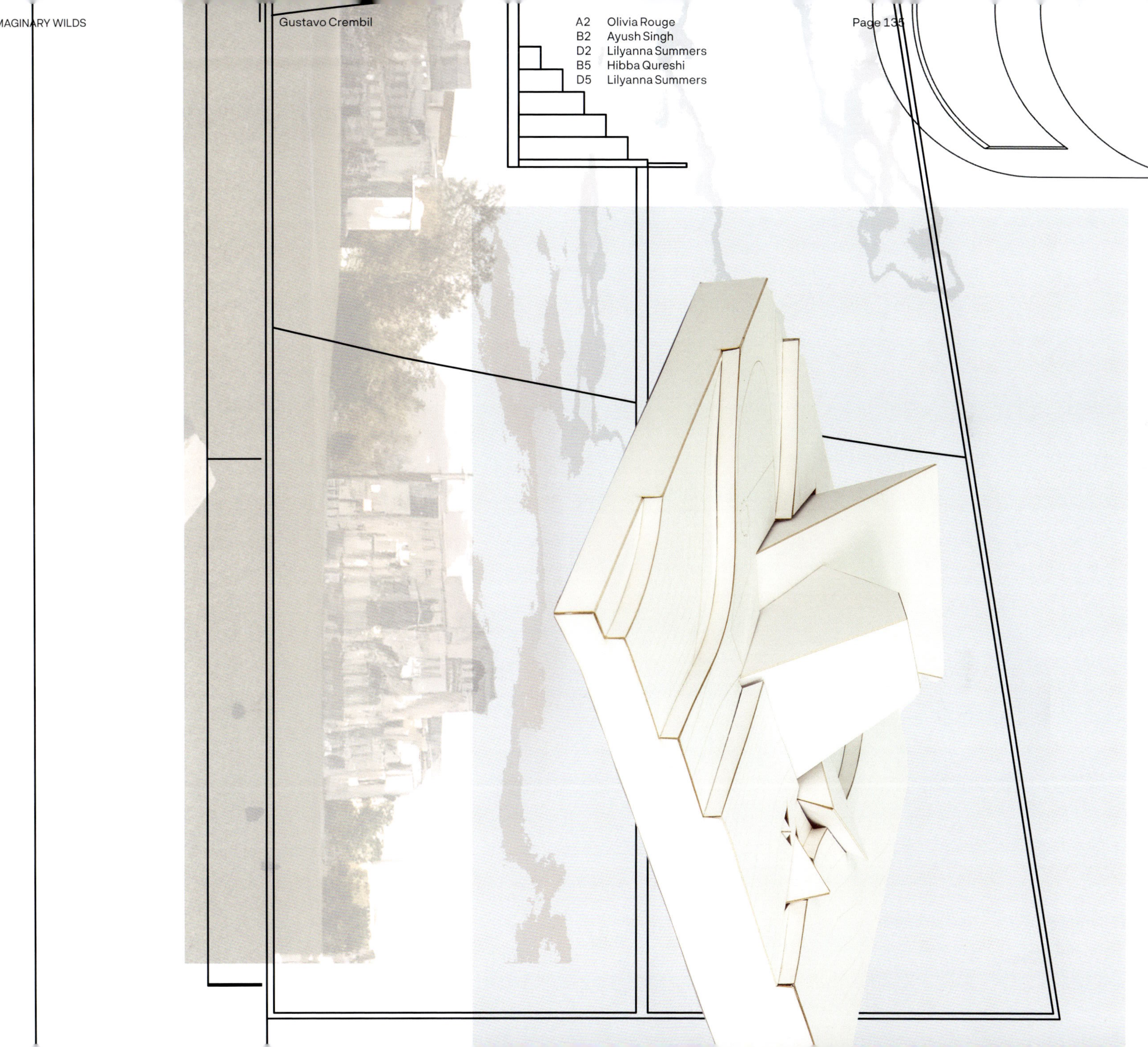
Gustavo Crembil
A2 Olivia Rouge
B2 Ayush Singh
D2 Lilyanna Summers
B5 Hibba Qureshi
D5 Lilyanna Summers
4
5
6

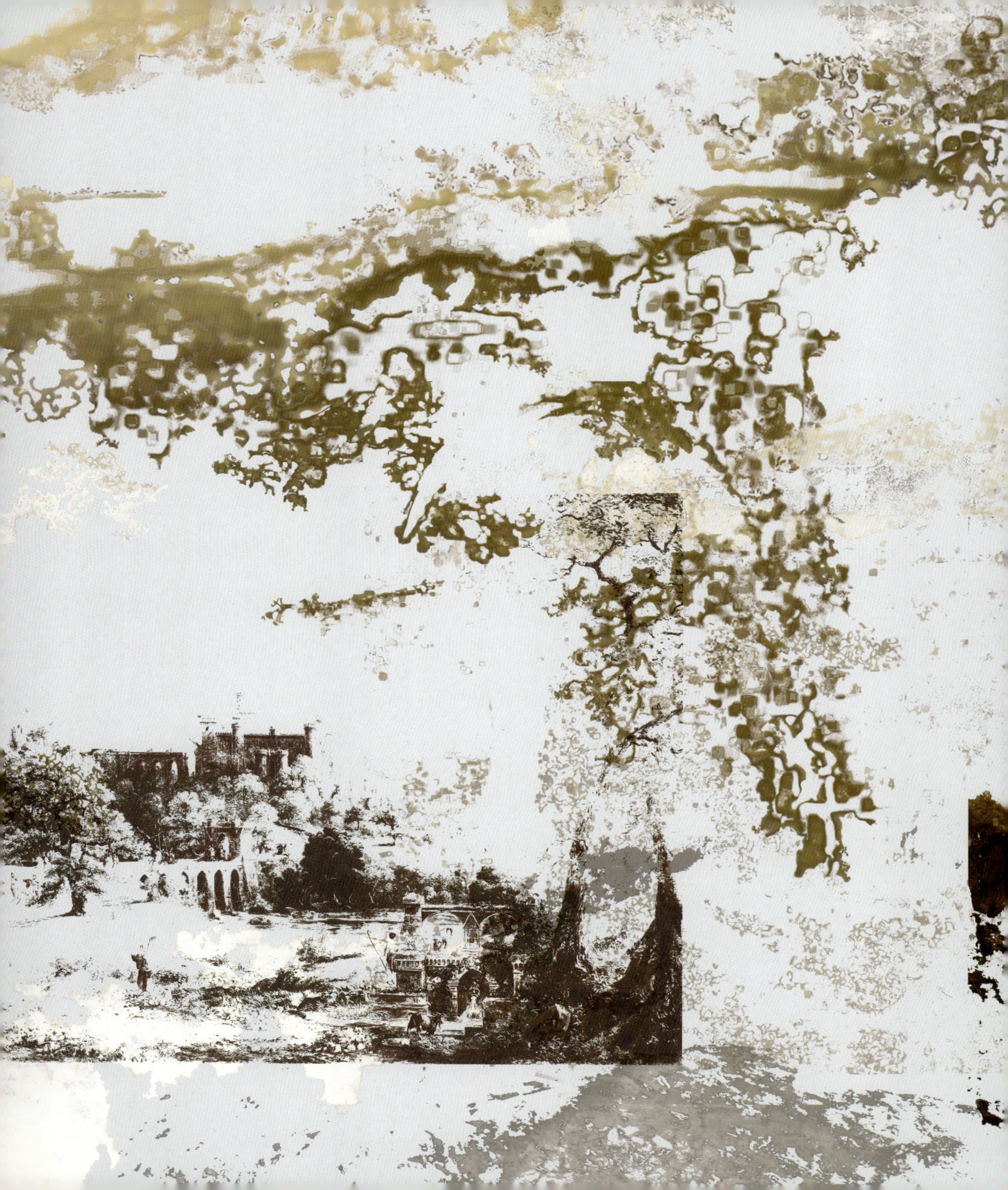

The Art of Being (Un)Original

Design Studio Instructor
Leandro Piazzi

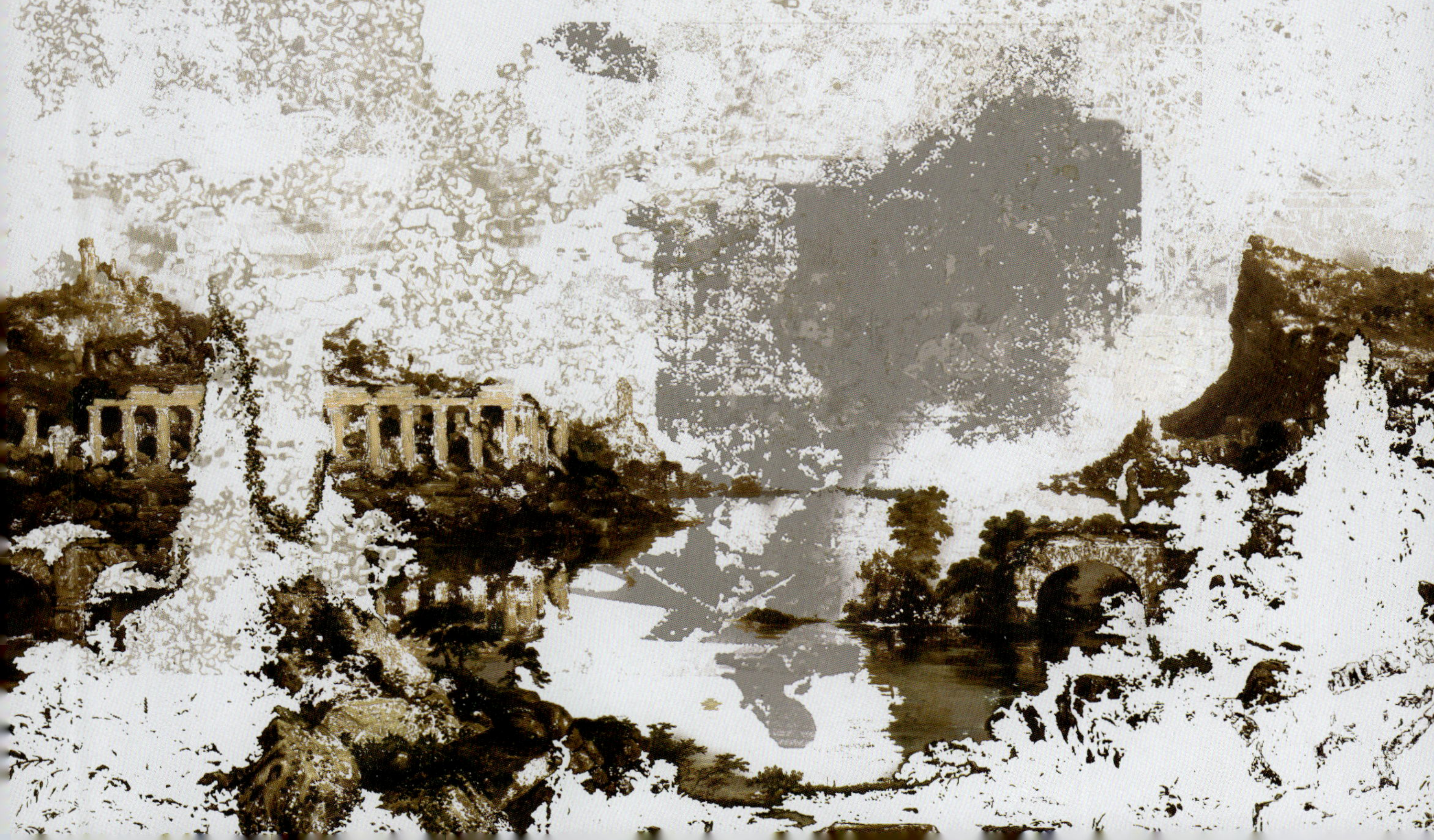

Art is a game among all people of all eras.
Marcel Duchamp

For architects Sebastián Adamo and Marcelo Faiden, the contemporary designer constantly engages in a dialogue with history. Without memory, their innovations become mere novelties. History provides their growth with direction. However, since memory is never perfect, each recollection becomes a composite or degraded image of a previous situation or moment. In this way, each memory always appears new, a partial and different construction from its origin, and, as such, possesses the potential for its own growth.[1]

Aligned with this perspective, the pedagogical strategies proposed for the studio fostered collective sensibilities capable of establishing dialogues that extended their field of action and knowledge beyond its autonomy. Students were consistently encouraged to draw upon history and references, not necessarily limited to architecture, as essential resources for providing direction and significance to their endeavors. Thus, during the design exercise, the aim was not to create architecture from scratch, but to work from projects already circulating in the cultural market, that is, projects already informed by others. In this sense, the concepts of originality (being at the origin of) and even creation (making something out of nothing) dissolved to form a new cultural landscape, where students were encouraged to borrow diagrams, plans, sections, elevations, and details from other projects, which, through exercises of manipulation and combination, nourished each stage of the design process.

Methods such as replication, extension, reduction, reconfiguration, juxtaposition, prolongation, multiplication, and reorganization, among others, guided the students throughout their exploratory journey. These methods facilitated the generation of unforeseen architectural formulations, instilling fresh meaning into each design phase. The iterative process fostered a reciprocal interplay between the generic and the specific, enabling the dialogical refinement of design iterations. Consequently, from the overarching master plan to the minutiae of architectural details, these design methods converged harmoniously with the particular demands of a museum program. The resultant designs expanded the architectural and cultural offerings of the Thomas Cole National Historic Site. Moreover, these designs diligently considered the specific qualities of the campus situated in Catskill, New York, as well as the technical requisites of a building suitable for exhibiting the artist's oeuvre.

The artistic question is no longer, What can we make that is new? but, How can we make do with what we have? In other words, how can we produce singularity and meaning from this chaotic mass of objects, names, and references that constitutes our daily life?[2]

Hence, although the primary objective of the course entailed designing a modest autonomous museum within the precincts of the Thomas Cole National Historic Site's campus, featuring a precise tectonic language, meticulously crafted interior spaces, and a discerning strategy for natural illumination, the studio transcended its academic aspirations by extending its inquiries beyond the mere architectural object. It emerged as a collective brain capable of instigating critical discourses concerning the present state of the discipline and its forms of production.

Finally, beyond the studio's own concrete production, the students allowed themselves to borrow objects from existing culture, manipulate them, and return them to the "universe of things," which is where they will remain until they are once again "appropriated" by others, in an infinite loop of consumption and postproduction.

1 Sebastián Adamo and Marcelo Faiden, *The Contemporary Constructor* (Valencia, Spain: TC Cuadernos, 2018), 254.

2 Nicolas Bourriaud, *Postproduction. Culture as Screenplay: How Art Reprograms the World* (Madrid, Spain: Fisuras de la cultura contemporánea. Cut & paste, 2011), 5-11.

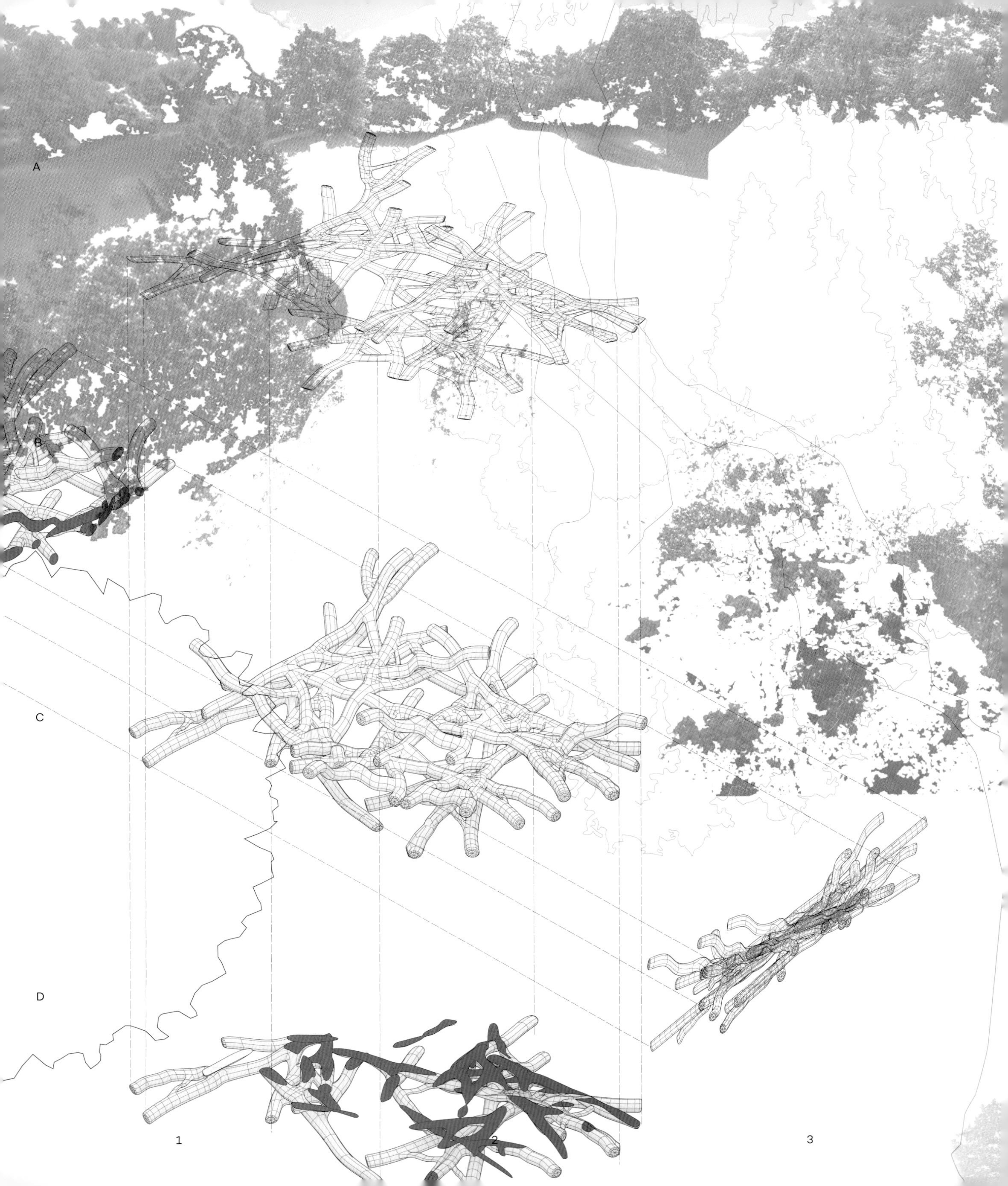
A
B
C
D
1
2
3

Leandro Piazzi

A2 Emily Zheng
B5 Emily Zheng

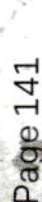

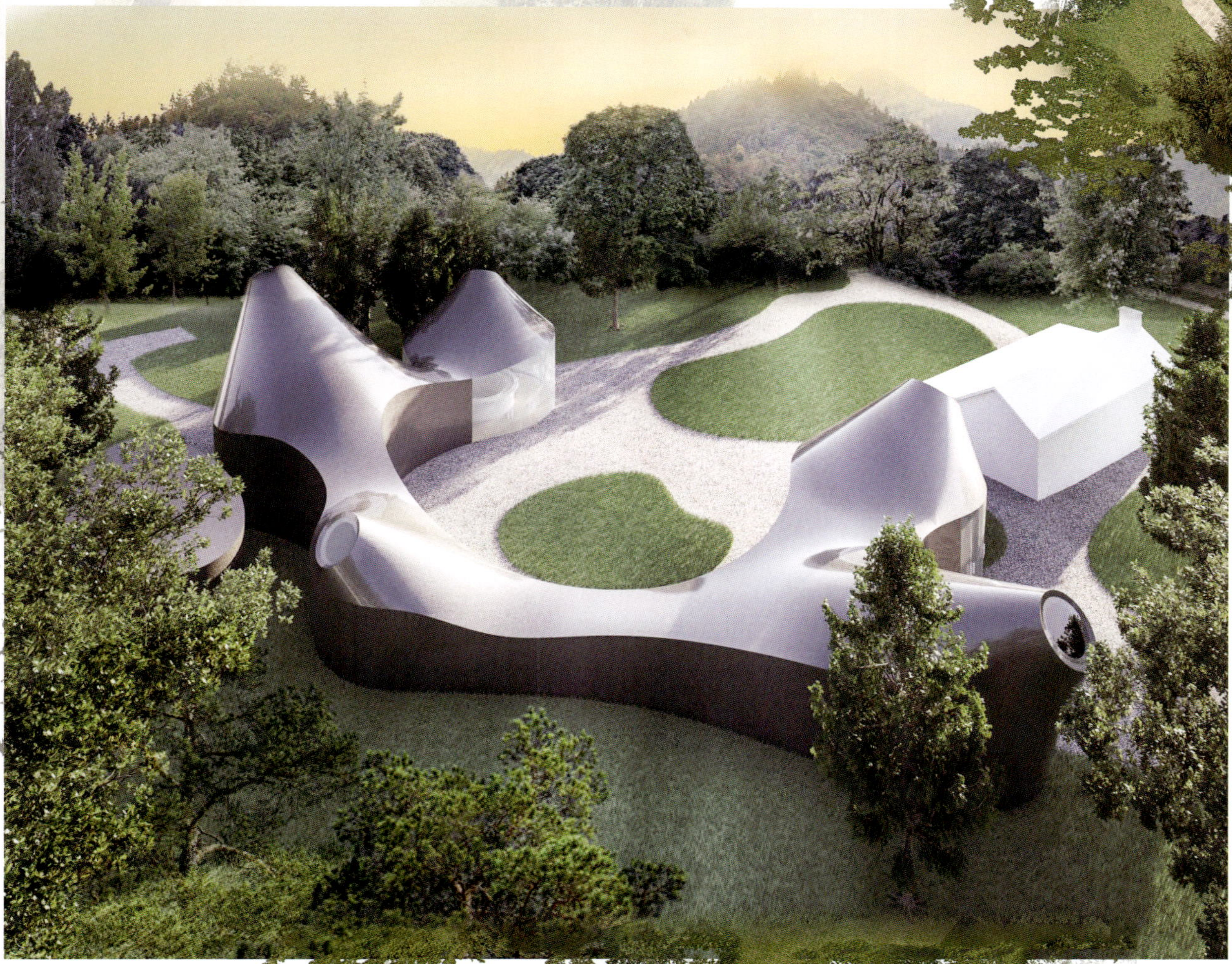

4 5 6

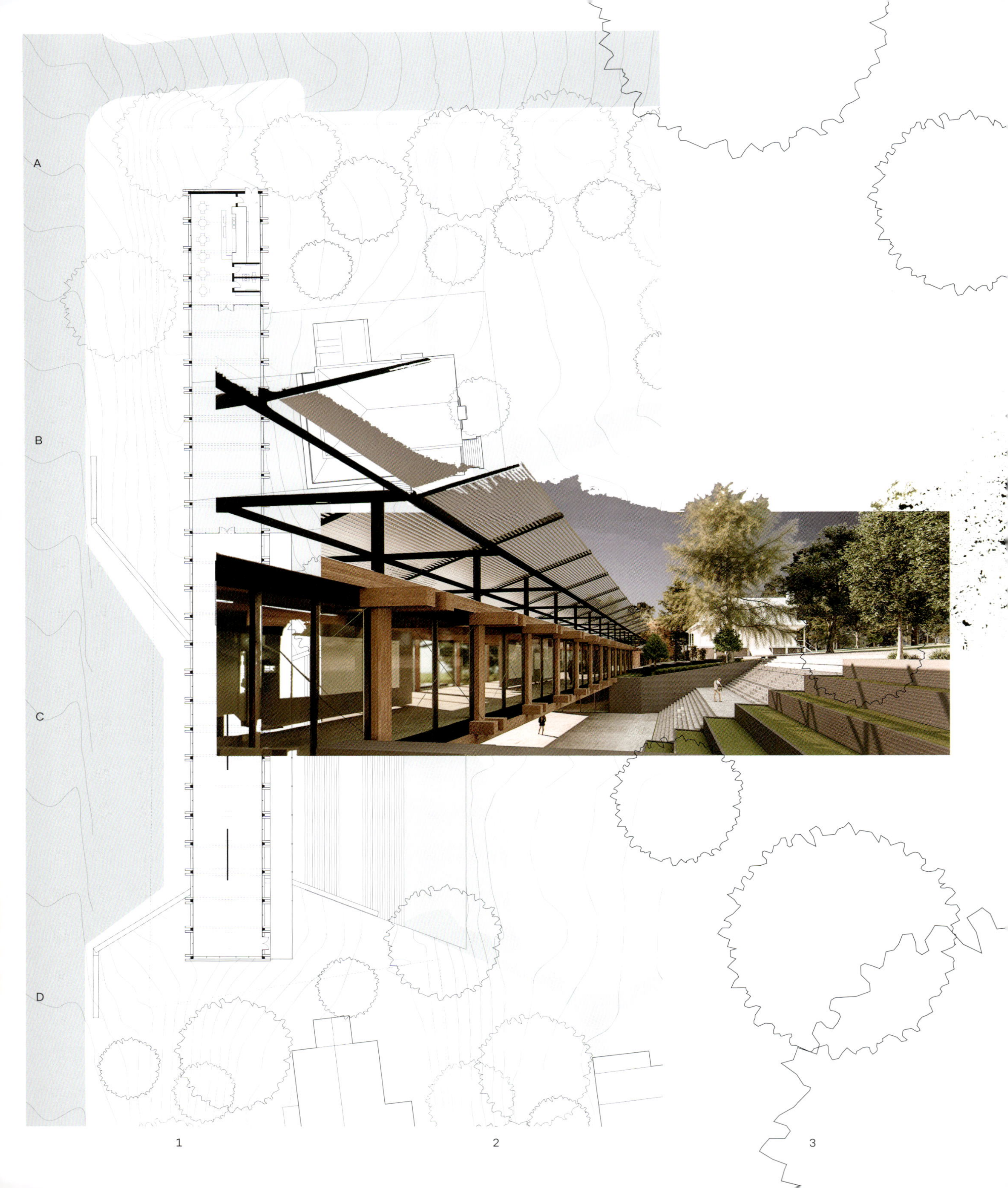
A
B
C
D
1
2
3

A1 Scott Sigmund
C2 Scott Sigmund
A5 Qi Han Zheng
B5 Ethan Aspiras

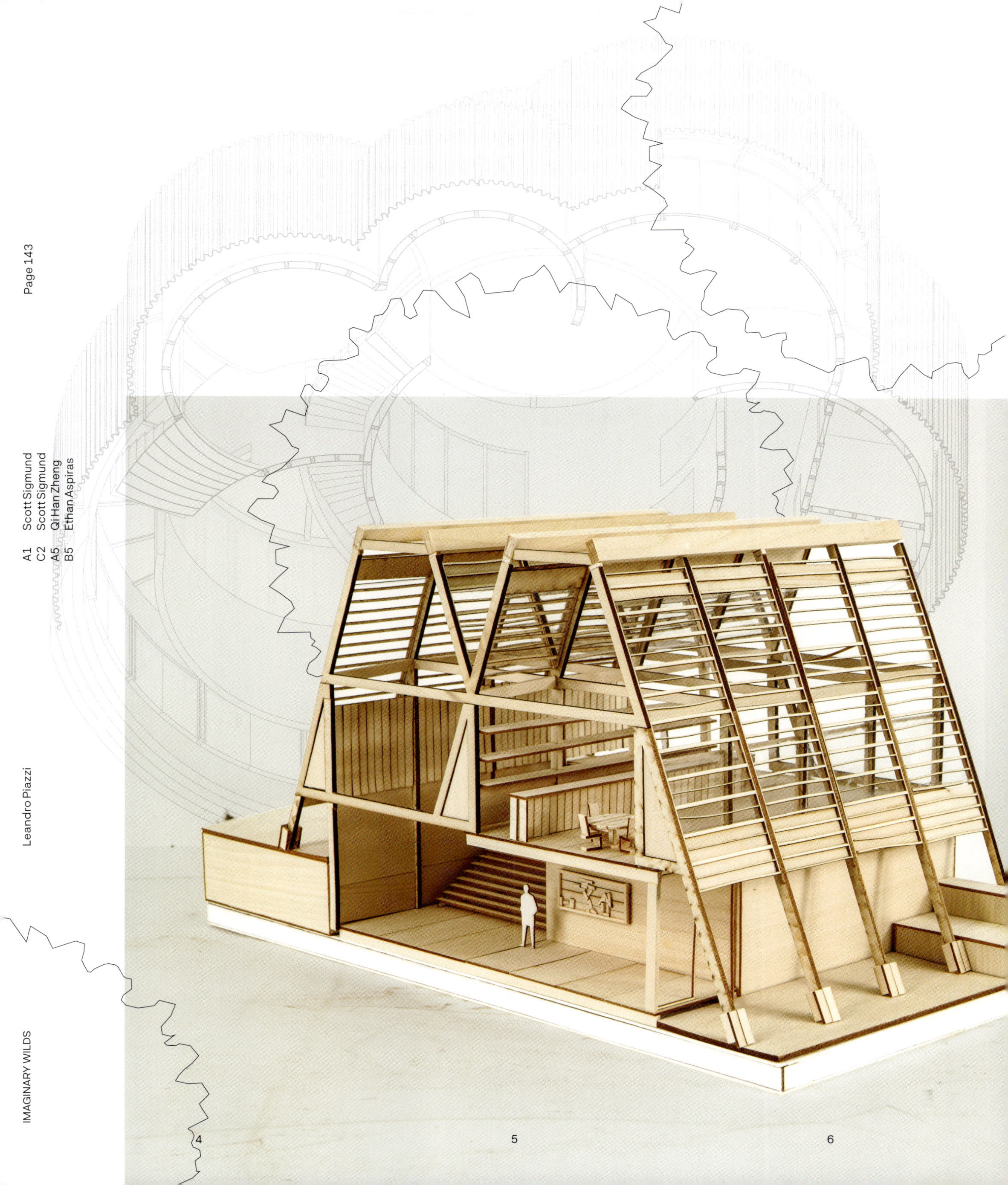

4 5 6

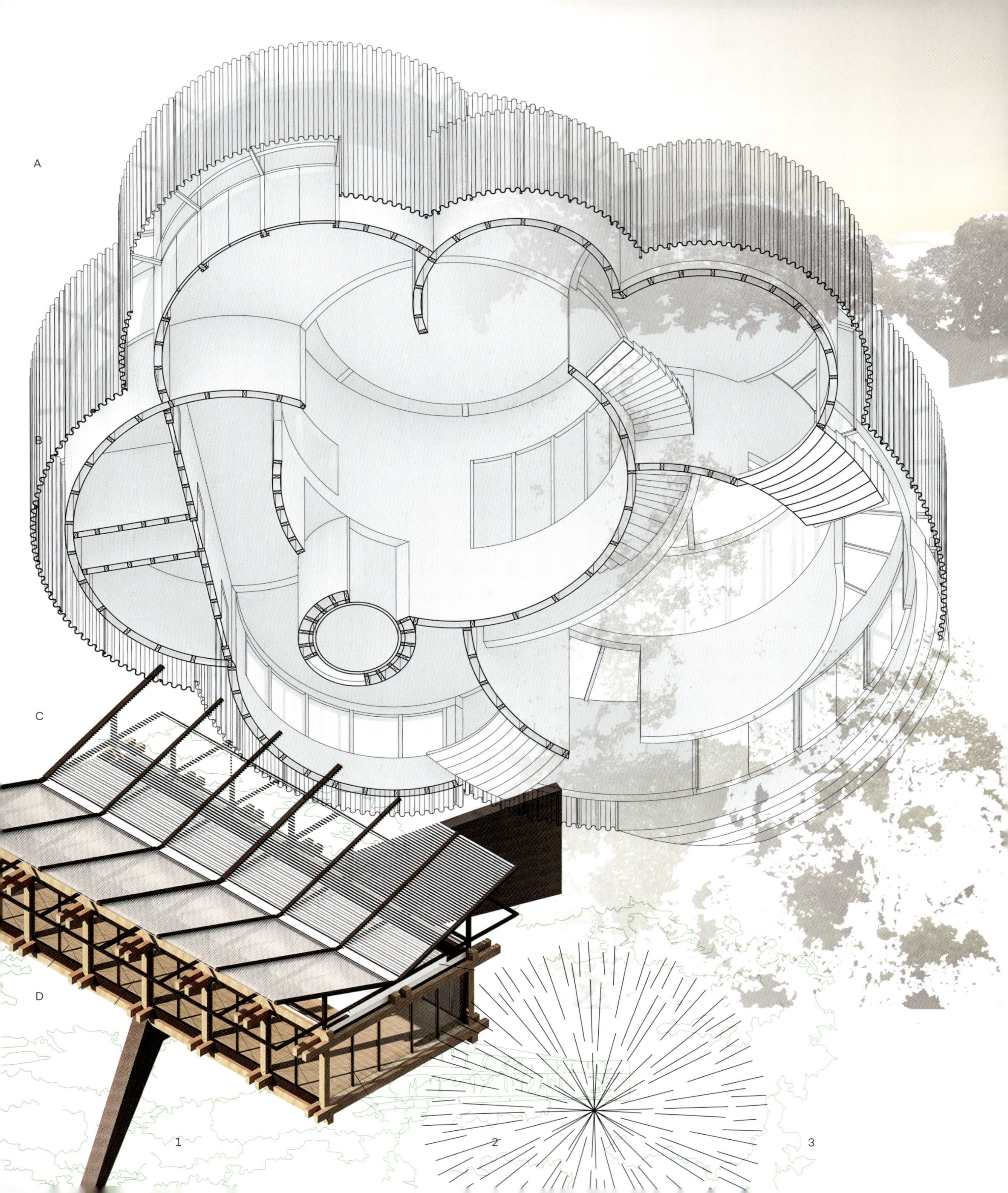

A
B
C
D
1
2
3

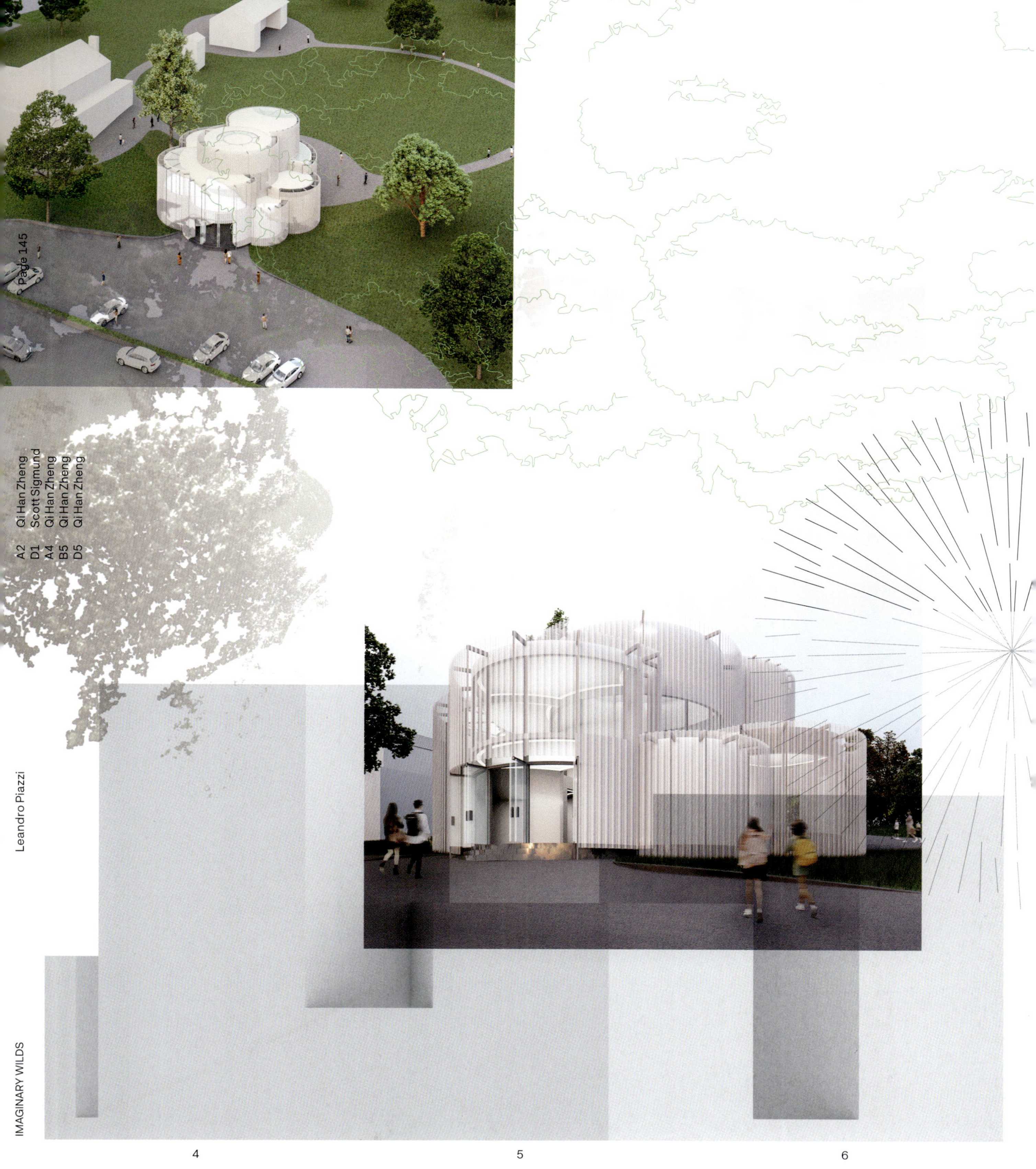

Leandro Piazzi

A2 Qi Han Zheng
D1 Scott Sigmund
A4 Qi Han Zheng
B5 Qi Han Zheng
D5 Qi Han Zheng

4

5

6

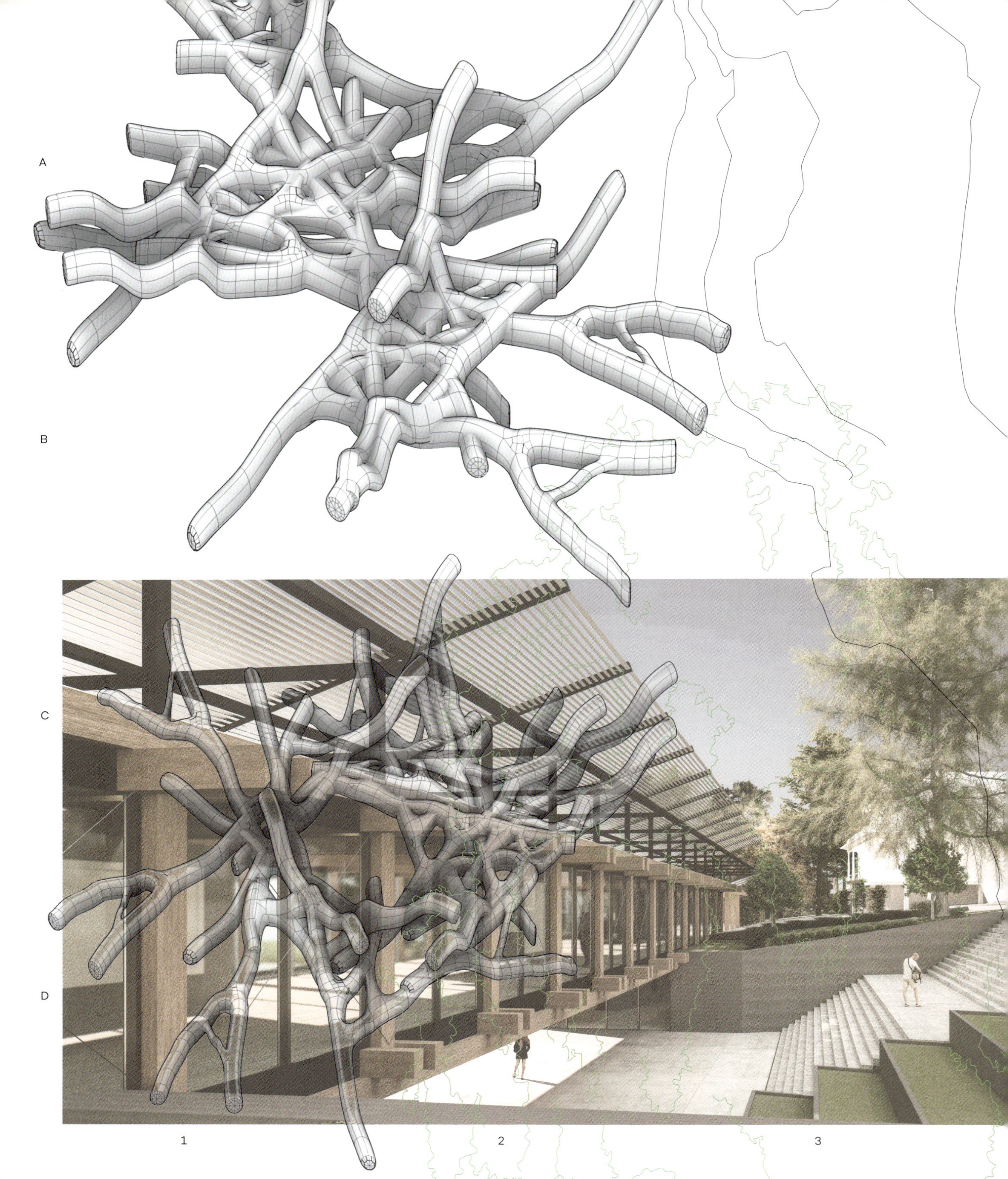
A
B
C
D
1
2
3

Leandro Piazzi

A1 Emily Zheng
C3 Scott Sigmund
A6 Vic Webb
D5 Vic Webb

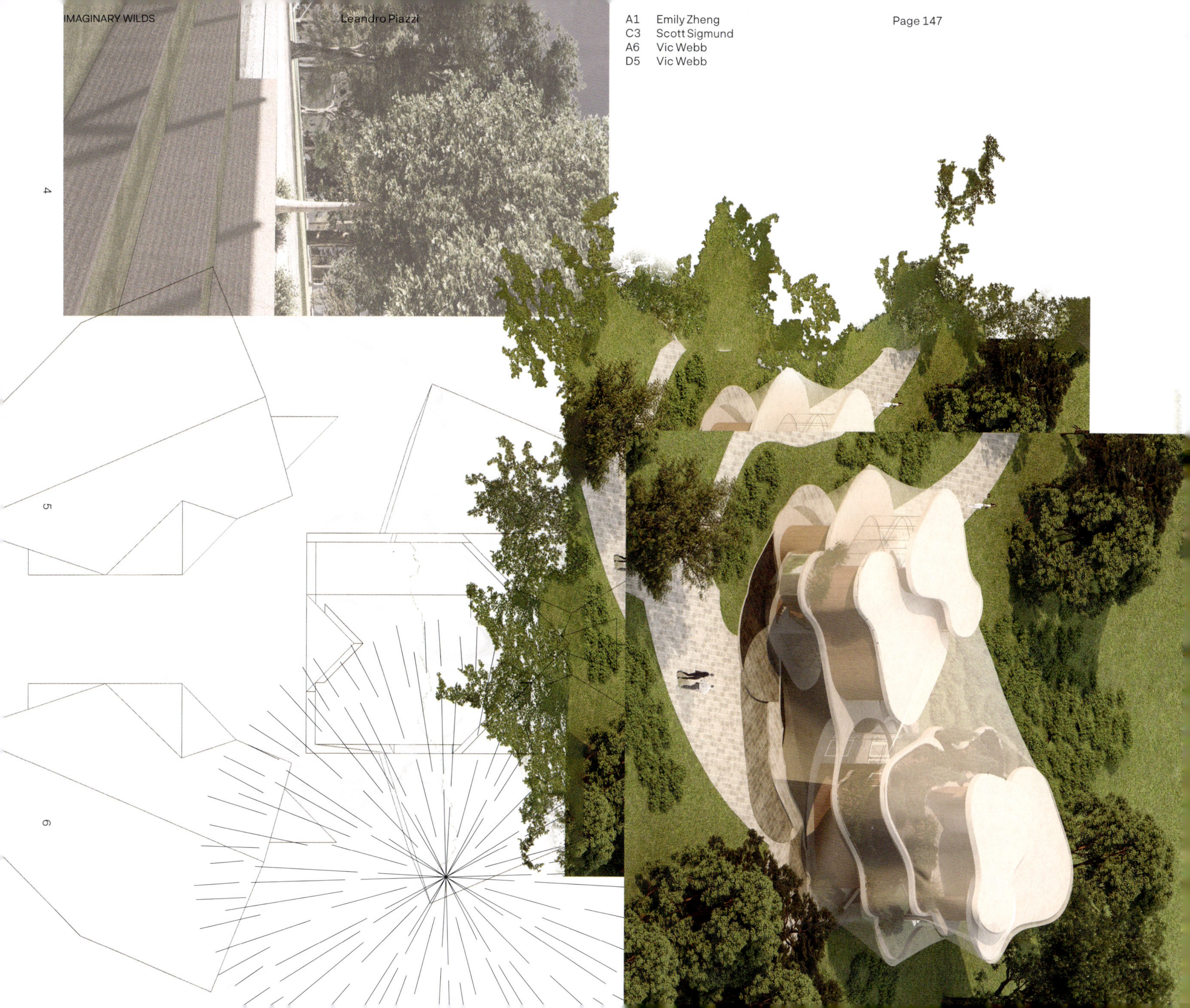

4

5

6

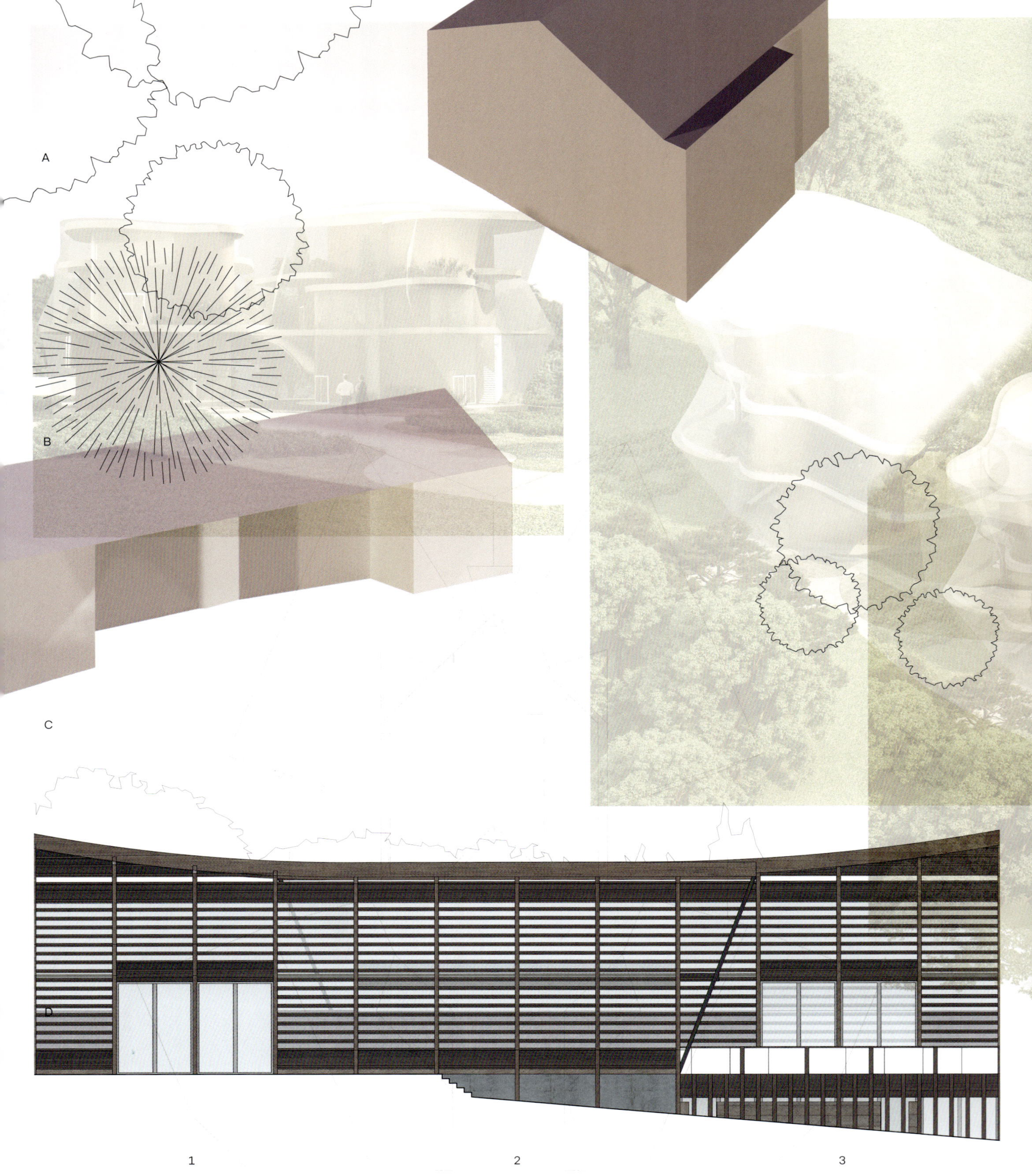
A
B
C
D
1
2
3

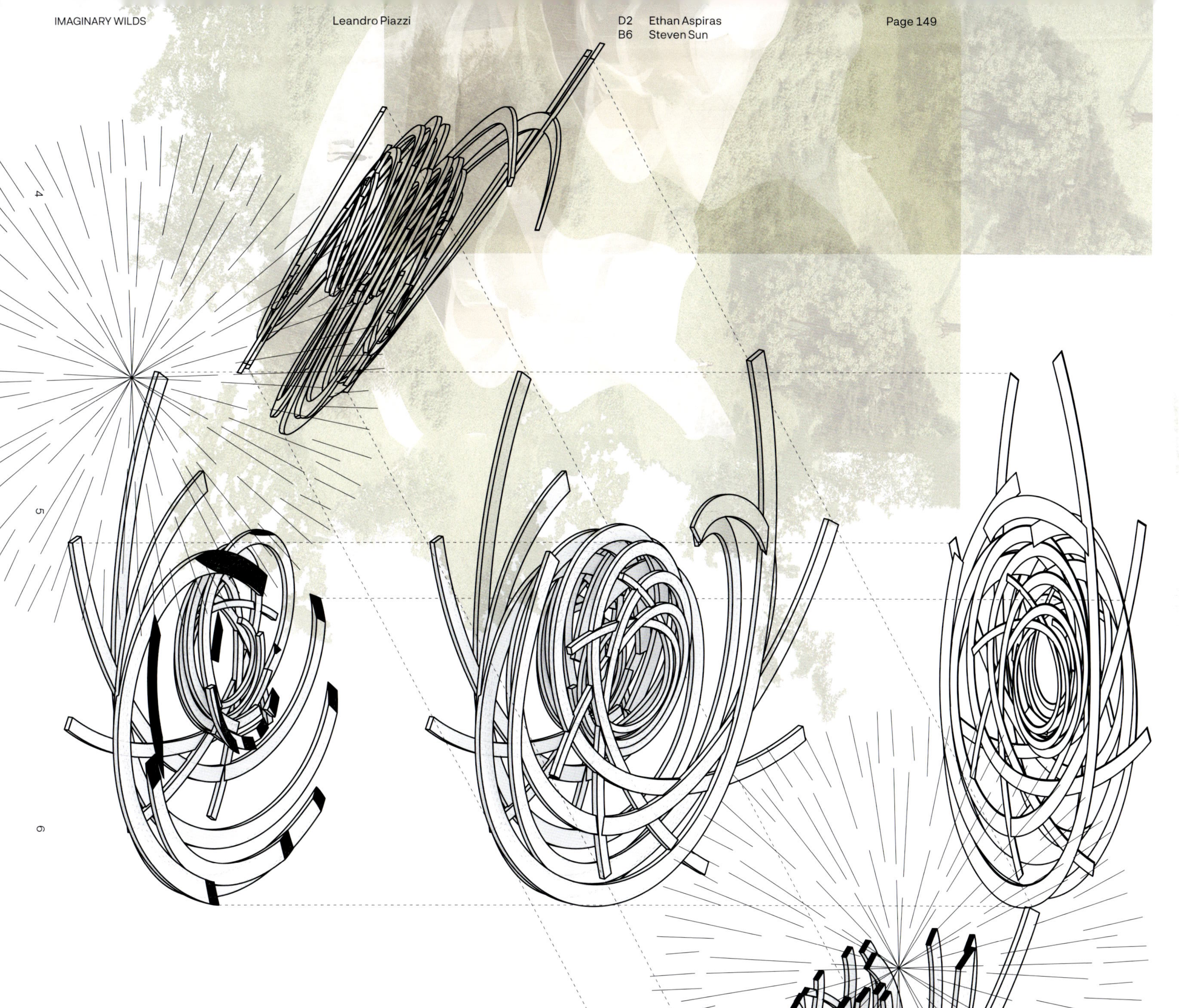
4
5
6

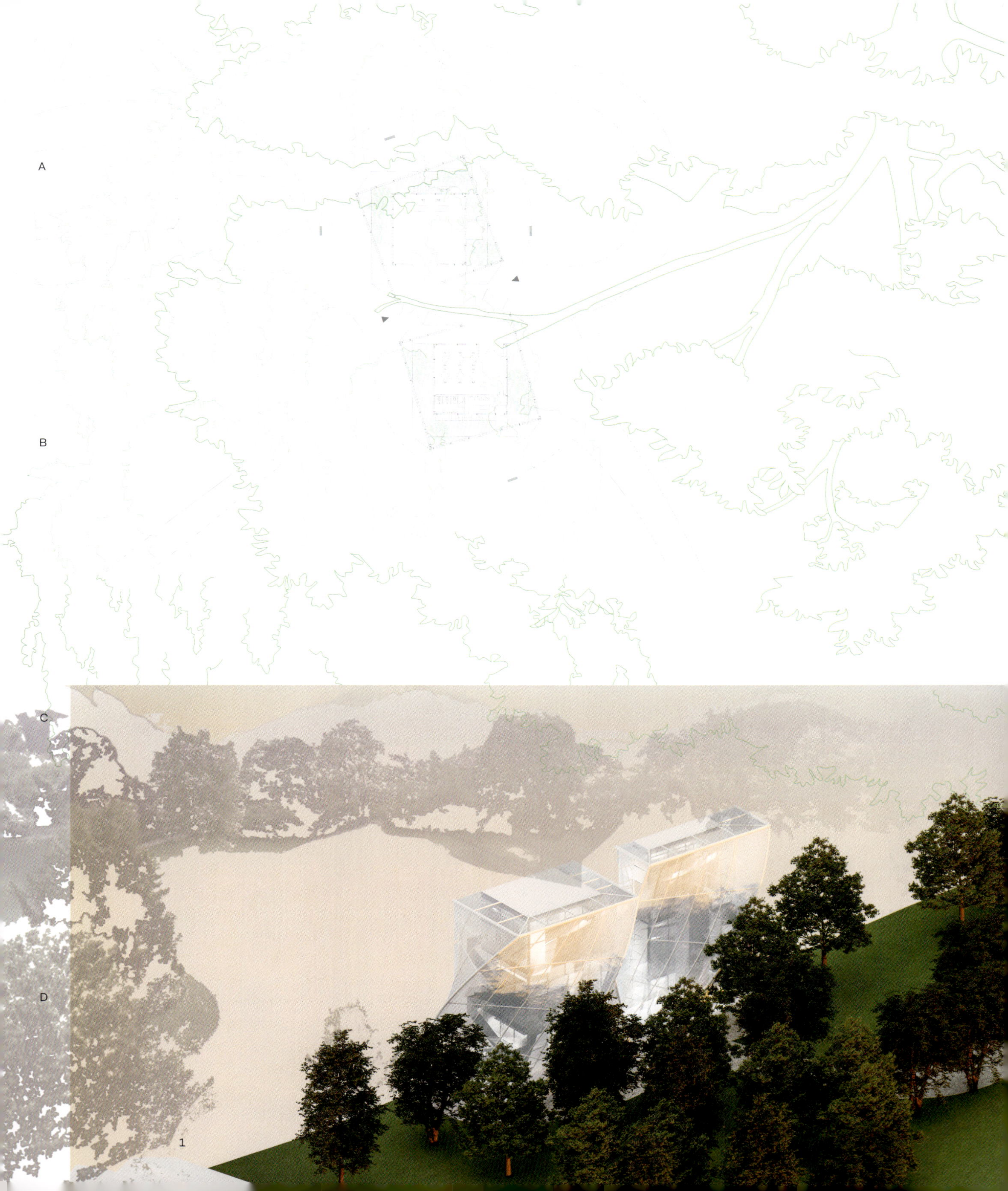
A
B
C
D
1

A1 Steven Sun
D2 Steven Sun
A6 Steven Sun
C5 John Xu

Leandro Piazzi

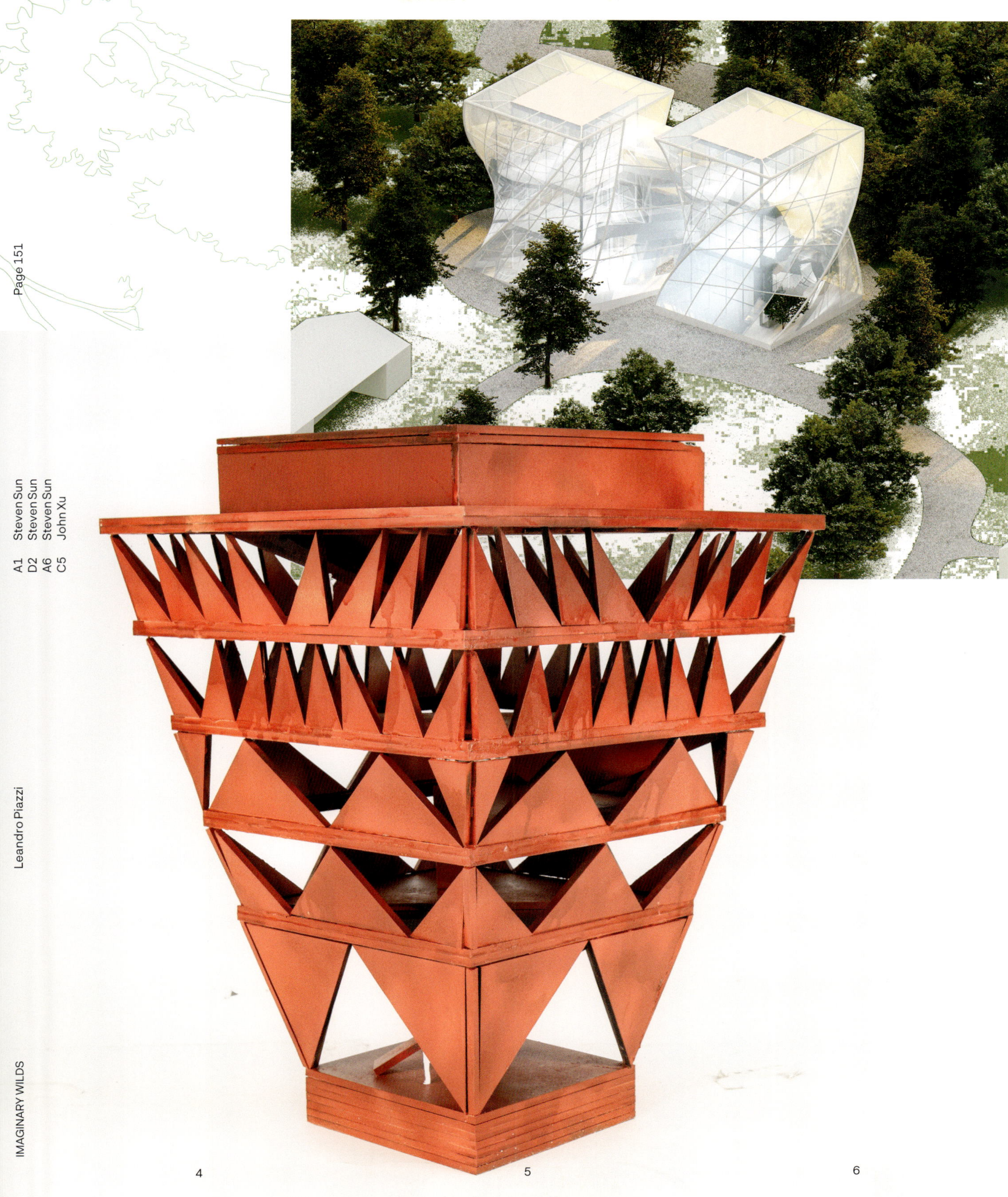

4

5

6

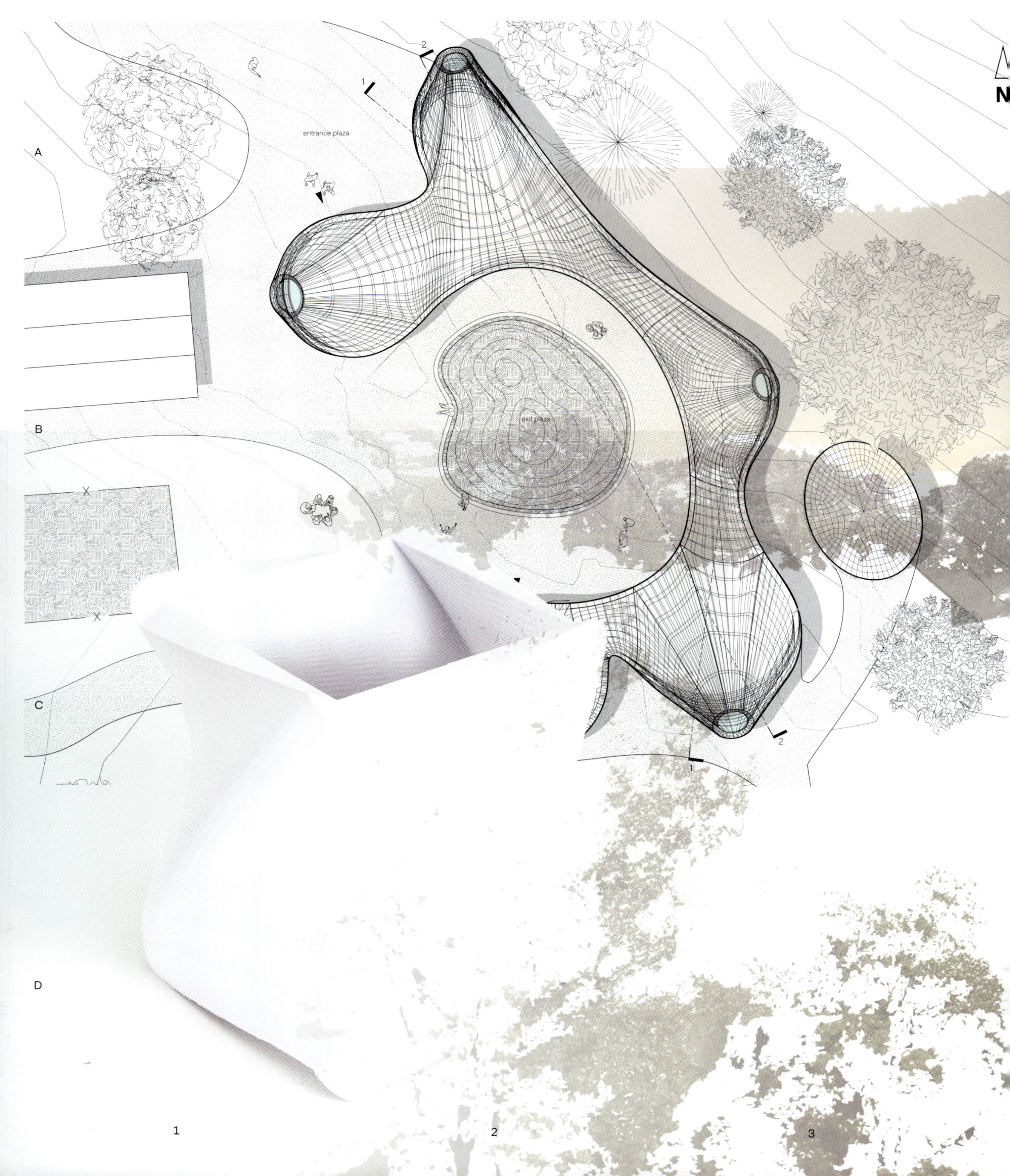

N
entrance plaza
exit plaza
A
B
C
D
1
2
3

A2 Emily Zheng
D1 Steven Sun
D5 Emily Zheng

Leandro Piazzi

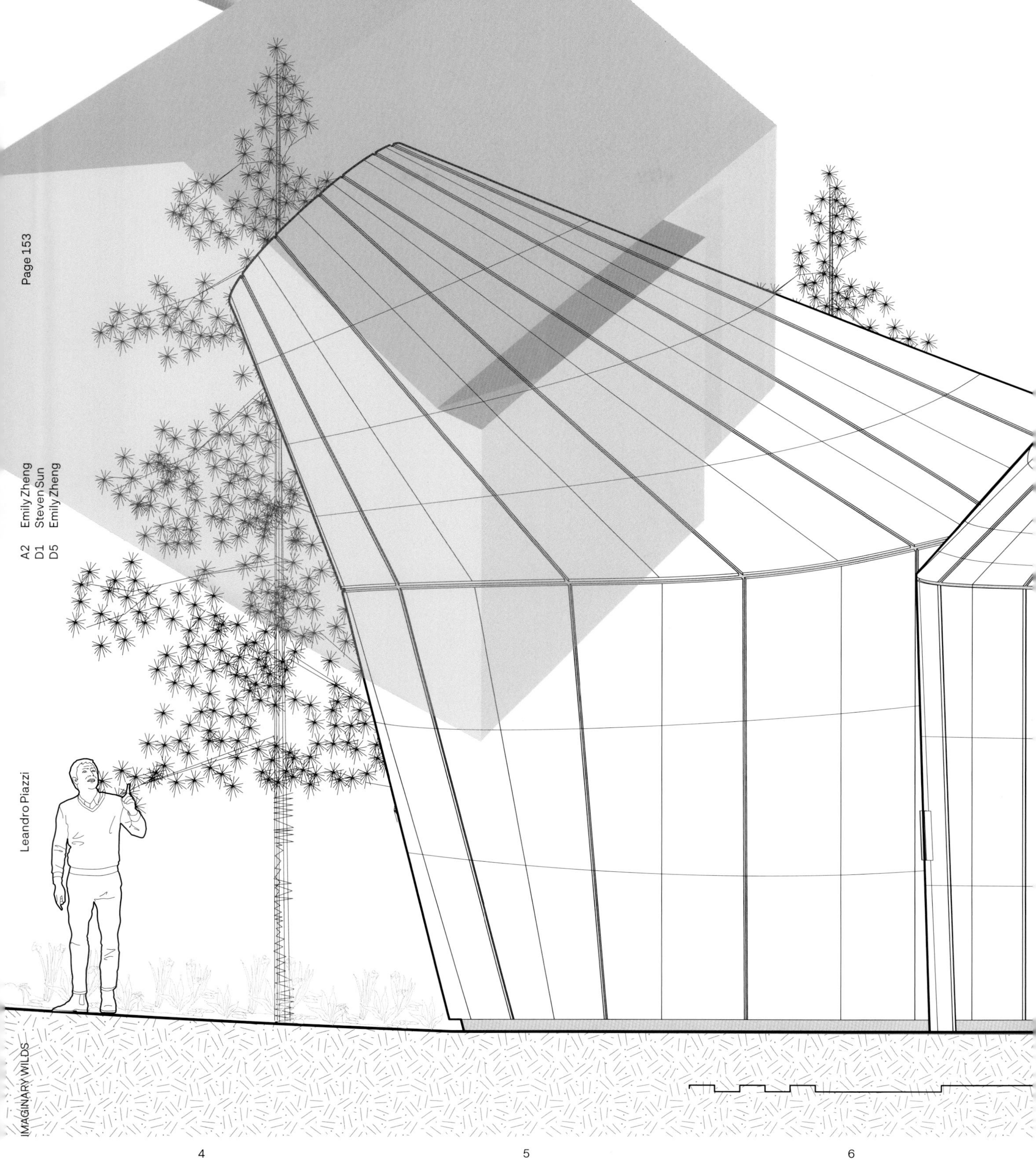

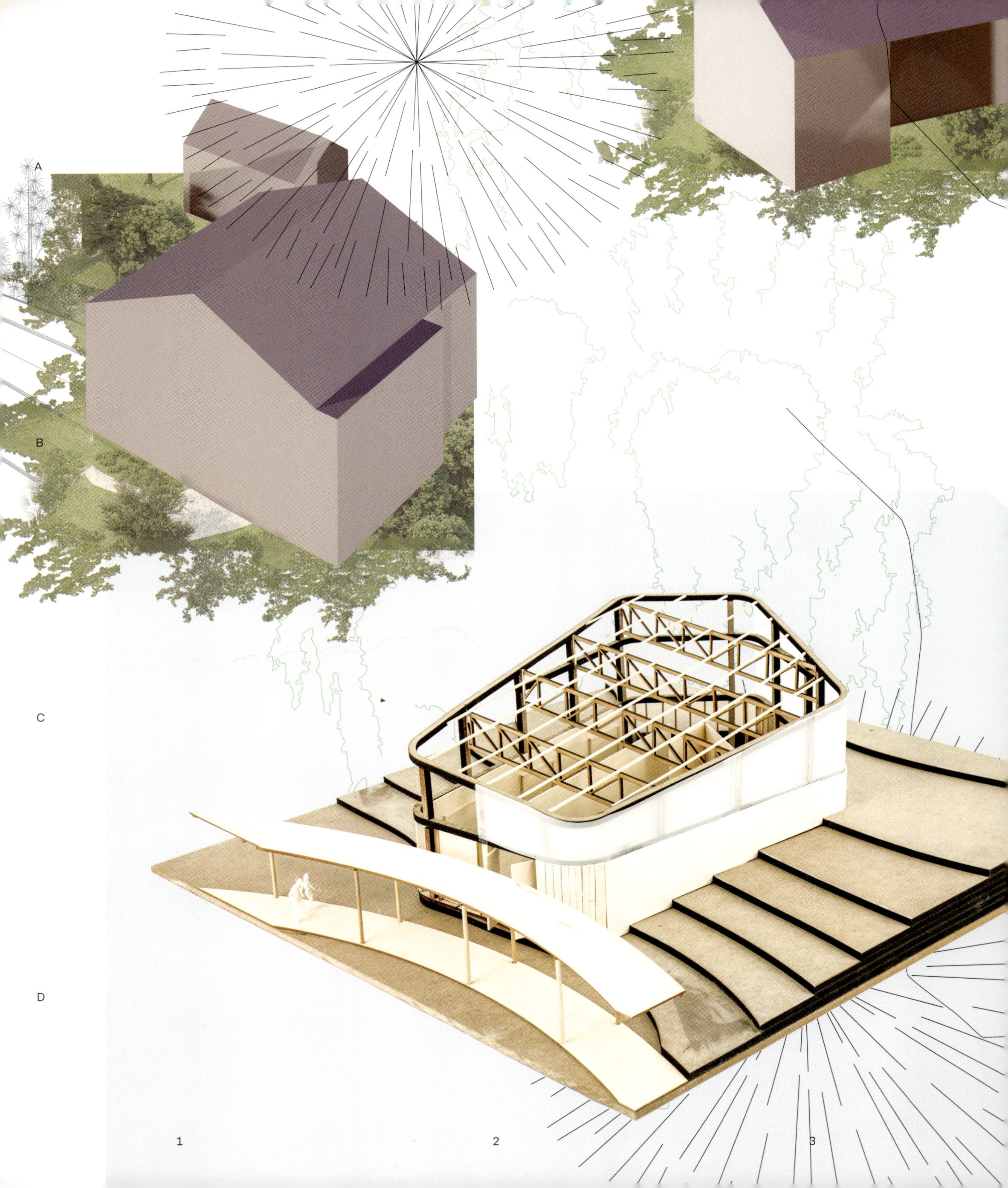
A
B
C
D
1
2
3

B1 John Xu
C2 Javier Torres
C4 John Xu
A6 Javier Torres
D6 Javier Torres

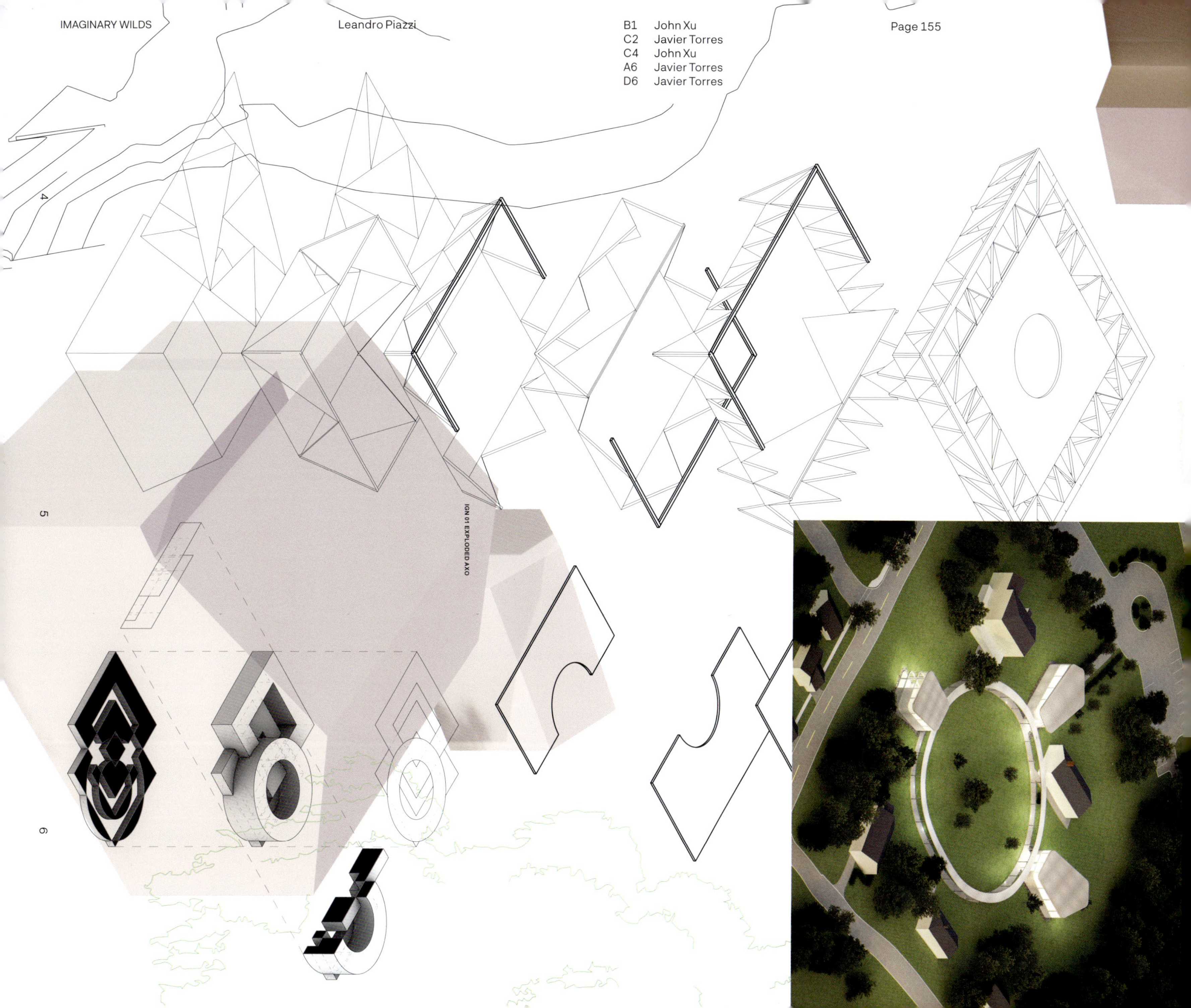

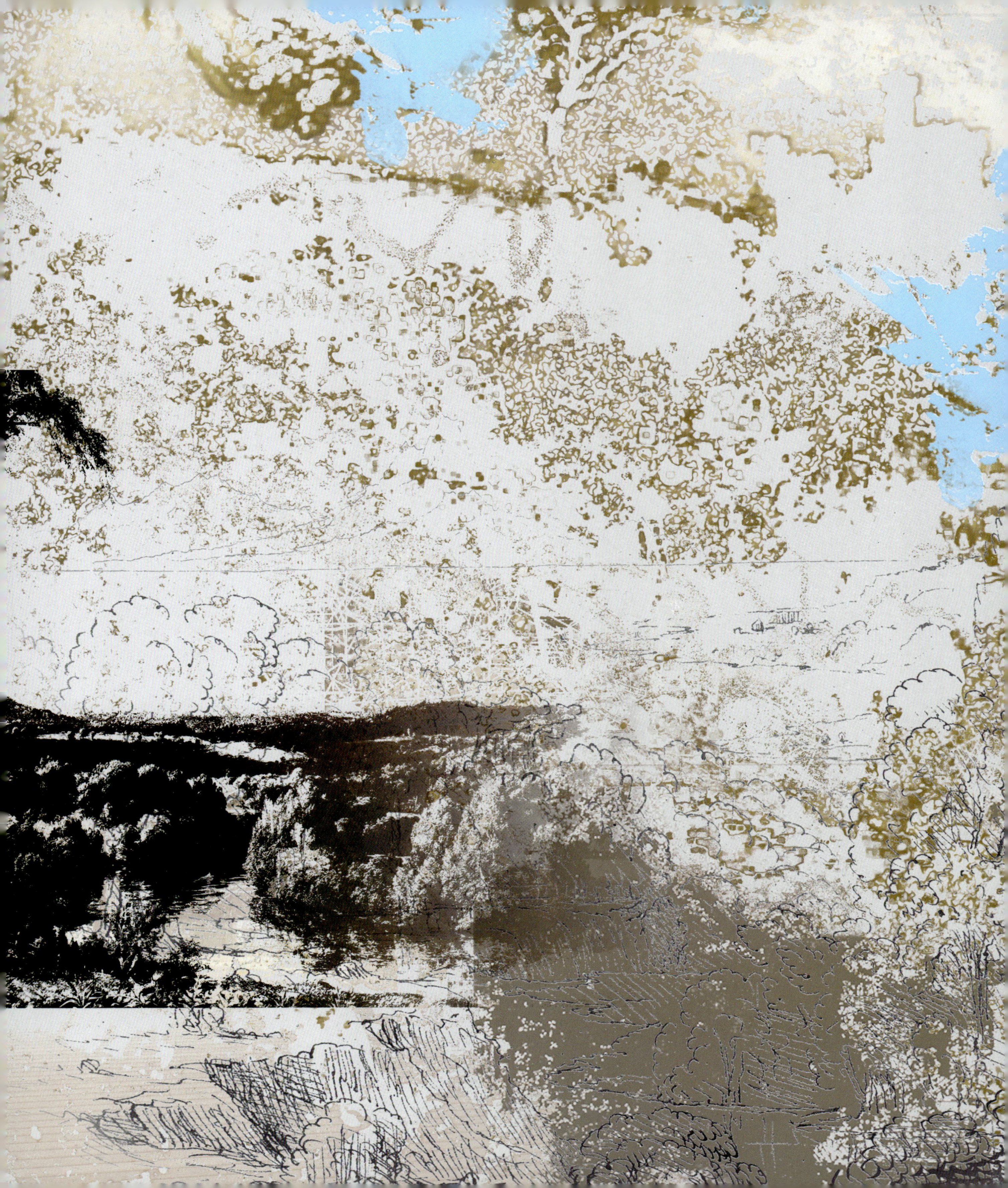

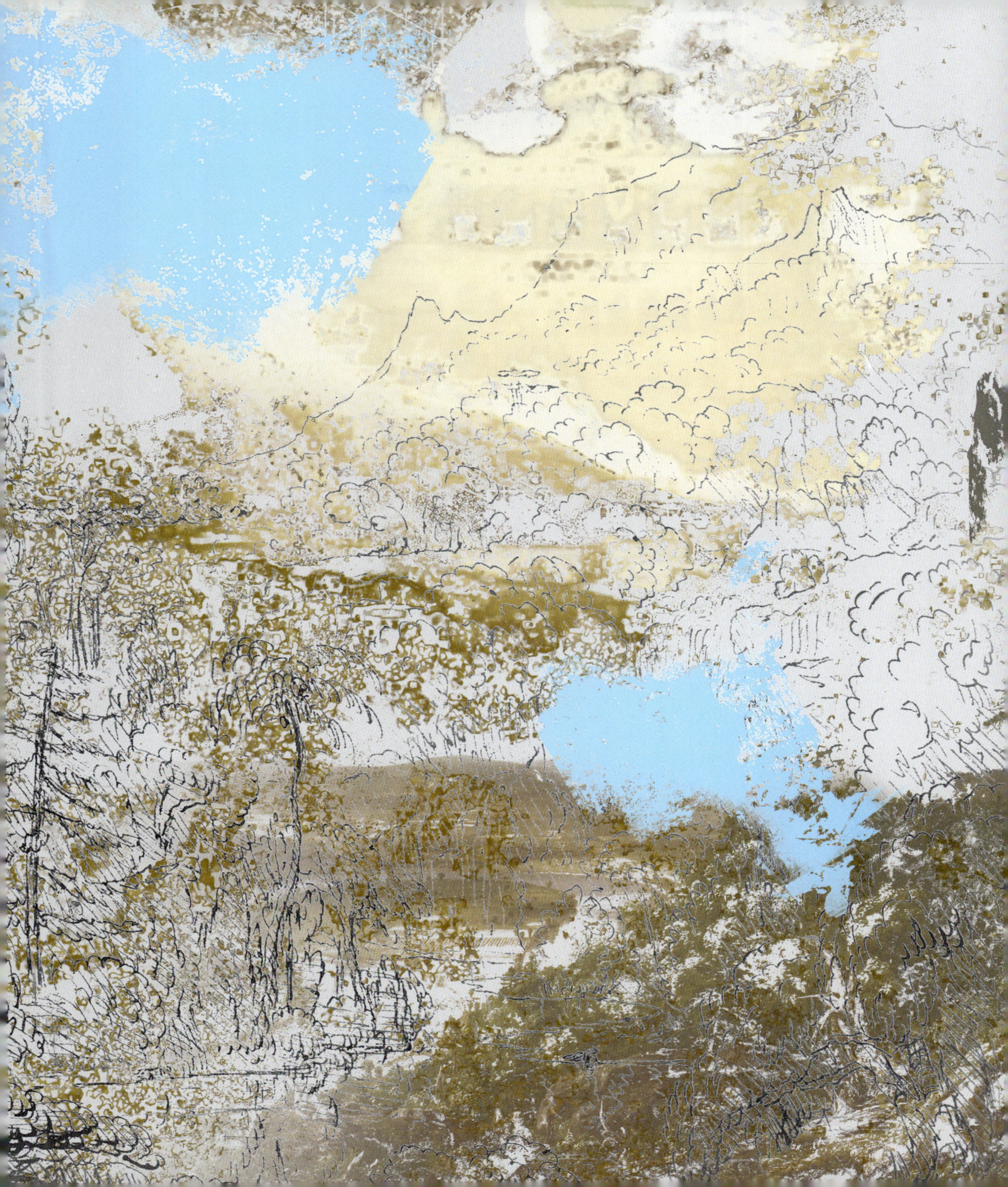

Design Studio Sections

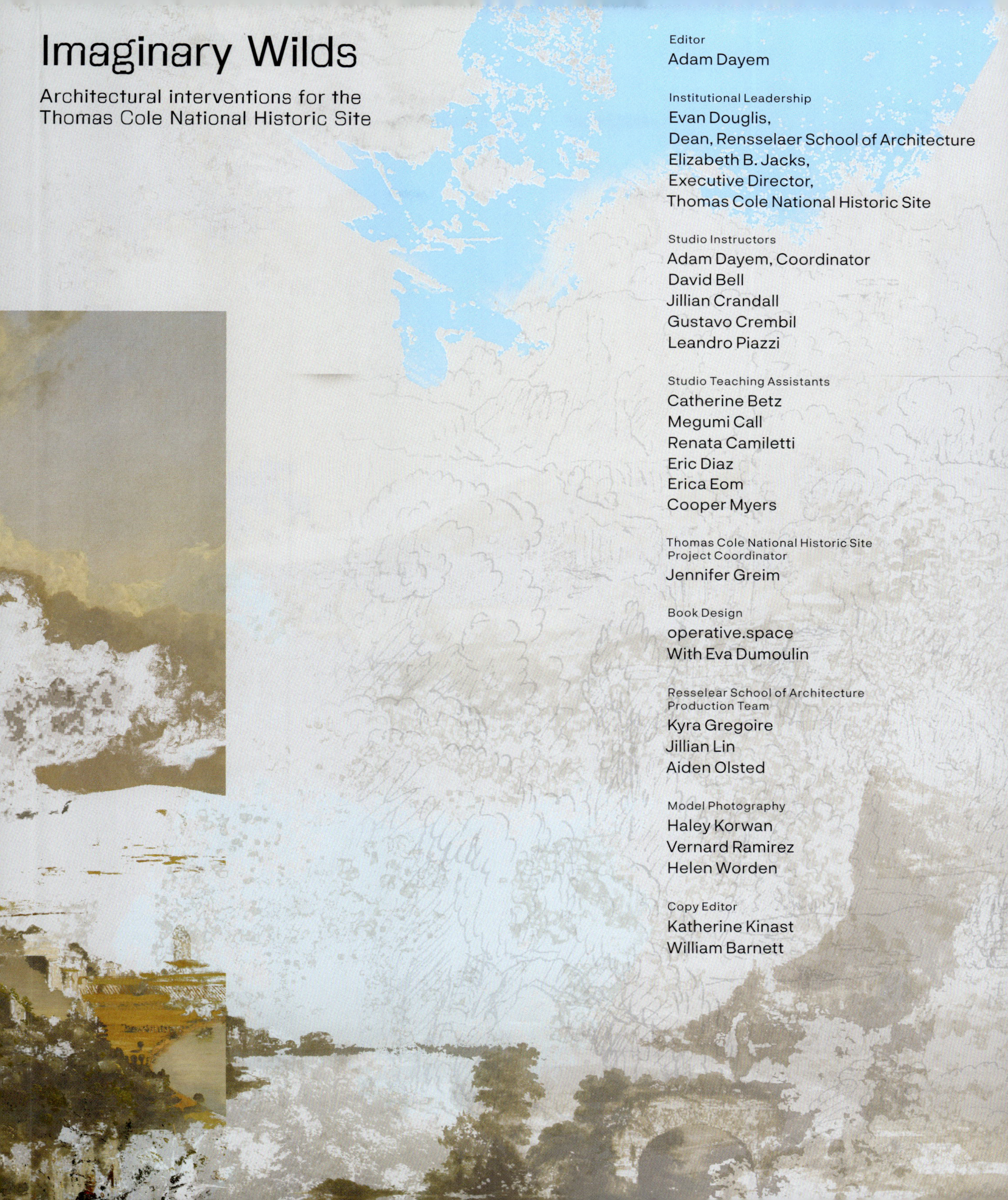

Imaginary Wilds

Architectural interventions for the Thomas Cole National Historic Site

Editor
Adam Dayem

Institutional Leadership
Evan Douglis,
Dean, Rensselaer School of Architecture
Elizabeth B. Jacks,
Executive Director,
Thomas Cole National Historic Site

Studio Instructors
Adam Dayem, Coordinator
David Bell
Jillian Crandall
Gustavo Crembil
Leandro Piazzi

Studio Teaching Assistants
Catherine Betz
Megumi Call
Renata Camiletti
Eric Diaz
Erica Eom
Cooper Myers

Thomas Cole National Historic Site
Project Coordinator
Jennifer Greim

Book Design
operative.space
With Eva Dumoulin

Resselear School of Architecture
Production Team
Kyra Gregoire
Jillian Lin
Aiden Olsted

Model Photography
Haley Korwan
Vernard Ramirez
Helen Worden

Copy Editor
Katherine Kinast
William Barnett

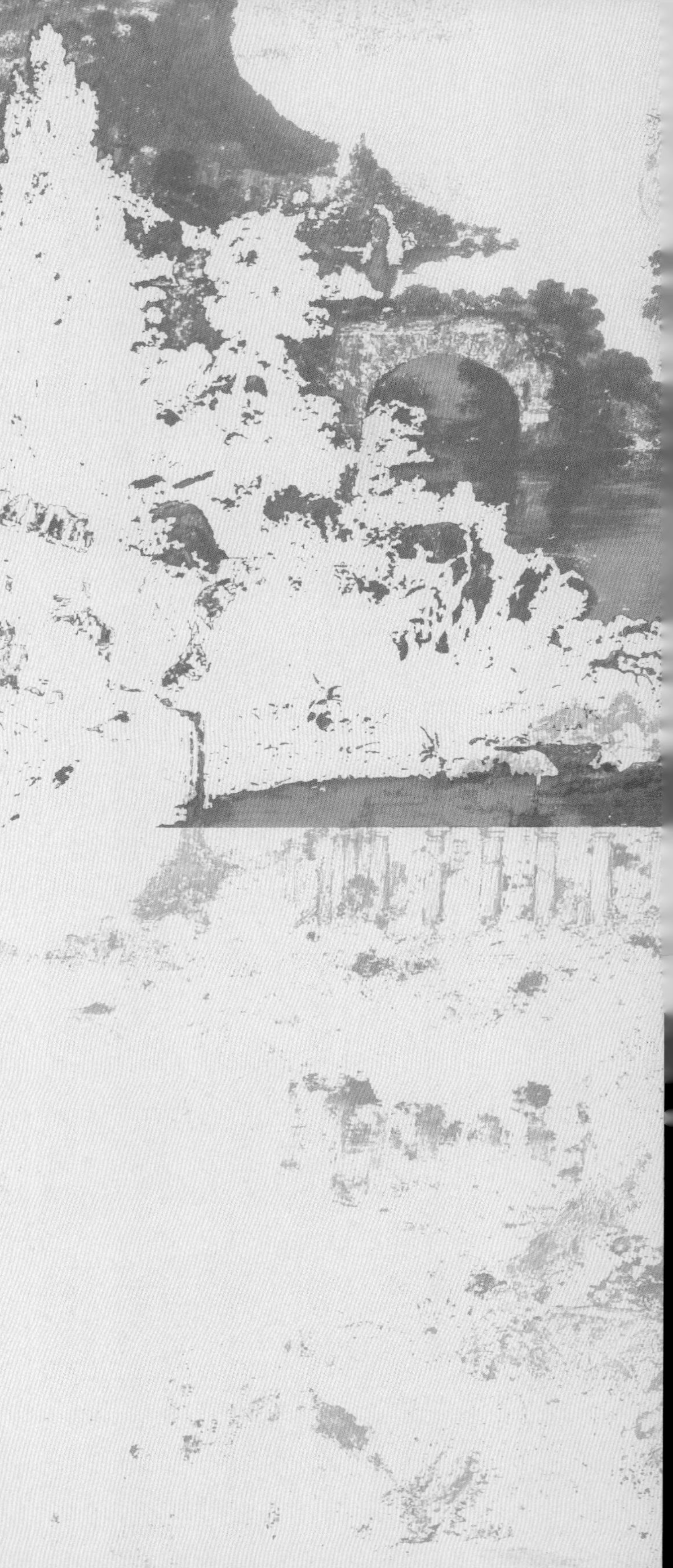

ORO Editions
Publishers of Architecture, Art, and Design
Gordon Goff: Publisher

www.oroeditions.com
info@oroeditions.com

Published by ORO Editions

Editor
Adam Dayem
With contributions by
David Bell, William L. Coleman, Jillian Crandall, Gustavo Crembil, Evan Douglis, Cathryn Dwyre-Perry, Elizabeth B. Jacks, Leandro Piazzi, and David Salomon
Book Design
operative.space (Berlin / Köln) with Eva Dumoulin
Project Manager
Jake Anderson

10 9 8 7 6 5 4 3 2 1 First Edition

ISBN: 978-1-957183-93-0

Color Separations and Printing: ORO Group Inc.
Printed in China

ORO Editions makes a continuous effort to minimize the overall carbon footprint of its publications. As part of this goal, ORO, in association with Global ReLeaf, arranges to plant trees to replace those used in the manufacturing of the paper produced for its books. Global ReLeaf is an international campaign run by American Forests, one of the world's oldest nonprofit conservation organizations. Global ReLeaf is American Forests' education and action program that helps individuals, organizations, agencies, and corporations improve the local and global environment by planting and caring for trees.